## Praise for
## The Writer's W[illegible]

"A brilliant publishing enterprise. One of the best elements in American culture is a genuine, welcoming interest in writing from other languages. Beginning with essential writers from Ireland, Mexico, and Poland, the series fills a vital need. Edward Hirsch is absolutely the right general editor to guide the series. In a time of clouds, anxieties, disasters, and blunders regarding our place among the nations, here is a beacon."

—ROBERT PINSKY

"These handsome, beautifully written, and thoughtfully edited volumes could not come at a more opportune moment. Even as our political borders are growing more rigid and fiercely defended, these welcome books remind us of the ways in which literature will always cross the most seemingly impermeable barrier and leap the highest wall."

—FRANCINE PROSE

"What an inspired way to engage other cultures: through the meditations of writers on the subject that they know best—writing. And what we discover in the essays collected in The Writer's World is that for all of our seeming differences and genuine divisions, we are bound by words, which in every language offer windows through which to glimpse the heart of the matter: what it means to be alive."

—CHRISTOPHER MERRILL

"The Writer's World is a wonderfully intriguing and exciting series. Each book is like a conference of great writers and thinkers brought together to consider matters essential to culture and society. There's nothing like it."

—C. K. WILLIAMS

# CHINESE WRITERS
## *on Writing*

Drawing from essays, poems, fiction, and interview excerpts, this anthology features pieces by forty-one Chinese writers working between 1917 and the present in China, Taiwan, Canada, France, the United Kingdom, and the United States. More than half are newly translated or appear in print for the first time in English. The contributors—the oldest of whom was born before the Boxer Rebellion—are the products of a tumultuous history of colonialism, isolationism, revolution, and engagement with the West, both psychically and linguistically.

### Contributors

Ai Qing
Bei Dao
Bian Zhilin
Can Xue
Chang, Eileen (Zhang Ailing)
Chen Li
Dai Wangshu
Ding Ling
Gao Xingjian
Gu Cheng
Haizi
Hsia Yü (Xia Yu)
Hu Shi
Ji Xian
Jia Pingwa
Lao She
Leung Ping-kwan (Liang Bingjun)
Li Ang
Liang Shiqiu
Lo Fu (Luo Fu)
Lu Xun
Mao Dun
Mao Zedong
Mo Yan
Shang Qin
Wang Anyi
Wang Ping
Wen Yiduo
Xi Chuan
Xi Xi
Yan Li
Yang Lian
Yang Mu
Yu Hua
Yu Jian
Zang Di
Zhai Yongming
Zhang Dachun
Zhang Er
Zhou Zan
Zhou Zuoren

## The Writer's World
Edward Hirsch, series editor

The Writer's World features writers from around the globe discussing what it means to write, and to be a writer, in many different parts of the world. The series collects a broad range of material and provides access for the first time to a body of work never before gathered in English. Edward Hirsch, the series editor, is internationally acclaimed as a poet and critic. He is the president of the John Simon Guggenheim Memorial Foundation.

*Chinese Writers on Writing* (2010)
edited by Arthur Sze

*Hebrew Writers on Writing* (2008)
edited by Peter Cole

*Irish Writers on Writing* (2007)
edited by Eavan Boland

*Mexican Writers on Writing* (2007)
edited by Margaret Sayers Peden

*Polish Writers on Writing* (2007)
edited by Adam Zagajewski

Trinity University Press gratefully acknowledges the following Patrons of The Writer's World:

Sarah Harte and John Gutzler
Mach Family Fund, Joella and Steve Mach

The press also thanks the Lannan Foundation and the Henry Luce Foundation, Inc., for their generous support of this book.

# CHINESE WRITERS

# *on Writing*

EDITED BY
*Arthur Sze*

TRINITY UNIVERSITY PRESS
*San Antonio, Texas*

Published by Trinity University Press
San Antonio, Texas 78212



Complete copyright information continues on page 291.



Cover design by Kristina Kachele Design, llc
Book design by BookMatters, Berkeley
Cover illustration: *My Dream,* by Xu Mangyao, 1988

The paper used in this publication meets the minimum requirements of the American National Standard for Information Sciences—Permanence of Paper for Printed Library Materials, ANSI Z39.48-1992.

*Library of Congress Cataloging-in-Publication Data*
Chinese writers on writing / edited by Arthur Sze.
p. cm.—(The writer's world)
Includes index.

*Summary*: "With more than half the works appearing in English for the first time, this is the first collection that brings together material by writers reflecting on their work, processes, and challenges of writing under China's political system" —Provided by publisher.

ISBN 978-1-59534-062-7 (alk. paper); ISBN 978-1-59534-063-4 (pbk. : alk. paper)
1. Authorship—Literary collections. 2. Authorship—Political aspects—China—Literary collections. 3. Chinese literature—Translations into English. 4. Authors, Chinese—Biography. 5. Chinese literature—History and criticism—Theory, etc. 6. Authors, Chinese—Political and social views. 7. China—Intellectual life—20th century.
I. Sze, Arthur.

PL2516.5.A87C45 2010
808'.04951—dc22 2009043341

14 13 12 11 10 5 4 3 2 1

# *Contents*

*Pieces marked with an asterisk appear in English for the first time.

Unless otherwise stated, footnotes are reproduced from the original English-language edition of the text.

# *Preface*

*I*

"Literature is an international enterprise—there has never been a culture without it—and one must be an intrepid traveler, crossing geographic, historical, and linguistic borders to experience its depths, the breadth and richness of what it has to offer," writes series editor Edward Hirsch about the Writer's World.

The vast literature of China is still not as well known as it should be, and although a handful of writers and texts are renowned, the full range and depth have yet to be appreciated. In determining the scope of *Chinese Writers on Writing*, I first considered such ancients texts as the *Lao-zi* and *Zhuang-zi*, as well as Lu Ji's "Essay on Literature," but quickly decided any attempt to draw on three thousand years of writing was an impossible task. I next considered that there are a number of collections of modern Chinese literature, but few focus on essays by the writers themselves.

This collection, *Chinese Writers on Writing*, features essays, as well as supporting poems, fiction, and interview excerpts, by forty-one writers first published between 1917 and 2010. It should be clear that this is only one out of many possible selections, and, as editor, I have had to make many difficult choices. I have included such landmark essays as Lu Xun's "Preface to *Call to Arms*" and Eileen Chang's "Writing of One's Own"; but I also wanted to commission translations of existing essays that have never before appeared in English as well as new essays that would enrich the discussion. The result is that more than half of the work included here is appearing in English for the first time.

My initial selection process led me to consider only essays written in Chinese, but when I encountered Steve Bradbury's interview with Hsia Yü, I discovered that, in her latest book, she collaged poems together from various sources in English, ran them through a computer translation program into Chinese, and then back into English. Because Hsia Yü enlarged the arena of linguistic experimentation, I decided to include an existing essay in English by Wang Ping, which discusses writing in both languages. I also commissioned Zhang Er to write a piece in English on Chinese women's poetry. While all the other essays were written in Chinese, this collection includes writers who lived or live in China, Taiwan, Canada, France, the United Kingdom, and the United States.

Although many anthologies of modern Chinese literature use *pinyin* spellings for all of the writers, a few writers, due to dialect or personal choice, have different, preferred spellings. In those cases, I have followed their choices and have included the *pinyin* in parentheses. For instance, because Leung Ping-kwan lives in Hong Kong and prefers this spelling, I have included the *pinyin* (Liang Bingjun) in parentheses. In addition to the issue of spelling, I also need to address pseudonyms. Of the forty-one writers included here, I count eighteen pseudonyms, and one poet has employed more than one pseudonym. In the headnotes to each writer, I have used pseudonyms wherever applicable. An analogous case in Western literature would be the great Chilean poet, Pablo Neruda: readers know him by his pseudonym rather than by his given name, Neftalí Ricardo Reyes.

## *2*

The Chinese writers included in this collection lived through enormous upheavals and transformations. To give the general reader some historical background, I want to begin in 1842 when, at the culmination of the 1839–42 Opium War, China signed the Treaty of Nanjing and formally opened five Chinese cities to the British. From that time on, Western powers dominated China and forced the Qing rulers to sign ever more humiliating treaties. From 1850 to 1864, the Taiping Rebellion, led by Hong Xiuquan, advocated a Christian community and destruction of the Qing, but the movement eventually collapsed. From 1894 to 1895, China was defeated by Japan, and, in the Treaty of Shimonoseki, China ceded Taiwan and the Liaodong region of southern Manchuria. Successive treaties irrevocably weakened the Qing, and in 1911 an uprising in Wuchang spread across the country. In 1912 the Republic of China was formed, and a provisional government took over.

At the end of the First World War, when the terms of the Versailles Conference revealed that Western powers, instead of rewarding China for its contribution to the Allies' effort, supported Japan's claims to Shandong province, there was widespread dissent. On May 4, 1919, student representatives drew up resolutions protesting the terms of the Treaty of Versailles and called for a mass demonstration. Defying police orders, about three thousand students protested. The May Fourth Movement grew from this demonstration at Tiananmen Square in Beijing into a national call for social, political, and cultural transformation.

In the early 1920s, while the Chinese Communist Party was nascent, Sun Yat-sen led the Nationalist Party (Guomindang). In 1925, after Sun's death, Chiang Kai-shek became the new leader. The Communist Party grew in strength, and the Nationalists initiated a series of encirclement campaigns against the Communists. In 1934 the Communists broke out of the last encirclement and began their Long March. After a trek of over three thousand miles, the Communists regrouped in Yan'an, in desolate northwest China. In 1935 the Communists and Nationalists formed, for the second time, a united front to fight the Japanese. In 1945, after Japan surrendered at the end of the Second World War, the Communists and Nationalists severed their makeshift alliance and started a civil war. The Communists prevailed, and Chiang Kai-shek retreated to Taiwan. On October 1, 1949, in Beijing, Mao Zedong proclaimed the People's Republic of China.

After the Communists took power, Mao enacted a series of five-year modernization plans, although the Great Leap Forward (1958–60), a disastrous effort to industrialize China, ended early. It was followed by the Cultural Revolution (1966–76), during which schools and universities were closed. Students were organized into Red Guard bands, and they arrested and even executed suspected counterrevolutionaries. When Premier Zhou Enlai died in April 1976, there was a public outpouring of grief at Tiananmen Square. After Mao's death and the emergence of Deng Xiaoping as the new leader, the authorities briefly allowed freedom of expression at Democracy Wall in Beijing. The underground literary journal *Today*, co-founded by Bei Dao and Mang Ke, published, in several issues from 1978 to 1980, a new generation of poets that became known as the Misty School.

In the looser 1980s, a new generation of fiction writers, including Mo Yan, Yu Hua, Can Xue, and Wang Anyi, rose to prominence. In the spring of 1989 students congregated in Tiananmen Square in support of democratic rights, but on June 4, 1989, their protest was crushed. Many writers went into exile. Since 1990, China has gone through yet another transformation into a market economy, and the country has experienced prodigious growth. In 2008, when it hosted the Summer Olympics, China took pride in its stature as a world power.

During these chaotic and tumultuous years of modern Chinese history, countless Chinese writers died or went into exile. Wen Yiduo was assassinated in 1946, hours after he gave a speech denouncing the Guomindang. In 1966, at the outset of the Cultural Revolution, Lao She and Zhou Zuoren were targeted and killed by Red Guards. In 1989 Haizi committed suicide by lying down in front of a train near Jiayu Gate at the western end of the Great Wall. In 1993, in New Zealand, Gu Cheng killed his wife and hanged himself. Although the personal tragedies of these writers are not the subject of this collection, they suggest the high cost of what it means to be a writer writing in Chinese.

## *3*

Before discussing the selections that form *Chinese Writers on Writing*, I need to provide some linguistic as well as literary background to distinguish classical Chinese poetry from modern Chinese poetry. One needs to know, first, that the Chinese language is composed of characters. Unlike the Western alphabet, which utilizes 26 letters to generate the entire lexicon, the traditional Chinese language utilizes 214 radicals, or root elements. The radicals move, more or less, from simplicity toward complexity. The first radical, for instance, is a single horizontal stroke and represents the number one. The 214th radical, written in seventeen strokes, is the word "flute" or "pipes." Some of the radicals, such as "sun," or "moon," are also characters, but most Chinese characters have radicals and phonetic components. Some radicals can be juxtaposed to create new characters. For instance, "sun" juxtaposed with "moon" creates the character "bright." Or "tree" juxtaposed to "tree" creates the character "forest." In China, after 1949, written characters were simplified so that it was easier for everyone to read and write. In Taiwan and Hong Kong, however, the traditional characters are still used. In terms of sound, Chinese is a tonal language. Modern Mandarin utilizes four pitched tones (as well as a toneless tone). A character may be pronounced with the level (first), rising (second), dipping (third), or falling (fourth) tone. For instance, the character "horse" is pronounced *ma,* with the third tone.

The two earliest collections of poetry in China are *The Book of Songs* (*Shi-jing*) and the *Songs of Chu,* also called *Songs of the South* (*Chu-ci*). *The Book of Songs* was compiled sometime after 600 B.C.E., and is composed of songs, hymns, and ballads from northern China. These poems, *shi*, are predominantly composed of four-character lines. The *Songs of Chu* were compiled several centuries later and include a long poem, "Encountering Sorrow," by Qu Yuan (ca. 340–278 B.C.E.), the first poet we know anything about. The poems in the *Songs of Chu* utilize a new meter with a caesura marked by an exclamatory syllable *xi* (like "O" in English). Qu Yuan diversified the rhythmical possibilities and utilized as many as thirteen characters to a line.

During the Han dynasty (206 B.C.E.–220 C.E.), a new form, *fu*, emerged. This form featured rhymed lines, except for introductory and concluding passages in prose, where the number of characters per line and number of lines varied greatly. In addition to the *fu*, another related form, the *yue-fu*, emerged. The *yue-fu* was originally the name of the Music Bureau that collected folk songs, and when music from Central Asia was introduced into China, *yue-fu* were composed to follow the new melodies. In addition to these forms, the *shi* form of poetry rose to prominence and featured a five-character line. It largely replaced the four-character form from *The Book of Songs*, and this new form featured a regular caesura between the second and third characters, 1-2 / 3-4-5. Tao Yuanming (365–427) was one of the great early poets who frequently used this five-character line, and his "fields-and-gardens" poems are imbued with contemplative insight.

In the Tang dynasty (618–907), many of the greatest Chinese poets, including Li Bo (701–62), Du Fu (712–70), and Wang Wei (701–61), brought poetry to new heights. While Li Bo often drew on Han *shi* and *yue-fu* poetic forms, Du Fu excelled at a new form, the regulated verse, *lu-shi*, which utilized an eight-line structure. The poetic line was either five or seven characters long. A seven-character line had two caesuras, 1-2 / 3-4 / 5-6-7. An example in English translation would be the opening line to Zhang Ji's "Mooring at Night by the Maple Bridge." Here it's possible to use a one-syllable word in English for each Chinese character: moon sinks / crows cry / frost full sky. In regulated verse, the two middle couplets had to incorporate parallelism, and there were complex requirements in the choice of tones. The first two tones were considered "level," while the third and fourth tones were called "oblique." (A fifth tone existed in older times, but that fifth tone was also considered an oblique tone.) Tonal requirements in the *lu-shi* created an intricate tapestry of sound, and even-numbered lines rhymed. Although Wang Wei also wrote some poems in regulated verse, he excelled at utilizing the five-character quatrain, the *jueju*. A late Tang poet, Li Shangyin (813–58) utilized oblique images to create rich, layered poems. Finally, it is important to know that the *shi* form of poetry utilizes sound and silence and is unaccompanied by music.

Toward the end of the Tang dynasty, a new lyric form, *ci*, emerged. The *ci* forms were based on popular songs, and the titles to *ci* poems refer to particular melodies for which the poems were composed. For instance, in the Song dynasty (960–1279), when the *ci* form rose to prominence, the great female poet Li Qingzhao (1084–1151) has a *ci* titled "To the Tune of Intoxicated in the Shadows of Flowers." The *ci* lyrics utilized lines of irregular length, and they were sung and accompanied by music. In the Yuan dynasty (1280–1368), the ruling Mongols promoted opera, and a new form of opera song (*xiqu*) emerged. Other songs (*sanqu*), independent of the operas, also began to be written. These short songs utilized lines of unequal length and made extensive use of colloquial language.

Of all poetic forms, the *shi* best represented the classical tradition; but after the Opium Wars awakened China to its many weaknesses, there was a torrent of translations of Western literature, philosophy, politics, and science. Many late–Qing dynasty (1644–1912) writers began to realize how restricted and removed classical Chinese poetry was. Poets began tentative experiments by injecting new vocabulary, which often consisted of transliterations of foreign words, into classical forms. One of the poets who articulated a new style was Huang Zunxian (1848–1905); he wrote that his hands followed the language that he spoke, and his poetry became an important bridge between classical poetry and the new vernacular poetry of the twentieth century.

## *4*

In making selections for *Chinese Writers on Writing*, I have tried to track the progression of modern Chinese literature by juxtaposing different points of view, by developing mini-conversations, and by creating a large web of thematic interconnections. It is of course impossible to include all the leading literary figures. This collection begins with an excerpt from Hu Shi's essay "Some Modest Proposals for the Reform of Literature," because its publication in 1917 caused a sensation and helped initiate a literary revolution. In the ensuing New Culture Movement (1917–23), the vernacular language displaced classical language in all areas of literature and writing. Hu Shi's book of poetry, *Experimental Verses*, was the first collection of modern Chinese poetry written in the vernacular, and I've included one poem from it.

The first selection of prose is by Lu Xun, the preeminent writer of twentieth-century vernacular prose. As background, it is important to know that outstanding short stories were written as early as the Tang dynasty, and such great novels as *The Water Margin* by Shi Nai'an (ca. 1296–1372) and *Dream of the Red Chamber* by Cao Xueqin (1715?–63) had been written in the vernacular long before 1917, so that the New Culture Movement's changes were far less controversial in fiction than in poetry. Lu Xun's 1922 preface to *Call to Arms* describes how he went to Japan to study medicine so that he could help the Chinese people, but one day when he saw, in class, slides of a Chinese man executed by the Japanese, he realized the need to take up the pen to awaken people. Lu Xun's opening to "The True Story of

Ah Q," imbued with irony and social critique, constitutes a chapter-long riff. It foreshadows Gao Xingjian, who many years later, in his novel *Soul Mountain*, disrupts the narration with his own chapter-long riff, "This isn't a novel!" Gao Xingjian responds frequently to Lu Xun's work, but it comes many years later; so a reader is invited to consider the essays, not just in their immediate sequencing, but also, thematically, across time.

From 1917 through 1945, the selections are, roughly, in chronological order. Mao Dun's "Literature and Life" asserts that Chinese literary criticism is historically lacking in discussing what literature is, what kinds of issues it treats, and how it relates to other fields of knowledge. His position exemplifies that of many Chinese writers who felt the literary tradition was bankrupt. Looking to Western literature, Mao Dun appears to absorb some deterministic thinking about a writer's race, environment, and era, but he leaves room for subjective creativity in discussing a writer's personality.

In 1926 a group called the Crescent Moon Society was re-formed in Shanghai. Xu Zhimo, Wen Yiduo, Liang Shiqiu, and Hu Shi were among its leaders, and they favored experimentation with new formal patterns in poetry. Although vernacular free-verse poetry had now established itself, Wen was distressed by the results. He thought most of it "a random and disordered jumble." Wen wanted the free-verse lines of the New Poetry to be rhythmically rigorous and architecturally pleasing. His innovations were in meter, where he developed a line "composed of three disyllabic units and one trisyllabic unit, so that each line has the same number of characters." One can see that Wen, with a profound knowledge of classical Chinese poetry (the Tang five- and seven-character lines have morphed into a nine-character line), is one of the great innovators.

The Nationalists and Communists had split by 1927, and Chinese intellectuals vehemently debated issues of Marxist class struggle and a literature that would promote revolutionary change. The excerpt from Liang Shiqiu's 1928 essay, "Literature and Revolution," picks up many issues discussed by Mao Dun and creates a mini-conversation about literature and social background. Whereas Mao Dun espouses a deterministic relationship between writers and the era they live in, Liang Shiqiu asserts, "*Writers do not give expression to any spirit of the times, it is rather that the times reflect the spirit of writers.*"

"Dai Wangshu's Poetic Theory" creates a dialogue with Wen Yiduo. He introduces French symbolist preoccupations into the discussion of modern Chinese poetry. Whereas Wen stresses rhythmical musicality, Wang prioritizes the nuances of poetic mood, yet both emphasize the discovery of new forms.

In 1936, when the Nationalists and Communists fought the Japanese as a united front, Zhou Zuoren was well aware of the political and social chaos, but he upheld the artistic integrity of the writer with, "I cannot lightly truckle to others." While Zhou also amusingly criticizes himself, Lao She extends self-criticism into significant artistic insight. Lao She stresses clarity and power and asserts, "Experience enriches imagination; imagination determines experience."

By 1942, the Japanese controlled all the coastal areas of China, along with most of the urban and industrial centers, while the Chinese Communist Party was entrenched in northwest Yan'an, and the Guomindang had moved to southwestern Chongqing. During these dark times, Ding Ling published "We Need the Zawen Essay" and asserted the writer must write "for the sake of the truth" and speak up against tyranny; yet one can see the politicization of the writer and the writer's roles when she asserts that "Lu Xun's essays have become China's greatest ideological weapon." While Ding Ling complained about the treatment of women in Yan'an, other writers criticized the lack of free expression and party abuses. Mao Zedong responded with his "Talks at the Yan'an Forum on Literature and Art." In the excerpts, Mao sharply criticizes Liang Shiqiu and Zhou Zuoren, and his position that art must serve the people became law for the 1950s and '60s, when a state-sanctioned propagandistic literature held sway.

Two years after Mao's "Talks," in occupied Shanghai, Eileen Chang composed a seminal essay, "Writing of One's Own." In it, Chang rejects the model of heroic literature and focuses on small intimacies between men and women. When she writes, "This era . . . constitutes my artistic material," she is in conversation with Mao Dun. Eileen Chang empowers the writer more and introduces the idea of equivocation as an artistic tool: "I utilize equivocal contrast as a means of writing the truth beneath the hypocrisy of modern people."

After 1945, it becomes increasingly difficult to follow a linear chronology, and I have deliberately juxtaposed varying voices and visions. The

1950s and '60s were a barren time in China, but writers in Taiwan continued to evolve and grow. On February 1, 1956, Ji Xian proclaimed, in *Modern Poetry*, the formation of the Modernist School (1956–62). His six tenets were a manifesto, and the second tenet—that new poetry entailed "horizontal transplantation" rather than "vertical inheritance"—was especially important. Horizontal transplantation meant drawing inspiration and sustenance from Western literature, while vertical inheritance meant drawing inspiration and sustenance from the tradition of classical Chinese literature.

In Bian Zhilin's 1978 introduction to his collected poems, he affirms "the ancient for modern use, the foreign for Chinese use," in clear contrast with Ji Xian. Ji Xian conceived of an either/or situation in regard to Western and classical Chinese literature, which was appropriate for its time; but Bian Zhilin, writing many years later, wants to utilize both. When Bian discusses rhythm and meter, Wen Yiduo's influence is apparent, but he develops his own prosody with the emphasis on an "*interior* musical meter and rhythm." Ai Qing's brief comments approach poetry from an inspirational point of view and introduce "the way of the imagination."

In the next essays, three leading poets from Taiwan approach poetry from differing viewpoints, but they share a commitment to experimentation. Lo Fu declares that literary tradition can only be continued through innovation. Shang Qin's prose poem, "The Lock Electric," is innovative in making the simple acts of turning a key, opening a door, and stepping inside an *ars poetica*. And Yang Mu states, "Far from being marginal, Taiwan's literature is an avant-garde of unstoppable force."

The next three fiction writers, Jia Pingwa, Li Ang, and Gao Xingjian, present very different aesthetic issues. Jia Pingwa articulates a kind of fiction that is deeply rooted in place. Li Ang focuses on what it is like to be a woman writer, and, like Ding Ling, she asserts the writer's responsibility to tell the truth. Gao Xingjian considers how fiction has moved beyond plot and character to disassemble the notion of a narrator as a single, unified character or voice. In doing so, he shows how far his aesthetic concerns have shifted away from Eileen Chang.

After the Cultural Revolution, Bei Dao and Mang Ke launched *Today* and published a new group of poets, including Gu Cheng, Duo Duo, Shu

Ting, and Yang Lian. Unlike the social-realist poetry of the recent past, their poems employed nuanced, oblique images, and, because they were considered difficult to understand, their poems were called Misty poetry. For many years, Bei Dao was a poet in exile, and insightful comments—"true resistance lies in allowing poetry to separate itself from politics"—are scattered throughout his memoirs. Gu Cheng's interview on Misty poetry (*menglongshi*) makes clear how this movement values suggestion and layering. He also articulates a vision of nature as his poetic teacher and inspiration.

The next group of essays and interviews by four female poets begins by discussing feminine consciousness but quickly moves into discussing issues that expand the range of all contemporary poetry. Zhai Yongming's essay is a manifesto from 1985 that foregrounds inner conflict and the creation of a "Black Night Consciousness." Zhou Zan's essay touches on voice, prosody, language, and memory, and proposes poetic language as a form of landscape. Zhang Er's essay looks at Chinese women's poetry and suggests that the male-dominated poetic tradition can be widened and enriched by drawing on the tradition of female folk songs. In Taiwan, Hsia Yü's linguistic experimentation involves estranging language from its source and provides yet another way contemporary poetry can be made new.

Several more post-Misty poets follow. Haizi extols Hölderlin but is of course articulating his own priorities as a lyric poet. Zang Di's highly influential essay draws on Western critical theory; when he says "accuracy, simplicity, clarity, power, symmetry, and completeness" are applicable to all modern poetry, he is foregrounding post-Misty poetics. Yu Jian's "The Brown Notebook" is a manifesto that advocates rejecting metaphor in order to restore "poetry's naming power," but his later interview qualifies that position. Although Yan Li is associated with the Misty poets, "Thanks for That" is thematically linked to post-Misty poetics in its declarative mode and clarity. I should add that not all the poems included here explicitly mention writing or the writing process. Zhai Yongming's poem exemplifies the Chinese imagination that draws on tradition but also transforms it. Other poems exemplify and clarify various aesthetic positions.

The next essays by Wang Anyi, Can Xue, Xi Xi, Zhang Dachun, Yu Hua, and Mo Yan form a conversation on writing and its sources.

Historically, after the Cultural Revolution, in the 1980s a "root-seeking literature" movement emerged. The writers included Jia Pingwa, Mo Yan, Han Shaogong, and Ah Cheng. These writers sought to find the roots of literature in ancient mythical and philosophical sources and also deep in the countryside. A few years later, a group of experimental writers, such as Yu Hua, Can Xue, Ge Fei, and Su Tong emerged. Although Wang Anyi has early work that fits in the "root-seeking literature," she evolved away from it. In the first essay, Wang describes how she was searching "for a way out" and that as she fell in love with writing, she was "delivered from all of those years of aimless wandering." Can Xue believes in "the grandness of the original power" and, also completely devoted to writing, asserts, "While writing, you have to endure everything, you have to give up all worldly things." Whereas Wang Anyi's essay is personal and unfolds across time, Can Xue's is archetypal and focuses on the moment of creation. Xi Xi, who lives in Hong Kong, inventively brings reading and writing together: "a book is a goatskin raft on the river of . . . life." And Zhang Dachun, who lives in Taiwan, conflates news and fiction into a genre that is "an attempt to interweave 'reality' with 'fiction.'" Yu Hua describes how the impulse of his novel *To Live* is from an American folk song, "Old Black Joe," and although the characters in the song and in his novel are worlds apart, Yu Hua makes an imaginative leap and finds connection in all literature. Mo Yan shows how his grandfather's brother was a magical storyteller by telling stories inside his story, and he also snipes at the literary obsession with innovation.

The final group of essays by Wang Ping, Chen Li, Leung Ping-kwan, Xi Chuan, and Yang Lian form a conversation about language, translation, and poetry. Wang Ping discusses how Chinese as a mother tongue tells her "what to see, where to go," whereas, writing in English, she can "bypass the old ways of seeing and thinking." Living in Taiwan, Chen Li affirms that traditional characters are richer in implication than the simplified ones, and he demonstrates it in "Breakfast Tablecloth." Leung Ping-kwan lives in Hong Kong and describes how translating avant-garde works from the West helped him make his writing "more colloquial, folk-like, and accented with magical symbols." For many years Xi Chuan taught Western literature at the Beijing Art Institute, but in the last five years he has switched to teaching classical Chinese poetry. He distinguishes classical Chinese from modern Chinese and says the gulf is so wide that translating from the first to the second is as difficult as translating from a Western language into modern Chinese. Yang Lian questions this position but ends up in agreement. In another sign that vertical inheritance is reasserting itself, Xi Chuan discusses a great Du Fu poem, while Yang Lian extols and provides an in-depth analysis of another one. Yang Lian believes the ultimate principle of poetry is "to express one's own feelings in one's own words." He ends by saying Du Fu "is marvelous—but what about us?" It is too soon to know. There is no question that from 1917 to 2008, China has undergone astonishing transformations, and the writings included here manifest such change.[1]

In October 2007 I participated in the Pamir Poetry Journey at Huang Shan Mountain. During the one-week festival in Anhui province, intense discussions between Chinese and English-language poets took place. When I returned to the United States, I was haunted by the interlacing of past and present and wrote the following poem, which I hope will help readers envision how all the writers in this collection are part of a cultural flow.

PIG'S HEAVEN INN

Red chiles in a tilted basket catch sunlight—
we walk past a pile of burning mulberry leaves
into Xidi Village, enter a courtyard, notice
an inkstone, engraved with calligraphy, filled
with water and cassia petals, smell Ming
dynasty redwood panels. As a musician lifts
a small *xun* to his mouth and blows, I see kiwis
hanging from branches above a moon doorway:
a grandmother, once the youngest concubine,
propped in a chair with bandages around
her knees, complains of incessant pain;

1. For readers who would like to learn more about modern Chinese literary history, *Modern Chinese Literary Thought: Writings on Literature, 1893–1945*, edited by Kirk A. Denton (Stanford University Press, 1996), and *The Literature of China in the Twentieth Century*, by Bonnie S. McDougall and Kam Louie (Columbia University Press, 1999), are excellent resources.

someone spits in the street. As a second
musician plucks strings on a zither, pomelos
blacken on branches; a woman peels chestnuts;
two men in a flat-bottomed boat gather
duckweed out of a river. The notes splash,
silvery, onto cobblestone, and my fingers
suddenly ache: during the Cultural Revolution,
my aunt's husband leapt out of a third-story
window; at dawn I mistook the cries of
birds for rain. When the musicians pause,
Yellow Mountain pines sway near Bright
Summit Peak; a pig scuffles behind an enclosure;
someone blows his nose. Traces of the past
are wisps of mulberry smoke rising above
roof tiles; and before we too vanish, we hike
to where three trails converge: hundreds
of people are stopped ahead of us, hundreds
come up behind: we form a rivulet of people
funneling down through a chasm in the granite.

*Arthur Sze*
*Santa Fe, New Mexico, 2009*

# *Acknowledgments*

I would like to thank the following people who so generously supported this book: John Balcom, Jody Beenk, Michael Berry, Steve Bradbury, Rosemary Catacalos, Chang Fen-ling, Chen Li, Michael Collier, Kirk Denton, Murray Edmond, Jennifer Feeley, Forrest Gander, Howard Goldblatt, David Hinton, Brian Holton, Andrew Jones, Lucas Klein, Mabel Lee, Sylvia Li-chun Lin, Andrea Lingenfelter, Gerald Maa, Denis Mair, Christopher Mattison, Carol Moldaw, Shin Yu Pai, Simon Patton, Pascale Petit, Frank Stewart, Zona Yi-Ping Tsou, Paula Varsano, Wang Ao, Wang Ping, Eliot Weinberger, Xie Guixia, Yang Lian, Michelle Yeh, Zhang Er, Zhao Si, and Zhou Zan. I would like to thank all the authors who wrote new essays; the translators who shared resources, made new translations, and checked some of my headnotes; and Michelle Yeh for insightful comments to my general introduction.

I would like to thank Barbara Ras and Sarah Nawrocki for their invaluable help and care. And thanks to Edward Hirsch, for inviting and entrusting me to serve as editor. Finally, I would like to thank the Lannan Foundation for their generous support.

# Hu Shi

*(1891–1962)*

Hu Shi was born in Shanghai. In 1910 he received a scholarship to attend Cornell University and initially planned on studying agriculture but, two years later, formally changed his major to literature and philosophy. In 1914 he received his A.B. degree and was accepted into the Ph.D. program at Columbia University, where he studied philosophy with John Dewey. He became Dewey's translator and was strongly influenced by Dewey's empirical and pragmatist thinking. He came to believe that China's modernization must involve writing in the spoken language—rather than in the classical manner—and changing traditional ways of thinking. In 1917, while at Columbia, he published "Some Modest Proposals for the Reform of Literature" in the Chinese journal *New Youth*. Hu's essay helped initiate a literary revolution.

After receiving his Ph.D., Hu returned to China to lecture at Beijing University. He became a leading intellectual and advocated reforms on a great variety of social, political, and literary issues. The Sino-Japanese War interrupted his academic career, and, from 1938 to 1942, he served as Chinese ambassador to the United States. In 1946 he returned to China to become chancellor at Beijing University, but in 1949 had to flee. He returned to the United States, then moved to Taiwan in 1958 to become president of the Academia Sinica Research Institute.

The following excerpt from "Some Modest Proposals for the Reform of Literature" contains Hu's opening statement with his eight tenets, along with his commentary on the first tenet. The rest of the essay goes on to expand on each of the following tenets, but a reader will find here his characteristic style, erudition, and exposition. In Hu Shi's book of poetry *Experiments*, published in 1920, he consciously struggled to elevate the vernacular as the appropriate form for writing poetry. "Dreams and Poetry" was controversial in its time and exemplifies, in his own words, his "poetic empiricism."

## Excerpt from "Some Modest Proposals for the Reform of Literature"

Those engaged in the present discourse on literary reform are myriad. How am I, unlearned and unlettered, qualified to speak on the subject? Yet I have over the past few years, with the benefit of my friends' argumentation, pondered and studied this matter a fair degree, and the results achieved are perhaps not unworthy of discussion. So I summarize the opinions I hold and list them in eight points; I have divided them in this fashion for the investigation of those interested in literary reform.

It is my belief that those wishing to discuss literary reform today should begin with eight matters, which are as follows:

1. Writing should have substance
2. Do not imitate the ancients
3. Emphasize the technique of writing
4. Do not moan without an illness
5. Eliminate hackneyed and formal language
6. Do not use allusions
7. Do not use parallelism
8. Do not avoid vulgar diction

### *1. Writing Should Have Substance*

The greatest malady of letters in our nation today is language without substance.[1] All one ever hears is "If writing is without form, it will not travel

1. The expression *yan zhi you wu* comes from the *Book of Changes* in which the gentleman is exhorted to "have substance in his words" in order to have "stability in his actions";

far."[2] But nothing is said about language without substance, nor what function form should serve. What I mean by substance is not the "literature conveys the *Dao*" [*wen yi zai dao*] of the ancients. What I mean by substance are the two following points:

A. *Feeling.* In the "Great Preface" to the *Book of Songs* is written: "Feelings come from within and are shaped through language. If language is insufficient to express one's feelings, then one may sigh; if sighing is insufficient, then one may chant or sing; if chanting or singing is insufficient, then one may dance with one's hands and feet." This is what I mean by feeling. Feeling is the soul of literature. Literature without feeling is like a man without a soul, nothing but a wooden puppet, a walking corpse. (What people call aesthetic feeling is only one kind of feeling.)

B. *Thought.* By "thought" I mean one's views, perceptions, and ideals. Thought need not depend on literature for transmission, but literature is enriched by thought and thought is enriched by the value of literature. This is why the prose of Zhuang-zi, the poetry of Tao Yuanming and Du Fu, the lyric meters of Xin Qiji, and the fictional narratives of Shi Nai'an are eternal. As the brain is to man's body, so is thought to literature. If a man cannot think, though he be attractive in appearance and capable of laughter, tears, and feelings, is this really sufficient for him? Such is the case with literature. Without these two kinds of substance, literature is like a beauty without a soul or a brain; though she have a lovely and ample exterior, she is nonetheless inferior.[3] The greatest reason for the deterioration of literature is that the literati have become mired in poetics and are without any kind of far-reaching thought or sincere feeling. The harm of an overly formalist literature lies in this so-called language without sub-

---

in *The I Ching, or Book of Changes*, trans. Wilhelm / Baynes (Princeton: Princeton University Press, 1977), 144.

2. Citation of Confucius in the *Zuozhuan* (Zuo commentary), Duke Xiang 25: "yan zhi wu wen, xing zhi bu yuan." The passage has been translated by Owen (1992: 29) as "If the language lacks patterning, it will not go far."

3. Liu Kai (b. 968), an early proponent of the Ancient-Style Prose, also uses this metaphor of woman as text: "Now it is bad if a woman's outer appearance is more cultivated than her inner virtue, but not bad if her inner virtues are more highly cultivated than her appearance. Likewise, with writing it is bad if the words are more splendid than the reasoning, but not bad if the reasoning is more splendid than the words"; cited in Ronald Egan, *The Literary Works of Ou-yang Hsiu* (1007–72) (Cambridge, Eng.: Cambridge University Press, 1984), 15–16.

stance. And should we wish to save it from this fault, we must save it with substance, by which I mean only feeling and thought.

*Translated by Kirk A. Denton*

## Dreams and Poetry

All are ordinary experiences,
All ordinary images;
By chance they surge into a dream,
Turning out many original patterns.

All are ordinary feelings,
All ordinary words;
By chance they encounter a poet,
Turning out many original verses.

Only one who has been drunk knows the strength of wine;
Only one who has loved knows the power of love.
You cannot write my poems
Just as I cannot dream your dreams.

*Translated by Michelle Yeh*

# Lu Xun

*(1881–1936)*

Lu Xun is generally considered the greatest writer of early-twentieth-century China. He was born in Shaoxing, Zhejiang. As a child, he read from his family's library and, later, began reading Chinese classics in school. From 1898 to 1899, he attended the Jiangnan Naval Academy and then attended the School of Mines and Railways. Here he encountered Western learning and read J.S. Mill's *On Liberty.* In 1904 he was the first foreign student to enroll at Sendai Medical Specialty School in Japan to study medicine. He found his studies tedious, however, and abruptly left in March 1906. He moved to Tokyo but, in 1909, when funds ran out, returned to China. In 1912, with the establishment of the Republic of China, he accepted a counselorship at the Ministry of Education in Beijing. In the May 1918 issue of *New Youth,* he published a short story, "A Madman's Diary," and its sharp criticism of antiquated Chinese cultural traditions established him as a leading writer. In 1920 he took part-time teaching positions at Beijing University and Beijing Women's Normal University. "The True Story of Ah Q" was published in serialized form in the *Morning Post Supplement* between 1921 and 1922, and this story became his most famous work. His early short stories were published in *Call to Arms* (1923) and *Wandering* (1926), while early prose poems were collected in *Wild Grass* (1927). From 1927 until his death, Lu Xun lived in

Shanghai, where he co-founded the China League of Left-Wing Writers and was involved in many literary debates. Although he never joined the Chinese Communist Party, he was posthumously canonized.

Lu Xun's preface to *Call to Arms*, which contains fourteen stories written between 1918 and 1922, is a locus classicus. In it, he candidly describes how he went to Japan to study medicine but realized that the most important thing was to awaken people's spirits. In taking up the pen, Lu Xun wrote with clarity and mordant wit. In "The True Story of Ah Q," which is of course fiction, the narrator makes a series of digressions that include the impossibility of ever knowing which characters stand for Ah Q's name.

Ah Q becomes an embodiment of the Chinese spirit. And, finally, when Ah Q becomes a scapegoat and is executed for a robbery he didn't commit, Lu Xun connects his death to the failures of the Republican Revolution, in which the poor are no better off.

## Preface to *Call to Arms*

*Beijing, December 3, 1922*

When I was young I, too, had many dreams. Most of them I later forgot, but I see nothing in this to regret. For although recalling the past may bring happiness, at times it cannot but bring loneliness, and what is the point of clinging in spirit to lonely bygone days? However, my trouble is that I cannot forget completely, and these stories stem from those things which I have been unable to forget.

For more than four years I frequented, almost daily, a pawnshop and pharmacy. I cannot remember how old I was at the time, but the pharmacy counter was exactly my height and that in the pawnshop twice my height. I used to hand clothes and trinkets up to the counter twice my height, then take the money given me with contempt to the counter my own height to buy medicine for my father, a chronic invalid. On my return home I had other things to keep me busy, for our physician was so eminent that he prescribed unusual drugs and adjuvants: aloe roots dug up in winter, sugarcane that had been three years exposed to frost, original pairs of crickets, and ardisia that had seeded . . . most of which were difficult to come by. But my father's illness went from bad to worse until finally he died.

It is my belief that those who come down in the world will probably learn in the process what society is really like. My eagerness to go to N— and study in the K— Academy seems to have shown a desire to strike out for myself, escape, and find people of a different kind.[1] My mother had no choice but to raise eight dollars for my traveling expenses and say I might do as I pleased. That she cried was only natural, for at that time the proper thing was to study the classics and take the official examinations. Anyone who studied "foreign subjects" was a social outcast, regarded as someone who could find no way out and was forced to sell his soul to foreign devils. Besides, she was sorry to part with me. But in spite of all this, I went to N— and entered the K— Academy; and it was there that I learned of the existence of physics, arithmetic, geography, history, drawing, and physical training. They had no physiology course, but we saw woodblock editions of such works as *A New Course on the Human Body* and *Essays on Chemistry and Hygiene*.[2] Recalling the talk and prescriptions of physicians I had known and comparing them with what I now knew, I came to the conclusion that those physicians must be either unwitting or deliberate charlatans; and I began to feel great sympathy for the invalids and families who suffered at their hands. From translated histories I also learned that the Japanese Reformation owed its rise, to a great extent, to the introduction of Western medical science to Japan.

These inklings took me to a medical college in the Japanese countryside.[3] It was my fine dream that on my return to China I would cure patients like my father who had suffered from the wrong treatment, while if war broke out I would serve as an army doctor, at the same time promoting my countrymen's faith in reform.

1. N— refers to Nanjing, and K— to the Kiangnan (Jiangnan) Naval Academy where the author studied in 1898.

2. Two English books about physiology and nutrition, the former was translated into Chinese and published in 1851, the latter in 1879.

3. This refers to the Sendai Medical College where Lu Xun studied from 1904 to 1906.

I have no idea what improved methods are now used to teach microbiology, but in those days we were shown lantern slides of microbes; and if the lecture ended early, the instructor might show slides of natural scenery or news to fill up the time. Since this was during the Russo-Japanese War, there were many war slides, and I had to join in the clapping and cheering in the lecture hall along with the other students. It was a long time since I had seen any compatriots, but one day I saw a newsreel slide of a number of Chinese, one of them bound and the rest standing around him. They were all sturdy fellows but appeared completely apathetic. According to the commentary, the one with his hands bound was a spy working for the Russians who was to be beheaded by the Japanese military as a warning to others, while the Chinese beside him had come to enjoy the spectacle.

Before the term was over I had left for Tokyo, because this slide convinced me that medical science was not so important after all. The people of a weak and backward country, however strong and healthy they might be, could only serve to be made examples of or as witnesses of such futile spectacles; and it was not necessarily deplorable if many of them died of illness. The most important thing, therefore, was to change their spirit; and since at that time I felt that literature was the best means to this end, I decided to promote a literary movement. There were many Chinese students in Tokyo studying law, political science, physics and chemistry, even police work and engineering, but not one studying literature and art. However, even in this uncongenial atmosphere I was fortunate enough to find some kindred spirits. We gathered the few others we needed, and after discussion our first step, of course, was to publish a magazine, the title of which denoted that this was a new birth. As we were then rather classically inclined, we called it *Vita Nova* (*New Life*).

When the time for publication drew near, some of our contributors dropped out and then our funds ran out, until there were only three of us left and we were penniless. Since we had started our venture at an unlucky hour, there was naturally no one to whom we could complain when we failed; but later even we three were destined to part, and our discussions of a future dream world had to cease. So ended this abortive *Vita Nova*.

Only later did I feel the futility of it all. At that time I had not a clue. Later it seemed to me that if a man's proposals met with approval, that should encourage him to advance; if they met with opposition, that should make him fight back; but the real tragedy was for him to lift up his voice among the living and meet with no response, neither approval nor opposition, just as if he were stranded in a boundless desert completely at a loss. That was when I became conscious of loneliness.

And this sense of loneliness grew from day to day, entwining itself about my soul like some huge poisonous snake.

But in spite of my groundless sadness, I felt no indignation; for this experience had made me reflect and see that I was definitely not the type of hero who could rally multitudes at his call.

However, my loneliness had to be dispelled because it was causing me agony. So I used various means to dull my senses, to immerse myself among my fellow nationals and to turn to the past. Later I experienced or witnessed even greater loneliness and sadness, which I am unwilling to recall, preferring that it should perish with my mind in the dust. Still my attempt to deaden my senses was not unsuccessful—I lost the enthusiasm and fervor of my youth.

In S— Hostel was a three-roomed house with a courtyard in which grew a locust tree, and it was said that a woman had hanged herself there.[4] Although the tree had grown so tall that its branches were now out of reach, the rooms remained deserted. For some years I stayed here, copying ancient inscriptions. I had few visitors, the inscriptions raised no political problems or issues, and so the days slipped quietly away, which was all that I desired. On summer nights, when mosquitoes swarmed, I would sit under the locust tree waving my fan and looking at specks of blue sky through chinks in the thick foliage, while belated caterpillars would fall, icy-cold, on to my neck.

The only visitor to drop in occasionally for a talk was my old friend Jin Xinyi. Having put his big portfolio on the rickety table, he would take off his long gown and sit down opposite me, looking as if his heart was still beating fast because he was afraid of dogs.

"What's the use of copying these?" One night, while leafing through the inscriptions I had copied, he asked me for enlightenment on this point.

4. The Shaoxing Hostel where Lu Xun stayed in Beijing from 1912 to 1919.

"There isn't any use."

"What's the point, then, of copying them?"

"There isn't any point."

"Why don't you write something? . . ."

I understood. They were bringing out *New Youth*,[5] but since there did not seem to have been any reaction, favorable or otherwise, no doubt they felt lonely. However I said:

"Imagine an iron house having not a single window and virtually indestructible, with all its inmates sound asleep and about to die of suffocation. Dying in their sleep, they won't feel the pain of death. Now if you raise a shout to wake a few of the lighter sleepers, making these unfortunate few suffer the agony of irrevocable death, do you really think you are doing them a good turn?"

"But if a few wake up, you can't say there is no hope of destroying the iron house."

True, in spite of my own conviction, I could not blot out hope, for hope belongs to the future. I had no negative evidence able to refute his affirmation of faith. So I finally agreed to write, and the result was my first story, "A Madman's Diary." And once started I could not give up but would write some sort of short story from time to time to humor my friends, until I had written more than a dozen of them.

As far as I am concerned, I no longer feel any great urge to express myself; yet, perhaps because I have not forgotten the grief of my past loneliness, I sometimes call out to encourage those fighters who are galloping on in loneliness, so that they do not lose heart. Whether my cry is brave or sad, repellent or ridiculous, I do not care. However, since this is a call to arms I must naturally obey my general's orders. This is why I often resort to innuendoes, as when I made a wreath appear from nowhere at the son's grave in "Medicine," while in "Tomorrow" I did not say that Fourth Shan's Wife never dreamed of her little boy. For our chiefs in those days were against pessimism. And I, for my part, did not want to infect with the

5. This magazine played an important part in the May Fourth Movement of 1919 by attacking feudalism, advocating the New Culture Movement and spreading Marxist ideas. Jin Xinyi is an alias for Qian Xuantong, one of the editors of *New Youth*. Lu Xun was an important contributor to the magazine.

loneliness which I had found so bitter those young people who were still dreaming pleasant dreams, just as I had done when young.

It is clear, then, that my stories fall far short of being works of art; hence I must at least count myself fortunate that they are still known as stories and are even being brought out in one volume. Although such good fortune makes me uneasy, it still pleases me to think that they have readers in the world of men, for the time being at any rate.

So now that these stories of mine are being reprinted in one collection, for the reasons given above I have chosen to entitle it *Call to Arms*.

*Translated by Yang Xianyi & Gladys Yang*

## Chapter I from "The True Story of Ah Q"

### *Introduction*

For several years now I have been meaning to write the true story of Ah Q. But while wanting to write I was in some trepidation too, which goes to show that I am not one of those who achieve glory by writing; for an immortal pen has always been required to record the deeds of an immortal man, the man becoming known to posterity through the writing and the writing known to posterity through the man—until finally it is not clear who is making whom known. But in the end, as though possessed by some fiend, I always came back to the idea of writing the story of Ah Q.

And yet no sooner had I taken up my pen than I became conscious of tremendous difficulties in writing this far-from-immortal work. The first was the question of what to call it. Confucius said, "If the name is not correct, the words will not ring true"; and this axiom should be most scrupulously observed. There are many types of biography: official biographies, autobiographies, unauthorized biographies, legends, supplementary biographies, family histories, sketches . . . but unfortunately none of these suited my purpose. "Official biography"? This account will obviously not be included with those of many eminent people in some authentic history. "Autobiography"? But I am obviously not Ah Q. If I were to call this an "unauthorized biography," then where is his "authenticated biography"? The use of "legend" is impossible because Ah Q was no legendary figure. "Supplementary biography"? But no president has ever ordered the National Historical Institute to write a "standard life" of Ah Q. It is true that although there are no "lives of gamblers" in authentic English history, the well-known author Conan Doyle nevertheless wrote *Rodney Stone;* but while this is permissible for a well-known author it is not permissible for such as I. Then there is "family history"; but I do not know whether I belong to the same family as Ah Q or not, nor have his children or grandchildren ever entrusted me with such a task. If I were to use "sketch," it might be objected that Ah Q has no "complete account." In short, this is really a "life," but since I write in vulgar vein using the language of hucksters and peddlers, I dare not presume to give it so high-sounding a title. So I will take as my title the last two words of a stock phrase of the novelists, who are not reckoned among the Three Cults and Nine Schools.[6] "Enough of this digression, and back to the *true story*"; and if this is reminiscent of the *True Story of Calligraphy* of the ancients, it cannot be helped.[7]

The second difficulty confronting me was that a biography of this type should start off something like this: "So-and-so, whose other name was so-and-so, was a native of such-and-such a place"; but I don't really know what Ah Q's surname was. Once, he seemed to be named Zhao, but the next day there was some confusion about the matter again. This was after Mr. Zhao's son had passed the county examination and, to the sound of gongs, his success was announced in the village. Ah Q, who had just drunk two bowls of yellow wine, began to prance about declaring that this reflected credit on him too, since he belonged to the same clan as Mr. Zhao and by an exact reckoning was three generations senior to the successful candidate. At the time several bystanders even began to stand slightly in awe of Ah Q. But the next day the bailiff summoned him to Mr. Zhao's house. When the old gentleman set eyes on him, his face turned crimson with fury and he roared:

"Ah Q, you miserable wretch! Did you say I belonged to the same clan as you?"

6. The Three Cults were Confucianism, Buddhism, and Taoism. The Nine Schools included the Confucian, Taoist, Legalist, Mohist, and other schools.

7. A book by Feng Wu of the Qing dynasty (1644–1911).

Ah Q made no reply.

The more he looked at him the angrier Mr. Zhao became. Advancing menacingly a few steps he said, "How dare you talk such nonsense! How could I have such a relative as you? Is your surname Zhao?"

Ah Q made no reply and was planning a retreat, when Mr. Zhao darted forward and gave him a slap on the face.

"How could *you* be named Zhao? Are you worthy of the name Zhao?"

Ah Q made no attempt to defend his right to the name Zhao but, rubbing his left cheek, went out with the bailiff from whom, once outside, he had to listen to another torrent of abuse. He then by way of atonement paid him two hundred cash. All who heard this said Ah Q was a great fool to ask for a beating like that. Even if his surname *were* Zhao—which wasn't likely—he should have known better than to boast like that when there was a Mr. Zhao living in the village. After this no further mention was made of Ah Q's ancestry, thus I still have no idea what his surname really was.

The third difficulty I encountered in writing this work was that I don't know how Ah Q's personal name should be written either. During his lifetime everybody called him Ah Gui, but after his death not a soul mentioned Ah Gui again; for he was obviously not one of those whose name is "preserved on bamboo tablets and silk."[8] If there is any question of preserving his name, this essay must be the first attempt at doing so. Hence I am confronted with this difficulty at the outset. I have given the question careful thought. Ah Gui—would that be the "Gui" meaning fragrant osmanthus or the "Gui" meaning nobility? If his other name had been Moon Pavilion, or if he had celebrated his birthday in the month of the Moon Festival, then it would certainly be the "Gui" for fragrant osmanthus.[9] But since he had no other name—or if he had, no one knew it—and since he never sent out invitations on his birthday to secure complimentary verses, it would be arbitrary to write Ah Gui (fragrant osmanthus). Again, if he had had an elder or younger brother called Ah Fu (prosperity), then he would certainly be called Ah Gui (nobility). But he was all on his own;

8. A phrase used before paper was invented when bamboo and silk served as writing material in China.

9. The fragrant osmanthus blooms in the month of the Moon Festival. And according to Chinese folklore, the shadow on the moon is an osmanthus tree.

thus there is no justification for writing Ah Gui (nobility). All the other, unusual characters with the sound *gui* are even less suitable. I once put this question to Mr. Zhao's son, the successful county candidate, but even such a learned man as he was baffled by it. According to him, however, the reason why this name could not be traced was that Chen Duxiu had brought out the magazine *New Youth* advocating the use of the Western alphabet, hence the national culture was going to the dogs.[10] As a last resort, I asked someone from my district to go and look up the legal documents recording Ah Q's case, but after eight months he sent me a letter saying that there was no name anything like Ah Gui in those records. Although uncertain whether this was the truth or whether my friend had simply done nothing, after failing to trace the name this way I could think of no other means of finding it. Since I am afraid the new system of phonetics has not yet come into common use, there is nothing for it but to use the Western alphabet, writing the name according to the English spelling as Ah Gui and abbreviating it to Ah Q. This approximates to blindly following *New Youth*, and I am thoroughly ashamed of myself; but since even such a learned man as Mr. Zhao's son could not solve my problem, what else can I do?

My fourth difficulty was with Ah Q's place of origin. If his surname were Zhao, then according to the old custom which still prevails of classifying people by their district, one might look up the commentary in *The Hundred Surnames* and find "Native of Tianshui in Gansu."[11] But unfortunately this surname is open to question, with the result that Ah Q's place of origin must also remain uncertain. Although he lived for the most part in Weizhuang, he often stayed in other places, so that it would be wrong to call him a native of Weizhuang. It would, in fact, amount to a distortion of history.

The only thing that consoles me is the fact that the character "Ah" is absolutely correct. This is definitely not the result of false analogy, and is well able to stand the test of scholarly criticism. As for the other problems, it is not for such unlearned people as myself to solve them, and I can only

10. Chen Duxiu (1880–1942) was then chief editor of *New Youth*, the magazine which gave the lead in the movement for a new culture.

11. *The Hundred Surnames* was a school primer in which surnames were written into verse.

hope that disciples of Dr. Hu Shi, who has such "a passion for history and research," may be able in the future to throw new light on them. I am afraid, however, that by that time my "True Story of Ah Q" will have long since passed into oblivion.

The foregoing may be considered as an introduction.

*Translated by Yang Xianyi & Gladys Yang*

# Mao Dun

*(1896–1981)*

Mao Dun was a prolific and versatile novelist, literary critic, translator, playwright, essayist, and advocate of Chinese communism. He was born in Zhejiang Province and received his early, formative education from his mother. In 1913 he entered Beijing University, where he studied Chinese and Western literature. Due to financial problems, he left before graduating and moved to Shanghai, where he got a job as a proofreader for the Commercial Press. In 1920, as editor of *The Short Story*, he featured translations of Tolstoy, Chekhov, Balzac, Flaubert, and Zola and published new works by Lu Xun and others. He introduced Western masterpieces into China with the goal of invigorating and developing modern Chinese fiction. In 1921 he joined the Shanghai Communist Team and helped found the Chinese Communist Party. He lived in Shanghai and worked on a trilogy, *Eclipse,* which, published in 1928, received widespread acclaim. From 1949 to 1965, Mao Dun served as minister of culture. He did not produce any major works after 1949 but continued to write essays and encourage younger writers.

Mao Dun's fiction is written in a realistic vein and is notable for its objective observations. Much of his work presents social communities in China in the late 1920s and early 1930s on the eve of a revolution, and his complex, psychological depictions transcend any easy political agenda. His major works include *Rainbow* (1929), "Spring Silkworms" (1932), and *Midnight*

(1933). Mao's lecture "Literature and Life," given in 1922 and published in 1923, introduces the idea of literature as a reflection of life and discusses their connections by considering issues of race, environment, era, and the writer's personality.

My topic for today is literature and life.[1] The Chinese have always imagined that literature is not something needed by ordinary people. Only self-satisfied people of leisure and highbrow taste were thought of as concerning themselves with literature. To be sure, throughout its history there have been in China a great many works of literature, poetry, lyrics, fiction, etc. On the other hand, works that treated the questions of what literature is, of what kind of issues it treats, have been very few and far between: equally rare has been that type of work which instructs us how to read a piece of literature or how to critique one. Liu Xie's *Literary Mind and the Carving of Dragons* might be considered a specialized treatment of literary issues: on closer examination, however, it also falls short because Liu Xie did not come to grips with the problem of literariness, etc. He merely defined the various forms of literature by the application of subjective criteria. As for what is a regulated verse poem [*shi*], what is a prose poem [*fu*], *The Literary Mind and the Carving of Dragons* provides a subjective definition but fails entirely to analyze or study individual works. Nor do we find any treatment of questions such as "What does poetry convey?" in the *Twenty-four Moods of Poetry* of Sikong Tu.[2] However we look at it, the fact is that there are countless works of literature, but theoretical works about literature are very few indeed. Consequently, there has been no clear-cut

1. Shen Yanbing (Mao Dun), "Wenxue yu rensheng"; originally presented as a lecture in August 1922, to the Songjiang diyici shuqi xueshu yanjianghui and published in *Xueshu yanjianglu* (1923); reprinted in *Mao Dun zhuanji,* 2 vols. (Fujian renmin, 1982), 1, no. 2: 1052–56.

2. *Ershisi shipin* by Sikong Tu (837–908) is a series of twenty-four tetrasyllabic poems describing various poetic moods. James J. Y. Liu (1973: 35–36) sees this work as one of the leading examples of a metaphysical view of literature that stresses the poet's apprehension of the Dao.

demarcation in China between literature and various other fields such as philosophy or philology.

Those who have commented upon literature have done so mainly by criticizing its rhetoric and paying virtually no attention to its ideas. As for the relationship between literature and other fields of knowledge, this has not even been broached. In approaching this topic, there are almost no sources within Chinese writing to which one can refer. Thus I have little choice but to first discuss what some Westerners have written about literature and then take up the question of whether or not there has been any relationship between literature and life within China's literature.

One of the most prevalent formulations among Western experts writing about literature is "Literature is a reflection of life." How people live, their social conditions, these are all reflected by literature. For example, if we take life as a cup, literature would be the reflection of that cup in a mirror. Thus we may say, "The background of literature is society." By "background" is meant the place whence it derives. Take, for instance, a piece of fiction that describes the conditions under which a family prospers and then declines; would we not necessarily want to know during which dynasty this took place? Supposing the work had been set in the time of the Qianlong emperor of the Qing dynasty, we would then look at the writing and assess whether or not it actually achieved a convincing likeness of the Qianlong period. Only if the work met that criterion would it be deemed successful.

There is nothing extraordinary about what I have said in the last two sentences above. Even so, from these two sentences we probably can surmise what literature is, although it cannot be denied that included within literature are some works that transcend normal life and some that create idealized worlds. Literary works of this kind can be very good indeed, but all such works lack a social context. As we now consider the relationship between literature and life, it does not suffice to merely illustrate the "social context." We may discuss this further by subdividing it into the following four items:

1. *Race* [*renzhong*]. Literature and race are closely connected. Just as there are different races, so there are different modes of literary expression; each race has its own literature exactly as it has its own skin, hair, eyes, etc.

Generally speaking, each race has its own distinctive quality; the Oriental races [*minzu*] have a strong mystical streak, and their literature is thus also supernatural. By the same token the character of each race and its literature are interrelated. The Teutons are tough and stoic and moreover have the quality of moderation; the same is true of their literature. Even if they write a love story, when it reaches a sorrowful ending, the emotional intensity will never be as unbridled as would a Frenchman's. In their delineation of character and description of their characters' feelings, French writers are very passionate. Suppose a character has something weighing on his mind and wants a drink, an Englishman will just quaff some beer whereas the Frenchman will necessarily go for the more potent brandy. In comparing the English with the French, this makes for a very apt metaphor. Those points of comparison in literature are equally obvious.

2. *Environment.* We live here and are surrounded by what? Let's suppose we are Songjiang people, then Songjiang society is my environment. What kind of family do I have, what kind of friends—that is all part of my environment. The influence of environment on literature is extremely powerful. For people in Shanghai, a literary work will invariably take up the conditions of Shanghai; for people engaged in revolution, discourse is invariably imbued with revolutionary spirit; as for someone born into a wealthy family, even though he may ardently side with the common people, there will be times when a certain air of being highborn will unexpectedly manifest itself.

Each era has its own environment and also has its own literature belonging to that era and environment. Now, environment is not strictly limited to the physical world—contemporary ideological trends, the political situation, social customs, and practices all go into the environment of a given period. The influence of his environment is constantly and stealthily at work upon any writer, it being quite impossible for him to shake loose from it or become independent of it. Even in the case of a mystic poet who is probing the mysteries of the universe and whose literary creation seems to have no connection with his environment—that is to say, never even refers to the environment—the ideas in his work will nonetheless be directly related to his overall environment. Even if a poem is directly opposed to the ideological trends of the period, it is still related to them. Thus the poet's "anti" [stance] is a response to the stimulus of the era's dominant values, not something that just pops up out of nowhere.

As for positive examples, these are beyond counting throughout the history of literature. For instance, it was France that produced George Sand and that group of important writers who witnessed the second revolution and restoration; the characters they depicted were thus all situated in the environment of France of that time. Even though adherence to revolutionary ideals forced Sand to flee abroad, the flavor of France at this time nonetheless suffuses all of this writer's works. To cite an example from right in front of our noses, here in Shanghai what we see are streetcars and automobiles and what we listen to is mainly the intelligentsia; so in the case of fiction, it is simply out of the question for us to detach ourselves from our environment and to try to write about life in the mountains or villages.

The pastoral poetry of the English [*sic*] poet Robert Burns now is widely acclaimed by people for its excellence, its beauty and serenity, whereas writers who wrote about the conditions in large cities at the end of the nineteenth century are being called degenerate by some people. This is all a consequence of environment. By the same token, there were a great many poets in Germany at the same period who were fed up with urban life and went out to write about the countryside, but the fact that they were wistfully gazing at it from afar is instantly discernible. This example is but the other side of the same coin.

It is clear that there is an extremely close connection between environment and literature: only living within a certain environment can one create that environment in writing; nor can anyone living within a certain environment jump out of it to portray a different one successfully. There are those who claim that the scope of recent Chinese fiction is too narrow—that is, those works that deal with romantic love limit themselves to middle-school students, those that center on family life treat only the commonplace and trivial, and those of a humanitarian bent concern themselves with naught but accounts of rickshaw men hauling their passengers around, etc. Actually this is not because we Chinese lack the capability of writing better works than these; rather, it is because the writers' environment is like this. If a writer intends to write about the life of society's lower stratum and the only thing he sees is the rickshaw puller at work, how is he going to be able to write about something else?

3. *Era* [*shidai*]. Perhaps *shidai* is an inadequate translation. The sense of the English word, *Epoch*, even includes the intellectual trends of the times, the social conditions, etc. Possibly the word *shishi* [the trend of the times] would come closer. By now everyone has heard of this term, *shidai jingshen* [Zeitgeist, or spirit of the times]. The Zeitgeist governing politics, philosophy, literature, art, etc. is as inseparable from them as a shadow from shape. That the writers of each era have a distinctive appearance, necessarily share a common tendency, is the result of the Zeitgeist. Naturally there are exceptions, but in general this is the case.

We have often heard it said that the Han dynasty had its own literary style just as the Wei-Jin period had its own—this is precisely because the Han had its Zeitgeist and the Wei-Jin period had its Zeitgeist. Modern Western literature is realist because science forms the spirit of the times. Because the scientific spirit emphasizes the pursuit of truth, literature also takes the pursuit of truth as its sole purpose. Just as the approach of the scientist emphasizes objective observation, that of the literary artist emphasizes objective description. In accordance with the pursuit of truth, in accordance with emphasizing objective description, it follows that whatever meets one's eye will determine what one writes. In our proper respect for individuality, it would be wrong to refuse to speak out merely for fear of being misunderstood or just because everyone else might consider something to be abnormal or bad. Our mouths should voice whatever we feel in our hearts. We need true honesty, not deception. This is an example of the modern Zeitgeist revealing itself in literature and art.

4. *The writer's personality* [*zuojia de renge*]. The writer's personality is of extreme importance. Revolutionaries will definitely write revolutionary literature; nature lovers will certainly suffuse their writings with nature. The resolute, unique personality of the Russian writer Tolstoy appears in his literature. The works of a major author, albeit influenced by the era and environment, will inevitably be imbued with the author's personality. In this vein it was the French writer Anatole France who claimed, "any work of literature, strictly speaking, is the autobiography of the author."

The above is Western critical thinking, and this line of thinking was not to be found previously in China. Nonetheless, Chinese literature can also serve to prove each of these four points. In the first instance, the temperament of the Chinese [race] is expressed by Chinese literature—we care not for reality, being partial rather to the mysterious and to seeking compromise in all things. Chinese fiction, no matter whether good or bad, must always conclude with a happy reunion: this is not evidence of taking things to extremes. Thus in the category of race, it may be stated that there is no contradiction here [i.e., Chinese literature conforms to Chinese cultural traits]. In the second instance, the category of environment is even more obviously confirmed. The environment of Chinese literature is, naturally, the Chinese family-centered society. In the third instance, although at first glance we might fail to detect any clear indication of the relationship between the era and Chinese literature, when we look closely, there it is. As has long been noted by those commenting on Chinese literature, the prose poem of the Han dynasty is not the same as the prose poem of the Wei and Jin dynasties. Likewise the regulated verse of the early Tang, the high Tang, and the late Tang dynasty differs each from the other. Any one of Li Shangyin's poems would never be placed among those of the four great poets from the early Tang. Whether in composition or prosody, because they derive from different eras, these works are completely distinct. The writing employed in *A New Account of Tales of the World* is quite different in syntax and in tone from that of other works;[3] the same is true of the Song *Dialogues.*[4] They, too, are different from *The Water Margin* and from the *Anecdotes from the Xuanhe Reign Period.*[5] These differences all stem from the differing atmosphere of each era. The works differ not only in ideology but in tone and prosody as well. The influence of the era is also very powerful.

As for personality, real authors (as opposed to those who will stoop to anything in the pursuit of fame) invest their works with something of their

3. *Shishuo xinyu*, by Liu Yiqing (403–444). Considered one of the most important collections of *zhiguai* stories, arguably the earliest of Chinese fictional narratives.

4. Mao Dun uses the title *Songren yulu*, which must refer to the *Er Cheng yulu*, collected dialogues of the Song neo-Confucianists Cheng Yi and Cheng Hao.

5. *Xuanhe yishi* is a semifictional Yuan work relating the events of the fall of the Northern Song dynasty. It is considered an important source for *The Water Margin*. For a translation of this work, see William O. Hennessey, *Proclaiming Harmony* (Ann Arbor: University of Michigan Center for Chinese Studies, 1981).

own personalities. Consequently, these four linkages between literature and life are also to be found in Chinese literature.

This, in a nutshell, explains the relationship of literature to life. From this, we should derive the following lesson: those who would study literature must at least possess a commonsense understanding of race, must at least understand the era and environment that produced this type of literary work, must at least comprehend the Zeitgeist in which it was produced, and moreover must at least understand the life and mentality of the person who created this type of literary work.

*Translated by John Berninghausen*

# Wen Yiduo

*(1899–1946)*

Wen Yiduo was born on November 24, 1899, in a small village in Hubei. He received a traditional education and, passing a government-sponsored examination, entered Qinghua College in Beijing. From 1913 to 1922, he followed a Western curriculum and acquired a great enthusiasm for the English Romantic poets, especially John Keats. During this time, he became involved with the May Fourth Movement. After the movement subsided, he wrote his first poem in the vernacular. In 1922 he came to the United States and studied painting at the Art Institute of Chicago. A year later, he transferred to Colorado College and studied English literature. While there, his first book of poetry, *Red Candle*, was published. In 1924 he moved to New York and entered the Arts Student League but attended no classes. In 1925 he returned to China to become the dean of the new Institute of Art in Beijing and thereafter held a succession of university positions. In 1928 his second, landmark book of poetry, *Dead Water*, was published. He co-founded the Crescent Moon Society and contributed essays on poetry. In 1932 he joined the faculty of Qinghua University in Beijing. In 1937, at the beginning of the Sino-Japanese War, he relocated to Kunming and taught at National Southwestern Associated University. He became politically active and, on July 15,

1946, gave an impassioned speech denouncing the Guomindang. He was assassinated later that day.

Although Wen Yiduo wrote in the vernacular, he had a keen interest in the Chinese classics, and his work shows a confluence of the two. As a leading proponent of the Crescent Moon school, he was interested in the musical, visual, and architectural elements of poetry. His essay "Form in Poetry," published in 1926, is a major statement on poetics that fully delineates his views about formal properties and "dancing in fetters." His poem "Dead Water," written in the vernacular, subverts some Tang dynasty imagery (Li Bo once wrote, "peach blossoms drop into flowing water") and marks the fulfillment of his innovative poetics.

## Form in Poetry

*I*

If we were to use "game theory" to explain the origins of art, we could compare poetry to chess; you can't play chess without rules, nor can you compose poetry without form. (We employ the Chinese term *gelü* here to stand in for the English term "form.") Although the word *gelü* has taken on some negative connotations of late, it wouldn't be appropriate to use the terms *xingti* ("shape") or *geshi* ("format") either. Furthermore, if we think of form and rhythm as similar, then there's really nothing wrong with translating "form" as *gelü*. If you were to set up your chess pieces at random and play without any rules, do you really think you'd have much fun? The pleasure of games comes from the sort of unexpected turns that happen only within the confines of a fixed set of rules. The pleasure of poetry is the same. If poetry didn't need form, wouldn't it be that much easier than a game of chess, or playing ball or mahjong? Small wonder that in recent years New Poetry has become "even more plentiful than bamboo shoots after the rain." This won't be music to everyone's ears, but Professor Bliss Perry is even more adamant: "Few poets, furthermore, will admit that they are really in bondage to their stanzas. They love to dance in these fetters, especially those of other poets."[1]

I am certain that if this statement were to make the rounds, a lot of people would jump to their feet and shout, "If that's poetry, then it's not for me!" To be perfectly honest, it would be just fine if these people didn't write poetry; because if they don't intend to don any fetters, their poetry will never achieve a very high level of accomplishment. Du Fu offers us these words of wisdom, and it would be worth our while to reflect on them: "In my old age, I've grown more attentive to the rules of poetry."

Revolutionaries in the Land of Poetry raise the cry "Back to Nature!" But in fact, they should recognize that form as it exists in the natural world, while sometimes no more than the tracery of spiderwebs and hoofprints, is always there if we look for it. Nonetheless, the forms found in nature are often flawed or incomplete and require art to make them whole. It follows that absolute realism amounts to nothing other than the bankruptcy of art. "Art begins where Nature leaves off." Oscar Wilde was right on the mark. Nature is not always beautiful. When there is beauty in Nature, it is a beauty akin to Art. The best proof of this is to be found in the plastic arts. Often, when praising a beautiful landscape, we say it's as pretty as a picture. Indeed, Chinese people apply the standards of Chinese landscape painting to their appraisal of beautiful scenery. In Europe, pre-Renaissance standards of feminine beauty, as we can see from the paintings of the period, are completely different from modern conceptions of feminine beauty; but current standards of feminine beauty are in accord with the ideals embodied in ancient Greek sculpture. This is because the excavation of Greek statues was the inspiration for Renaissance art; and ever since the Renaissance, Greek sculpture has been the blueprint for artistic representations of beautiful women, and has remade European conceptions of feminine beauty. I've noticed a similar observation in a poem by Zhao Yi (1727–1814):

1. Perry's original text reads: "And few poets, furthermore, will admit that they are really in bondage to their stanzas. They love to dance in these fetters, and even when wearing the same fetters as another poet, they nevertheless invent movements of their own, so that Mr. Masefield's 'Chaucerian' stanzas are really not so much Chaucer's as Masefield's." Bliss Perry, A Study of Poetry, Chapter Six.

Just like a basin filled with water, these gathered jade cliffs
Ornament the sky, these bamboo shoots of stone fill the river cove.
The forces of creation delight in creating new scenes as well,
Even patterning real mountains on the false.

This is a clear statement that Nature can imitate Art. Of course, Nature is not entirely lacking in beauty. One can also find beauty in Nature, but only should one happen upon it. We might also happen upon rhythms in speech that resemble poetry. This might tempt us to say that speech is poetry and that we may do away with meter, making poetry no different from speech—this would truly be a suicidal course for poetry. (Please note that by no means am I opposed to the use of colloquial language in poetry; in fact I believe that common speech is the province of our New Poetry, one with very fertile soil indeed. We will discuss this in more detail later. For the moment, we will simply note that colloquial language is something with which we can "compose" poetry; I use the word "compose" in order to elucidate the point that colloquial language must undergo a process of selection and tempering—must be tempered before it can become poetry.) The ability of poetry to stimulate feelings stems entirely from its rhythm; and rhythm is form. Throughout Shakespeare's plays, at moments of heightened dramatic tension, the playwright uses rhymes to convey this. Goethe used the same technique in *Faust* and even mentioned it in a letter to Schiller. As was once said of Han Yu (768–824), "when he found a challenging rhyme, he would not look for a way out; for difficulty brings out skill, and the narrower the confines the more marvelous the result . . ." I suspect that the stronger the writer, the greater the chance is that he won't be happy unless he is dancing in fetters, nor will he dance well without those fetters. Only those who cannot dance will fault the fetters for being an impediment, and only those who cannot write poetry will feel immobilized by form. For those who cannot write poetry, form represents an obstacle; but for a writer, form is a well-honed instrument of expression.

There are also those who hold aloft the banners of Romanticism in the assault against form. I have only one thing to say to such people: if they want to bandy about terms like "Romanticism" the way so many of them do these days, they might as well admit that they're not really sincere about creating art. Because if we look at what they've achieved, they simply haven't treated Art as important. Their objective is merely to reveal the unadorned Self. Narcissistic youths, to a man, think that there is nothing finer or more beautiful than themselves, and that all they have to do is bare all in order to create great art. Haven't you heard them singing their perpetual song of "Self Expression"? Indeed, all they are acquainted with are the raw materials of art, and they know nothing of the tools required to transform these raw materials into art. That they use words as tools for expression is purely accidental. The work that they find truly satisfying is exposing the "self," letting the world know how talented, artistic, and long-suffering "I" am. And oh, yes, they can gaze into the mirror of Art and see their untrammeled charm, along with a few deeply felt tears! How fascinating! How Romantic! But this is all the romance that there is in their "Romanticism," and it bears no relationship with a school of artistic thought. But since these people's objective isn't Art, following poetic form in their poetry is more than they can manage. Within the limits of poetic form, their poetry simply cannot be written; for under these circumstances how could they not abandon their original purpose of "doing as they please"? Stated more bluntly, we can treat such works of pseudo-Romanticism as a game, or we can treat them as a peep-show; but we can't treat them as Art. There's no order and nothing to discuss. They can protest form all they want, but we don't have to waste our time arguing with them.

We've already defined *gelü* as "form" above. Suppose we were to abolish form altogether—would we still have Art? Earlier in this essay, we also equated form with rhythm. It is here that we can see even more clearly the importance of form; because while it is possible to have prose with relatively minimal rhythm, there is no such thing as poetry without rhythm. Poetry has never departed from form and rhythm. Until now, no one had ever called this law of nature into question. Nowadays, do even laws of nature have to be proven before they can be accepted? How did we find ourselves engaged in such a fierce debate? Does everyone believe that poetry can turn its back on form? Perhaps it's a spirit of "anarchy," or a fashion-conscious mentality, or laziness, or maybe it's the fear of being exposed as utterly devoid of talent, or then again, perhaps it's . . . I have no idea!

*2*

We've talked a bit about why poetry can't do away with form. Let's take a moment to analyze the nature of form. Externally, we might be inclined to discuss form in terms of these two aspects: (1) the visual, and (2) the auditory. But in fact, we can't really treat them as separate from each other, for they are inextricably intertwined. For instance, form that is visual has a balance of stanzas, symmetry of lines. Form that is auditory has a pattern, metric feet, tones, and end-rhymes; and yet without a pattern, it would also lack balanced stanzas, meter, and symmetrical lines.

As for the question of pattern, meter, tones, and end-rhymes, this journal has already published a pair of essays by Rao Mengkan, "On Meter in New Poetry," that discuss this in great detail. However, his focus was on the auditory, and he didn't say anything about the two questions pertaining to the visual. Of course, the visual occupies a position of relatively secondary importance. Still, it cannot be ignored, especially in Chinese literature. Because our written language is pictographic, at least half of our appreciation of a work of literature is based on what comes in through our eyes. While literature, by its very nature, occupies both time and space, it cannot convey a concretely visual impression. This is a shortcoming of European literature, but the Chinese written language has the potential to create this sort of impression, and it would be a great pity if we didn't take advantage of it. In this regard, the way that New Poetry has adopted Western poetic lineation is quite relevant. Setting aside the question of what the person who initiated this practice intended, all of us owe him our gratitude. Because it has finally allowed us to see that the real power of poetry lies not just in its musical (metrical) and painterly (rhetorical) beauty, but also in its architectural beauty (the balance of stanzas and symmetry of lines). Hence poetry has been strengthened by these new reinforcements, and its power extended. Thus, if someone were to ask what distinguishes New Poetry, we would have to reply that one of its salient characteristics is that it has given poetry the potential for architectural beauty.

Lately, it seems that many people have been expressing skepticism toward balanced stanzas and symmetrical lines, seeing them as emblematic of a fusty and antiquated approach. This is a great misfortune for the ancients, especially for the ancients of the Republic of China! Don't you think it's a bit strange? Not only has Confucius been stripped of his honorific titles of "sage" and "master" in all the uproar, he's even been deprived of his proper name, and some people simply call him "Old Number Two." But Jesus is still Jesus Christ, and Socrates is still Socrates. It's all right to compose poems in the form of sonnets, but you'd better take extra care—you wouldn't want them to look too much like classical regulated verse. I don't honestly know what's so lowly and hateful about classical poetry! In any case, is it even possible to use everyday language to write poetry that truly resembles regulated verse? If we compose poems with symmetrical stanzas and lines today, are we really writing classical regulated verse?

In truth, regulated verse also has architectural beauty; but its potential to create this kind of beauty is vastly inferior to that of New Poetry. Regulated verse has to keep to one template, but the structures available to New Poetry are without limit. This is the first difference between regulated verse and New Poetry. No matter what your subject is, no matter what your artistic mood or conception, you still have to squeeze it into this fixed pattern. It's as if everyone, man, woman, and child alike, had to wear the same clothes. With New Poetry, on the other hand, each poem is tailor made. For example, you could no more set "Zhaojun Journeying Beyond the Borders" to the pattern of "Picking Lotus" or write "The Last Resolution" in the form of "The Railroad Song" than you could write "Seeking" in the form of "March 18th." If anyone can point to an example in any of these poems, where the form and content, or the spirit and outward shape, are not in harmony, I'd like to hear their reasoning. We might well ask ourselves—is the beauty of harmonious spirit and shape anywhere to be found in the printer's template of regulated verse, or in the random and disordered jumble of free verse, where thoughts flow unchecked from the pen?

There's no relationship between the form and content of regulated verse, but the form of New Style verse is based on the spirit of its content. That is the second point of difference between the two. The patterns of regulated verse were set for us by others, while the patterns of New Poetry are created out of our own artistic conception on an ad hoc basis. That is the third point of difference. We should be able to determine from these three points whether form in New Poetry marks a return to antiquated style or an innovation, if it constitutes a step backward or a step forward.

Currently, four-line stanzas with an equal number of characters per line have become very common. Lines with even character counts that look as though they've been sliced with a knife look especially odd to people who are used to the uneven edges of free verse. They think it's a lot of trouble to trim one's lines so tidily. It also occurs to them that if writing poetry requires that much work, won't poetic inspiration be destroyed? If inspiration is destroyed, where will poetry come from? There you have it—when inspiration is wiped out, poetry is ruined with it. But to hone one's words and lines with such care and precision isn't really so difficult a thing. It would take more than this one thing to deal a blow to inspiration.

I've asked a few poets who write a lot of this even-lined poetry, and they've all said the same thing: they agree that if their poem isn't good, the fault lies with their own lack of facility with the form. The form itself isn't to blame in the least. Let's look at the two following examples. One example has uneven lines; the other has even lines. Let's see if there's any relationship between orderly and disorderly lines and syllables and how beautiful the poem is—

I want to penetrate the mistiness of solitude, thin floating gauze,
Listen carefully to the hiss of fine rain quiet on the eaves, striking
    intensely as I face the sighing sound in the emptiness that blows
    from afar,
Aware of the white blossoms falling lightly one by one.

At this, the lamp outside made a sudden sound,
The look of the old man's face was changed;
The children watched, startled, his face
And he watched, startled, the coal fire's red glow.

When all is said and done, which one has the best syllabic rhythm—the one with ordered composition, or the one that lacks order? To take it even further, not only are orderly line-lengths no obstacle to meter, they can actually improve metrical harmony. There are those who will refuse to accept this. Let's analyze the preceding examples for a moment, and see if ordered lines and harmonious meter are one and the same.

The children / watched startled / his / face
He too / watched startled / the coal fire's / red glow

Haizimen / jing wangzhe / tade / lianse
Ta ye / jing wangzhe / fanhuo de / hong guang

Each of these lines can be divided into four metrical feet, with two three-beat lines per line and two two-beat lines, and even though the lines don't follow the same ordering of metric feet, each line still has to contain two trimeters and two dimeters. Writing like this is sure to make the meter sing, while maintaining an even word count. Thus orderly lines are the inevitable product of harmonious meter. For the meter to be harmonious, the words and lines must be even. (On the other hand, an even word count does not guarantee euphonious meter. This is because if all you have is an even number of characters per line, you wouldn't necessarily have paid attention to composing even metric feet—this sort of symmetry is merely ornamentation on the well-ordered but lifeless frame of a wooden mask. This isn't the rich and naturally ordered shape engendered by content.)

In this sense, an even word count is extremely important, because this external pattern conveys the inner spirit of the poem—the absence or presence of rhythm. If the reader is in need of further examples, we can apply a similar analysis to my poem, "Dead Water."

Beginning with its first line,

This is / a ditch / of hopeless / dead water
Zhe shi / yi gou / juewang de / sishui

Each line is composed of three disyllabic units and one trisyllabic unit, so that each line has the same number of characters. The result is that I think that this poem is my first satisfactory experiment in syllabics. Because many friends have expressed skepticism about poems like this one, which is laid out like mahjong tiles, today I will take the opportunity to elaborate a bit on "Dead Water." I hope that readers will see from the preceding analysis that New Poetry clearly already possesses a concrete syllabic methodology. With the discovery of this sort of metrical method, I assert that New Poetry will soon enter a new period of development. Come what may, we must acknowledge that this marks a sweeping change in the history of New Poetry.

Before long, the course of events will answer the question of whether this powerful wave constitutes forward movement or is a retreat.

*Translated by Andrea Lingenfelter*

## Dead Water

Here is a ditch of hopelessly dead water.
A cool breeze would not raise the slightest ripple on it.
You might throw in some scraps of copper and rusty tins,
or dump in as well the remains of your meal.

Perhaps the green on copper will turn into emeralds,
or the rust on tin will sprout a few peach blossoms.
Let grease weave a layer of fine silk-gauze, and
mould steam out a few red-glowing clouds.

Let the dead water ferment into a ditch of green wine,
floating with pearls of white foam;
but the laughter of small pearls turning into large pearls
is broken by spotted mosquitoes stealing the wine.

Thus a ditch of hopelessly dead water
can yet claim a bit of something bright.
And if the frogs can't endure the utter solitude,
let the dead water burst into song.

Here is a ditch of hopelessly dead water.
Here beauty can never reside.
You might as well let ugliness come and cultivate it,
and see what kind of world comes out.

*Translated by Arthur Sze*

# Liang Shiqiu

*(1903–1987)*

Liang Shiqiu was a prominent writer, literary critic, translator, and lexicographer. He was born into an affluent family in Beijing and, from 1915 to 1923, was educated at Qinghua College in Beijing. He began writing poetry and short stories there and became very interested in Oscar Wilde and other Romantic writers. In 1923 he came to the United States and first studied at Colorado College; a year later he went on to Harvard, where he studied literary criticism with Irving Babbitt. In 1925 he transferred to Columbia University and pursued further studies in English literature. In 1926 he returned to China and became a professor of English at a succession of universities. He was a co-founder of the *Crescent Moon Monthly* and served as editor from 1928 to 1933. During this era, he published a series of essays that championed the intrinsic value of literature, and he vehemently opposed the use of literature for propagandistic purposes. Lu Xun and other leftist writers attacked him, including Mao Zedong in his "Talks at the Yan'an Forum." In 1949 he went to Taiwan where he taught at Taiwan Normal University until 1966. From 1930 until 1968, he single-handedly translated the complete works of Shakespeare into Chinese. He brought out a series of Chinese-English and English-Chinese dictionaries and also wrote a multivolume, comprehensive history of English literature.

Liang Shiqiu's essays range widely, but "Literature and Revolution," published in 1928, is a major essay. In the excerpt included here, he asserts, *"literature rich in revolutionary spirit always appears before the actual revolutionary movement."* Although he sees writers in the vanguard, he rejects the polemics of revolutionary literature and states, "The creation of literature cannot undergo any form of coercion."

## Excerpt from "Literature and Revolution"

During a period of revolution, literature very easily takes on a particular shade. We certainly cannot say, however, that within a revolutionary period all writers must create "revolutionary literature." Why should this be? Poets, indeed all literary men, are those who stand at the forefront of the times. People's suffering, society's corruption, political darkness, false virtue: none feels these things earlier, or deeper, than the writer. It is not that people living under vile conditions, rich or poor, are without perceptions or unaware of suffering, but they cannot express what they feel, and even if they can give voice to it, then what they say does not conform to the rules of art; it is only writers who, because of their inherent nature and long-standing apprenticeship, are able to be the mouthpiece of all the people, to give expression to the sufferings of all peoples, and to use different kinds of artistic methods to express their dissatisfaction with the status quo. Writers of intense feelings might launch a direct attack on contemporary hypocrisy; writers rich in imagination might evoke a golden past; writers who are optimistic and indulge in fantasies will create their ideal paradise; but they are all equally dissatisfied with the present status quo. Writers have always been the unofficial representatives of the people, unconsciously representing their intimate pains and joy, thoughts and inclinations. Particularly in times of suffering, the stimuli writers receive are exceptionally heartfelt and thus their anguished cries are exceptionally moving. Because writers are the first among people to feel, the first to be aware, we know from a historical perspective that *literature rich in revolutionary spirit always appears before the actual revolutionary movement.* Thus, "revolutionary literature" prior to revolution is the first cool drop of sweet dew in people's souls, and it is the most intense, the most sincere, the most natural. Instead of saying, "First revolution, then 'revolutionary literature,'" say rather, "First 'revolutionary literature,' then revolution." After the actual revolution has broken out, the revolutionary coloring of literature naturally becomes increasingly intense, to the point where a great quantity of literature that comes close to rhetoric or propaganda is produced. *Writers do not give expression to any spirit of the times, it is rather that the times reflect the spirit of writers.* Of course, since writers cannot exist apart from real life and since the life of an entire revolutionary period is also not without commensurate stimuli for a writer, we must therefore begin by acknowledging that, during a revolutionary period (including the periods of "fermenting and erupting"), literature easily takes on a particular kind of coloring.

So why do I say again that writers do not need to create "revolutionary literature" in times of revolution? From a literary perspective, the term "revolutionary literature" is basically untenable. *In literature there is only "literature of a revolutionary period," and certainly no so-called revolutionary literature.* From the standpoint of an actual revolutionary, that is, from a utilitarian point of view, we could say that one thing is "revolutionary literature" and another "not revolutionary literature" and furthermore, using communist theory, we could extend this to say that "non-revolutionary literature" is "counter-revolutionary literature." However, in literary theory we divide literary categories according to the most basic qualities and tendencies, and external realities such as revolutionary movements or restoration movements cannot be borrowed to be used as standards by which to measure literature. Moreover, great literature is founded on a fixed universal human nature, and good literature is only that which flows forth from the depths of the human heart, for what literature finds hard to achieve is fidelity: fidelity to human nature. And it is unimportant what kind of connection results from the tide of the times; and whether it is influenced by the times or influences the times, or if it is integrated with revolutionary theory or is restricted by traditional thinking, bears no relationship to literature's value. This is because human nature is the sole standard for measuring literature. The term "revolutionary literature," even if not necessarily a concoction devised by revolutionaries, at the very least serves to add confusion to the understanding of literature. Furthermore, human nature's complexity and profundity need abundant experience before a commensurate understanding can be reached, and it is not necessarily the case that everyone will have revolutionary experience in a time of revolution (spiritual and emotional aspects of life also count as experience), and we definitely cannot compel those without revolutionary experience to write "revolutionary literature." The creation of literature cannot undergo any form of coercion. Literature containing revolutionary ideology is literature, and as literature it makes public the anxieties and feelings of a period.

*Translated by Alison Bailey*

# Dai Wangshu

*(1905–1950)*

Dai Wangshu, poet, essayist, and translator, was born near Hangzhou and graduated from high school there. In 1923 he attended Shanghai University, majored in Chinese literature, and attended a class taught by Mao Dun. From 1922 to 1924, he began writing New Poetry and developed a keen interest in French literature. He then transferred to Shanghai's Aurore University and took an intensive course in French. In 1926 he joined the Communist Youth League and helped edit a short-lived journal, *The Jade Necklace Trimonthly*. His first published poems appeared in this journal. In 1927 anti-Communist purges forced Dai to briefly go into hiding. In 1928 he published six poems, including "Rainy Alley," which, in its imagery and suggestiveness, showed the strong influence of the French symbolist poets. In 1930 he attended the founding meeting of the Chinese League of Left-Wing Writers; and, in 1932, Dai went to France and enrolled at the University of Lyons but spent a lot of time in Paris. He met André Malraux, André Breton, Max Jacob, and interviewed Jules Supervielle. In January 1935 he left France and returned to China. In 1937, after the outbreak of the Sino-Japanese War, Dai moved to Hong Kong and worked as editor of a leading newspaper. After Hong Kong fell to the Japanese, he was arrested, imprisoned, and tortured for his anti-Japanese sentiments. After the war, he returned to Shanghai and then moved to Beijing, where he worked in translation for the International News Bureau, the forerunner to today's Foreign Languages Press.

Dai Wangshu's poetry is rich in implication and musicality. His finest poems are haunting, employ synesthesia, and blend the imaginary and real. He translated Baudelaire's *Les Fleurs du Mal* and was the first to translate Federico García Lorca's poetry into Chinese. His short essay "Dai Wangshu's Poetic Theory," published in 1932, is notable for his championing of poetic nuance and for his assertion that "new poetry should have new emotions and new forms."

## Dai Wangshu's Poetic Theory

1. Poetry cannot rely on musicality and should discard its musical qualities.
2. Poetry cannot rely on the strengths of painting.
3. The mere composition of beautiful words is not a characteristic of poetry.
4. Those of the Symbolist school say: "Nature is a prostitute who has been debauched a thousand times." But who knows if a new prostitute will not be debauched ten thousand times? The number of times doesn't matter, what we need are new instruments and techniques for debauchery.
5. Poetic meter lies not in the melodiousness of the characters but in the melodiousness of the poem's emotion, the degree of the poetic mood.
6. What is most important for new poetry is the "nuance" of poetic mood and not the "nuance" of characters and phrases.
7. Rhyme and regularity of lines may obstruct poetic mood or deform poetic mood. If the emotion behind a poem is made to conform to stagnant and superficial old rules, it is like placing your own feet in the shoes of another. A fool will trim the foot to fit the shoe, whereas a rather more intelligent man will choose for

himself a better fitting shoe. A wise man, however, will make for himself a pair that fits his own feet.

8. Poetry is not a pleasure felt by a single sense alone but something felt by all the senses, or which transcends the senses altogether.
9. New poetry should have new emotions and new forms for expressing these emotions. And this so-called form is most certainly not the superficial arrangement of characters, nor the mere compilation of new words.
10. There is no need to necessarily have new objects as thematic material (although I am not opposed to this), for new poetic moods may be found in old poetic objects.
11. Diction of the old classics cannot be opposed when it bestows on us a new poetic mood.
12. One should not simply indulge one's fancy for resplendent adornment, for this will never be eternal.
13. Poetry should have its own *originalité*, but you must also give it a *cosmopolité* [*sic*] quality; neither is dispensable.
14. Poetry is born from reality passing through the imagination; it is neither only reality nor only imagination.
15. When poetry expresses its own emotions and causes people to feel something, it seems to take on a life of its own and is not a lifeless thing.
16. Emotion is not captured as with a camera, it should be brought out through description in an ingenious style. This style must be alive and ever-changing.
17. If one uses a certain language to write poems and the people of a country feel them to be good poems, they are not really good poems but at most the magic of language. What is good in a real poem is not just the strengths of language.

*Translated by Kirk A. Denton*

# Zhou Zuoren

*(1885–1967)*

Zhou Zuoren was an essayist, translator, and literary critic. He was the younger brother of Lu Xun, and in his early years followed his older brother's lead. Like Lu Xun, he enrolled in the Nanjing Naval Academy. In 1906 he went to Japan to study civil engineering but, once there, began writing cultural essays and translating world literature. He learned classical Greek from American missionaries in Tokyo and also developed an interest in Japanese burlesque comedy as well as folklore, natural history, psychology, and anthropology. When he returned to his hometown, Shaoxing, he taught English at a middle school. In 1917 he received a major promotion and was hired to teach literature at Beijing University. There, he contributed essays to many May Fourth journals, wrote some poetry, and made translations. He started a newspaper column, "One's Own Garden," declared his independence from competing political ideologies, and was the first writer in China to call attention to Dostoevsky and Blake. In 1939 he accepted an appointment, under Japanese occupation, as librarian at the reorganized Beijing University. He accepted other appointments, including director of the North China Office of Education. In 1945, after the war, he was arrested by the Guomindang for his Japanese ties during the occupation. Sentenced to fourteen years in Nanjing Prison, he was pardoned and released by the Communist government. He retired to Beijing and continued to translate. His works include pioneering translations of Euripides, Sappho, Sei Shonagon, and Lucian. Early in the Cultural Revolution, he was beaten by Red Guards and died on May 6, 1967.

Zhou Zuoren was astonishingly erudite and wrote essays on a great variety of subjects. The following excerpts from "My Own Compositions," published in 1936, show his irreverent, independent, insightful, slightly subversive, and amusing tones as a writer of personal essays for which he became famous.

## Excerpts from "My Own Compositions"

I understand a popular saying states that men always prefer other people's wives and their own compositions. Since this saying goes the rounds, there must be some truth in it—it shows nobody has found cause to object to it. However, in my view it does not say the last word. As to the first point, I have no experience, so we lay that aside for the time being. As to compositions, over the last forty years I have scribbled a lot of them in the classical and modern languages, so can claim some slight knowledge, but I have no sense at all that my hometown of Shaoxing is the nation's cradle of literary excellence and I myself am number one in the town. No, if you have read compositions, no matter of the *Anthology* or Tongcheng school, you do get a dim perception of quality, and when you write yourself you do get a glimmering of understanding that it is not all as easy as pie. You may derive no more than a tiny bit of knowledge from this, yet knowledge and belief don't go well together: since you know that composition may be good or bad, you naturally find it hard to believe that all your own compositions are good.

It is of course pleasurable to hear people praise my compositions, but this pleasure is for the most part like seeing the chief examiner's remarks on your paper: the honor is flattering but they do not necessarily tell the truth. Some people have very kindly said my compositions are even and temperate, which is very gratifying yet at the same time very disturbing. Evenness and temperateness is what I most lack. Though that tone has, I admit, been my ideal, in fact I have been entirely unable to come near to it, no doubt because one's ideals are actually what one most lacks and what one cannot achieve. It goes without saying that in writing essays nowadays one can no longer concern oneself with "the right method" and "structure and rhythm." The thought becomes paramount, but given that it is difficult enough to make the thought content sound and complete, it is even more difficult to express one's thoughts well. My only property is testiness, or to put it more agreeably, positiveness, but under either name it is impossible to produce good writing, I have to say. I wrote in my preface to *A Book of Rainy Days* in 1925:

> In my recent writing I have aspired to the state of temperateness and naturalness, but this kind of composition I have found only in classical or foreign literature, and I cannot imagine the day will ever come when I shall be able to achieve it, for it is bound up with character, situation, and age, and cannot be forced. A person of my mean and hasty temper, born in China at this time in history, can hardly hope calmly and unconcernedly to produce mild and temperate essays.

I went on:

> I am very opposed to literature in the service of morality, but I can never produce a work of literature in the service of literature. As a result I have only put together some collections of preaching, which is a highly comical contradiction. [. . .]

Another ten years on, in 1935, I said in the preface to *Bitter Tea Essays:*

> I feel quite ashamed that I was always so enthusiastic, so positive, and was still so after I already had a rough idea of how things stood—could I have believed in miracles? It was truly an egregious error. In future I should strictly set my mind on writing good compositions, pay no attention to the sordid doings of others, and take up the harmless topics of flora and fauna. Top priority!

It is obvious that once again this self-remonstrance was useless. Confucius said, "I cannot associate with birds and beasts. If not with this human race, with whom can I associate?" China is my home country, is the place where "I sing and I weep," but anyone can see it has gone to the dogs. Leaving aside the affairs of state, you just have to go out of your door to see women's tiny bound feet, and now as I write my ears are filled with the screeching of announcements and old opera from the radio of the house behind me: you can't help the bile rising within you. There is no chance of achieving an even and temperate style; it never comes from my hand, it only lives in my mind. [. . .]

In retrospect, if there is anything good about my essays, it would only be found where they fail to achieve temperateness and ease, that is to say, where they are given over to moralizing. I wrote in the second preface to my *Book of Rainy Days:*

> I have always detested moralists (or to use the new term, Pharisees), not realizing that was exactly because I myself was a moralist. I was out to destroy their false, immoral morality, but at the same time unconsciously wanted to set up the new morality I myself believed in.

My morality is, I have to confess, Confucian, but to the left and right there are some elements of Taoism and Legalism mixed up in it, and from outside has been added some common knowledge of modern science, like biology, anthropology, and psychology of sex, with the last being more important to me. Among our esteemed forebears there have been those who hit upon the truth while meditating facing a blank wall, and those who discovered the secret of writing from watching snakes fight, while I, on the other hand, conceived my morality from the "making of the beast with two backs," which would be certain to make all the old wives titter. But let all those who want to laugh laugh as they like, my opinions are solidly based on what I know, hence it follows that I cannot lightly truckle to others.

*Translated by David E. Pollard*

# Lao She

*(1899–1966)*

Lao She was born in Beijing of Manchu parents. His father, a palace guard, died in a street battle, and his mother raised him. He graduated from Beijing Normal School in 1918 and, from 1918 to 1924, worked as a teacher and administrator at several primary and secondary schools. From 1924 to 1929, he taught Chinese in the School of Oriental Studies at the University of London. There, he absorbed English literature and was particularly struck by the novels of Charles Dickens. He wrote three novels during his time in London: *The Philosophy of Lao Zhang*, *Zhao Ziyue*, and *The Two Mas*. In 1931 he returned to China and taught at Qilu University in Jinan. In 1936 his most famous novel, *Camel Xiangzi*, later translated by Evan King as *Rickshaw Boy*, was published. Within the next few years, he published two satiric novels, *Cat Country* and *Divorce*, along with such short stories as "Crescent Moon" and "Black Li and White Li." In *Rickshaw Boy*, Lao She describes the tragic life of a rickshaw puller in Beijing during the 1920s. In "Crescent Moon," he describes the misery of a mother and daughter as their lives spiral downward. From 1937 to 1945, during the Sino-Japanese War, he wrote several plays and headed the All-China Anti-Japanese Writers Federation. From 1946 to 1949, Lao She lived in the United States on a cultural grant from the State Department. In 1949 he returned to China and eventually became a deputy to the National

People's Congress, and served as vice-chairman of the All-China Federation of Literature and Art, and was extolled as a "People's Artist." His play *Teahouse* was written in 1956 and performed by the Beijing People's Art Theater in the following year. At the outset of the Cultural Revolution, he was publicly denounced and, on August 24, 1966, was killed by Red Guards.

Lao She's essay "How I Wrote My Short Stories" was included in *An Aging Ox and Dilapidated Cart*, published in Qingdao in 1936. In this engaging personal essay, he discusses the evolution of his writing and provides insight into the art of fiction.

## How I Wrote My Short Stories

I wrote my very first short story when I was teaching at Nankai Middle School, merely to please the editor of the school magazine. That was twenty or thirty years ago. Needless to say, it was hardly worth reading and played no significant role in my experience as a writer, since it failed to spark any interest in me to one day become a writer. My creative history must begin with the novel *The Philosophy of Lao Zhang*.

This is something worth talking about. Why? Because before I wrote novels I had no experience in writing short stories. That did not serve me well. One has to work extra hard on stories for them to turn out well, while there is always room to maneuver in longer works. If a novel can boast several well-wrought passages and a number of fine sentences in each passage, that will do just fine. It may not be how it should be, but it's the way things are. Even the reader will be unusually forgiving if that is all a novel has to offer—because it is a novel. The world tolerates novels that fall short of excellence, but will not permit the same leniency to short stories. I wrote five or six long works without the benefit of experience in short stories, so technical improvements came slowly—no surprise there. Technique is critical for short stories, a relatively new arrival on the scene; it is no exaggeration to state that technique is what makes it possible for them to exist as an independent genre. But my preparation for entering the field consisted only of full-length novels, which was a bit like trying to lift heavy stones before mastering the leg work in martial arts. Not getting crushed by the stones would have been enough to feel good about; but even if I'd lifted something many times my own weight, it would have been nothing but useless brute strength. This insight did not come to me until after I'd written a few stories.

I used the words "a few" in the previous paragraph advisedly. The twenty-five stories collected in *Going to Market* and *Yinghai ji*, plus some more recent stories, such as "Soul-slaying Spear" and "An Old Tragedy for a New Era," can be divided into three phases. The first includes the first four stories in *Going to Market* and two toward the end, "Mr. Jodhpurs" and "The Grandson." The second phase includes all those written between "By the Temple of Great Compassion" and "Crescent Moon." Finally, the stories "Crescent Moon," "Soul-slaying Spear," and "An Old Tragedy for a New Era" constitute the third phase.

I wrote the five or six stories in phase one as a lark. "May Ninth," the earliest, was thrown together for the *Qilu [Cheeloo] University Quarterly*. "Hot Dumplings" I wrote for the "Forest of Words" supplement to the *Yishi bao*, keeping it short because I was asked to. Both were written at a time when short stories were not in my future. "Thrown together" is a fitting description for them.

Following the January 28th Incident [1932], I realized that the time to turn my attention to short stories had arrived, owing in large part to the mushrooming of new magazines, all clamoring for manuscripts. Short stories fit the bill perfectly, since they were easier to deal with. That's right, easier to deal with, just that. At the time I still had a low opinion of short fiction, feeling it was a waste of my time, which is why I limited myself to comic pieces like "The Grandson." My attitude was: knock off a few comic pieces to save time for writing novels. I had it all planned out. But finding the time to write novels was getting harder and harder, while the demand for short pieces was on the increase. Time to move beyond humor and get serious about writing stories. "By the Temple of Great Compassion" and "Wei shen" began my second phase.

"Wei shen" and "Black Li and White Li" went through three drafts. Since I was done with "having fun" with short stories, I had to buckle down and do my best. Still, lacking the time to revise my work, I produced some terrible pieces. Given the paltry sums paid to writers at the time, output became an important consideration—more stories meant more income. Then, too, I did not want to offend friends, so I cranked out pieces they could publish. These two factors were decisive in my approach—and that of other writers, I suppose—that infrequent good writing was less appealing than frequent, if slipshod, writing. It was a necessity, not a strategy. I couldn't help feeling that I was failing my responsibility to quality literature, but offending friends and undervaluing money were not viable options. An editor friend named Wang once asked me to send him something he could use, so I wrote and I wrote, altogether more than 30,000 words, without actually creating a story. Afraid he might not believe me, I sent him everything, rejects and all. I recount this not as evidence of a serious attitude toward creative writing, but as an example of what I was up against. It could not be repeated, for if all attempts ended that way, I'd have either died of exhaustion or starved to death. Exhaustion is a quick, noble death, but starvation entails great suffering and a loss of dignity. For every 5,000 words I submitted I sacrificed as many as 30,000. At twenty yuan or less for 5,000 words, starvation became a real possibility. But enough about that.

Material for the dozen or more stories in the second phase came principally from four sources: first, personal experience or events and people I knew firsthand; second, stories I'd heard; third, imitations of other people's writing; and, fourth, ideas for which I then created characters and plots. Here's a list:

1. "By the Temple of Great Compassion," "Wei shen," "The Woman from Liu Tun," "The Eyeglasses," "No Distance Too Far, No Sacrifice Too Great," "Caterpillars," and "Neighbors"
2. "Also a Triangle," "Brother Yu Takes Office," "Liu Tun," and "An Old Man's Romance"
3. "Crooktails"
4. "Black Li and White Li," "The Tractor and the Sick Duck," "The Last Dollar," and "A Good Man"

Since the third group—imitations of others' writing—has only one story, I'll begin with it. "Crooktails" was written in imitation of J. D. Beresford's

"The Hermit." Wanting to use this curious story in my fiction class, I went ahead and translated it into Chinese. It stuck with me for a long time, and I wanted to write a story like it. But since I couldn't come up with a new scenario, I simply imitated Beresford. The material was mine, the core idea his.

Most of the stories in the first group re-created events I'd witnessed; only a couple involved my personal experience. I wouldn't have much to say about them, if not for the fact that "No Distance Too Far, No Sacrifice Too Great" was badly panned. Both the characters and the incident were taken from real life, but everyone who wrote about the story flayed it mercilessly, some even denying its claim to realism. I responded to such comments, as most people would, by stating that "it really happened." But then I went back and read it again, and I understood: It was indeed badly written. It wavered terribly; the second half of the story does not go far enough in aiding the first half. It was fragmented, revised as I went along, like making a quilt out of used cotton, patching one corner and then another. Truth is unreliable, since facts do not in and of themselves constitute fiction; it all depends on what you do with them. Placing too much emphasis on the material can cause a writer to neglect the artistic component.

The stories in the second group, conversely, were smoother, though they were based on stories and incidents related to me by friends. Since they were told to me by other people, I was especially attentive. There is nothing wrong with being cautious. Several stories in the fourth group are in the same vein, in that the people and events are imaginary, the offspring of a concept, an idea. The two characters in each of the stories "Black Li and White Li" and "The Tractor and the Sick Duck" clearly represent disparate concepts. The concepts preceded the characters, which meant that all the characters were restricted in terms of scope and courses of action, a considerable improvement over unbridled chaos, if you ask me. Experience enriches imagination; imagination determines experience.

The language in these stories is an improvement over that in my novels; some of that is a result of careful revision, some the inevitable result of being pressed to submit my work quickly. In the former, the passions are cooled (usually by deletion). The latter has nothing to recommend it. In general, however, I strove to retain both the "unrefined" and "idiomatic" style typical of my writing. In rhetorical terms, clarity has always been my prime consideration. If clarity is the fruit of thought, then it is power. I cannot say if my language is characterized by clarity and power, but that has always been my goal.

Here I ought to turn to the third group. Several of these stories—"Crescent Moon," "Sunbeams," "Soul-slaying Spear," and "An Old Tragedy in a New Era"—have no virtues worth talking about. One fact and one insight have led me to assign them to a separate category. Early on, I indicated that I wrote the stories in the first phase for fun. That they came out badly was preordained; only sheer luck could have caused them to come out well. Although the stories in the second phase were written with a sense of purpose, at the time I still felt as if short stories were somehow beneath me, that my real talent lay in writing novels. The third phase signaled a change in that attitude. External realities forced me to turn material intended for novels into short stories. The facts were, with increased demand for my writing and a limited amount of material, I could save the situation only by calling up material I'd planned to use for novels.

Needless to say, I was reluctant about having to convert wholesale to piecemeal. But when I used material intended for a novel of 100,000 words in writing a 5,000-word story, "Soul-slaying Spear," that reluctance turned to insight. I tell you, there is nothing more valuable than experience! Here is what I learned: nothing is lost by condensing material for a novel into a short story, because you select the best parts. Better to take a bite of a celestial peach than to eat a basketful of rotten apricots. Taking it even further, though novels may well have their core thought, owing to the complexity of events and profusion of characters, the descriptions and subplots are many-sided. But if only one of those sides is employed in the telling of a story, the obvious result is a tight and penetrating narration. Virtually any aspect of a novel can be turned into a fine short story, but if these aspects are scattered throughout a novel, the brilliance of any one of them may be difficult to spot. A novel ought to be well balanced, a short story needs to be concentrated. Take "Crescent Moon," for instance. It is but one part of the novel *Daming Lake*. After *Daming Lake* was destroyed in a fire, I happily abandoned everything but that one unforgettable part, which, it goes without saying, was the most interesting part of the entire novel. But while still a part of the novel, it wasn't nearly as complete or finished as the story it became. It was, you see, buried among so much other material it had no independent value. Looking back, I'm glad to have published "Crescent Moon" and have no regrets over losing *Daming Lake*. That's not to say it's a masterpiece of short fiction, but it is stronger alone than buried in a novel.

"Soul-slaying Spear" is another case in point. It is a single episode from the novel *Double-fisted Master*, a martial arts novel I planned but never got around to writing. I'll never know how that might have worked out, since only completed works count; trying to anticipate creative outcomes is folly. The story involves three characters and a single incident, all of which were gleaned from a pile of material I'd prepared; since I'd given the characters plenty of thought, I had no trouble making them work. The incident was one of many I'd planned for the novel, so it too was ready-made for the story. Focusing on a single incident that involved three fictional individuals made for an ideal story; everything fit just the way I wanted. As a result, a loss of material wound up making better art. Who's to say that 5,000 words isn't an improvement over 100,000? Art is not like a pig, where less is never more. On the other hand, a 100,000-word novel can be sold for as much as 500 yuan, whereas my 5,000-word story brought in only 19 yuan. This, I venture to say, is one argument against getting too familiar with art. Sacrifice in the name of art has a wonderful ring to it, but no one deserves to starve, and I wonder why people think it's all right for writers to go hungry. I don't get it!

If "Crescent Moon" hadn't been written, "Sunbeams" might have fared better with readers, some of whom considered it a failure of subject matter. Here is why *I* think "Sunbeams" is not as good as "Crescent Moon": as we have seen, "Crescent Moon" was a revised episode from the novel *Daming Lake*, and thus constitutes an organic whole, with nothing extraneous or forced. "Sunbeams," on the other hand, while intended as a part of a novel, had not been given much independent thought, so even though it was a short story, I threw in other things that occurred to me at the time, which made it stiff and unnatural. Take material you've nurtured over a long period of time, turning a complex matter this way and that until the characters and events come across as recognizable and familiar, then extract a portion to create a short story, and success is guaranteed. That's because the minute you put pen to paper, you will create something balanced and beautiful. That is the insight I gained upon finishing "Crescent Moon" and "Sunbeams."

There is another concern that deserves mention, and that is that creative work requires time. Which is to say, a creative writer must be prepared to spend lots of time at his craft if he is to write well. This being prepared can be characterized by one magnificent word—food. I often hear people proclaim that there are no great works, and every time I hear that, my thoughts turn to the type of person who would utter it, someone who probably believes that a writer is some little critter that can subsist on morning dew. I know I'm not a prodigiously talented writer and that I have no hopes of ever writing a great story or novel. But I believe that, given time and enough to eat, I could write pretty good stuff. You don't believe me? Come on, try me out!

"An Old Tragedy for a New Era" has many flaws, the most conspicuous of which is that you see the heads [beginnings] of many characters, but no tails [endings], no "we'll figure that out later." Why? Because it's a novella. I planned it as a full-length novel, but by keeping it at the more modest length, I was forced to concentrate on a single character, and had no choice but to toss in some secondary characters in order to submit a 30,000-word manuscript. If I'd have shortened it to story length, that problem might have been solved. My plan for the novel was to create three major characters: Old Man Chen and his two sons, plus someone named Song Longyun. Old Man Chen was to represent the past, his son Lianbo was to be roughly 70 percent old and 30 percent new, the brother Lianzong half old and half new, and Song Longyun the new. But in limiting myself to a novella, I had to delete three-fourths of the material and deal only with Old Man Chen. The others were mere shadow characters whose sole function was to prop up the framework of the story. A risky course of action, with little hope for a successful outcome. That said, there is vigor in Old Man Chen, and if I'd followed through with my plan to write a novel, he might not have been as stiff as he appears in the story. And so, I have no regrets about cannibalizing the material for my novel; in fact, I feel that it takes special skill to sing martial-arts opera in a lyrical style, dispensing with all the sound and fury.

The cost of this simple insight was the labor required to write thirty or so short stories. An insight, however, is one thing; putting it into practice by making the writing better is another. How my future short stories will turn out is something that makes me anxious. Who knows, maybe this "aging ox and dilapidated cart" will undergo a bit of rejuvenation someday.

During the War of Resistance against Japan [1937–45], owing to the fact that I was very busy and often sick, not to mention living an unsettled life, it was particularly difficult to write full-length novels; even my short-story output went into a decline. But a busy schedule, sickness, and an unsettled life were not the only reasons. At the time I'd begun trying my hand at writing plays and poetry. From 1938 to 1943 I wrote between ten and twenty short stories, which filled two collections, *The Fire Chariot* and *Anemia*. The title for *Anemia* was aptly chosen, since I have suffered from anemia from the winter of 1940 till now (spring 1944). Every winter even the slightest exertion makes me light-headed, and if I don't stop whatever I'm doing, my light-headedness leads to fainting spells or head-spinning vertigo. The symptoms lessen when the weather warms up, signaling a return to writing. It would make perfect sense for me to stop writing and simply rest for six months or a year, but I won't allow myself to be idle for a prolonged period while I'm still learning, nor am I ready to get by financially by borrowing money. So, when my body fails me, I take to my bed, and then when my health improves, I write. What that has led to is increasingly poor health and progressively bad writing. To my everlasting regret, you can hardly find a story in either *The Fire Chariot* or *Anemia* worth reading!

That being the case, why do I continue to publish short fiction? That's easy. As soon as I take to my bed, I can write nothing, not even junk. So bad though the stories I publish might be, writing is what I do, and poor health keeps me from that. So when I feel up to it, not to write, even for basic survival, is not an option. Now you see the reason for the existence of *The Fire Chariot* and *Anemia*.

*Translated by Howard Goldblatt*

# Ding Ling

*(1904–1986)*

Ding Ling was one of China's leading female writers during the early twentieth century. She was born in Hunan and was raised by her mother. She was greatly influenced by her mother's independent views. In 1921 she rejected an arranged marriage but also formally broke with her family. In 1922 she traveled to Shanghai and entered the Chinese department at Shanghai University, where Mao Dun was one of the lecturers. Two years later she moved to Beijing, where she audited Lu Xun's classes. In 1925 she met an aspiring poet, Hu Yepin, and together they moved to the Western Hills outside Beijing. She read Western literature and was particularly influenced by Flaubert's *Madame Bovary*. She began writing stories that featured an independent woman who was emotionally unfulfilled and sexually restless in a sinister city. Her first collection of short stories, *In the Darkness* (1928), was greeted with immediate success and contains her most famous story, "Miss Sophie's Diary."

In 1930 she and Hu Yepin moved to Shanghai and joined the League of Left-Wing Writers. Her husband joined the Chinese Communist Party, and she followed a little later. Her writing then shifted focus to emphasize the lives of workers, peasants, and revolutionaries. In 1931 Hu was arrested by the Guomindang and executed. Two years later Ding Ling was also arrested, but she eventually escaped and joined the Communists at Yan'an. There, she grew restive: on March 9, 1942, Ding Ling published an editorial in *Liberation Daily* that lamented how women were treated under Communist rule. A series of discussions ensued, and Mao Zedong decided to convene a literary conference to address unorthodox tendencies and issued his "Talks at the Yan'an Forum on Literature and Art." In 1951 her proletarian novel, *The Sun Shines over the Sanggan River*, received the Soviet Union's Stalin Prize. Yet despite her acclaim, she was on uneasy footing with the party because of her activism for women's rights. In 1957 she was denounced as a "Rightist" and traitor. During the Cultural Revolution, she was imprisoned but later released. After her "rehabilitation," she went on to become vice-president of the All-China Writers' Association.

Ding Ling's "We Need the Zawen Essay" was published in 1942. *Zawen* is a short, incisive, and topical essay that was used to great effect by Lu Xun. In this particular piece, Ding Ling's outspoken voice and vision come through.

## We Need the Zawen Essay

One day a theorist said to me, "It's very difficult to talk about the living. In the future, let's discuss only those who are dead." I see his point. Talking about the living often leads to conflict. Dead people, on the other hand, can never challenge you, let alone generate the sarcasm and denunciations that come from the petty rivalries of scholars, factional viewpoints, or personal feelings. To avoid trouble, it is no doubt wise to adopt a policy of prudent self-protection.

Other people, elsewhere, are saying things like, "It's best to be a good member of the group. Let's give our support to the accepted ideas—no matter what they are."

I have also heard many sullen complaints of a type that should have disappeared long ago: "Who am I anyway? Are my words even worth a fart?"

What all these viewpoints show is that we still don't understand how to put democracy into practice or develop self-criticism and free discussion. Clearly, we lack tolerance and the patience to listen carefully to the opinions of others. At the same time, we lack courage and willpower. We're afraid of trouble, afraid of rejection, afraid of sacrifice. The cause is sheer laziness—and we merely grumble behind each other's backs.

If someone is willing and, in fact, dares to speak out, even if the opinion is not absolutely correct, there will always be some overly sensitive people to say there's an ulterior motive behind it, that it expresses a partisan viewpoint, that it's attacking or defending this or that. They'll say it's destroying unity, it's frivolous . . . and surely no one will go along to support the person and argue to help perfect the theory. This is a disgrace in our lives.

When a person advocates an action or idea before it becomes widely understood, the first thing he is bound to encounter is criticism. Only someone who is persistent and unafraid of criticism can be successful. Lu Xun is the prime example.

Because Lu Xun wanted to cure the soul of mankind, he gave up his study of medicine for literature. And because he was able to diagnose clearly the ills of his age, he needed the sharpest scalpel, and so he turned from writing fiction to the *zawen* essay. The subjects of his essays touch upon all aspects of Chinese society. At the time they were written, his essays were not taken seriously by many envious and denigrating scholars who said he wrote them because he couldn't write fiction. But today, Lu Xun's essays have become China's greatest ideological weapon, works so splendid they are intimidating.

Obviously, if you are willing to write essays only if they're as good as Lu Xun's, you might as well decide at the outset not to write at all. But the more articles one writes, the better they become. Besides, they aren't written for fame or glory, but only for the sake of the truth.

Our era is not so different from Lu Xun's; we have corruption, tyranny, persecution, and assassination of progressive thinkers; the people aren't even freed to defend themselves in the War of Resistance. Yet all we can say is, "This is the time for a united front!" We don't realize that we can build an even more solid united front through criticism. As a result, we are abdicating our responsibility.

Even in the progressive regions of the country, where the beginnings of democracy are visible, we need, more than elsewhere, determination and vigilance. The feudalistic evils deeply ingrained in China for several thousand years are very difficult to uproot. The so-called progressive regions themselves did not just drop out of the sky. They have very close links to the old Chinese society. And yet in these progressive regions we say it is inappropriate to write *zawen*, that here we ought to depict only the democratic life and glorious work of construction.

Although it is not unusual to get carried away by small successes, to ignore the disease and avoid the doctor, such behavior is no more than cowardice and laziness.

Lu Xun is dead. People keep saying we should do this and that in his memory, but we lack the courage to learn from his fearless example. I believe that the best thing we can do today is to emulate his unfailing intellectual honesty, daring to speak out for truth and being afraid of nothing. Our age still needs the *zawen;* we must not cast this weapon aside. Take it up, and the essay will not die.

*Translated by Ruth Nybakken*

# Mao Zedong

*(1893–1976)*

Mao Zedong, the son of an affluent peasant, was born in Hunan. During his early years he received training in classical Chinese texts and developed a strong interest in poetry and historical novels. In 1918 he traveled to Beijing and was there during the May Fourth Movement. He worked as an assistant librarian at Beijing University and joined a Marxist study group. In 1920 he worked to establish a labor union for miners and, a year later, became a delegate who attended the clandestine Chinese Communist Party's founding congress in Shanghai. In 1923 he was elected one of five commissars of the Central Committee and returned to Hunan as an organizer. In 1927 he published "Report on an Investigation into the Peasant Movement in Hunan." This influential essay detailed a peasant revolt and presaged Mao's belief that China's Marxist revolution would be won by peasants and not by the urban working class.

In October 1934 the Communists broke out of the last encirclement campaign, and, as they began their Long March to Yan'an, Mao emerged as the leader. After the Second World War, the Communists fought the Nationalists and defeated them. On October 1, 1949, Mao proclaimed the People's Republic of China. From 1949 to 1976, Mao embarked on a series of initiatives to modernize China. From 1953 to 1958, he launched a first

Five-year Plan to end agricultural dependence and develop industry. In 1958 he launched the Great Leap Forward to collectivize agriculture and promote steel and infrastructure, but the movement became a disaster. A short period of liberalization ensued, but, in 1966, Mao launched the Cultural Revolution. Huge numbers of people died during the ensuing economic and social chaos. Although Mao declared the Cultural Revolution to be over in 1969, it is generally viewed as a ten-year period that only ended with his death.

During the Yan'an Era, Mao convened a major forum on art and literature. Given as two lectures to party cadres, "Talks at the Yan'an Forum on Literature and Art" (May 2, 1942) is very extensive; but in the two excerpts included here, Mao discusses how, in his view, art must serve the people and how revolutionary writers must go out among the masses. Throughout his life, Mao wrote poetry, and it is interesting to note that he chose to write in the traditional *shi* and *ci* forms.

## Excerpts from "Talks at the Yan'an Forum on Literature and Art"

The first problem is: literature and art for whom?

This problem was solved long ago by Marxists, especially by Lenin. As far back as 1905 Lenin pointed out emphatically that our literature and art should "serve . . . the millions and tens of millions of working people." For comrades engaged in literary and artistic work in the anti-Japanese base areas, it might seem that this problem is already solved and needs no further discussion. Actually, that is not the case. Many comrades have not found a clear solution. Consequently their sentiments, their works, their actions, and their views on the guiding principles for literature and art have inevitably been more or less at variance with the needs of the masses and of the practical struggle. Of course, among the numerous men of culture, writers, artists, and other literary and artistic workers engaged in the great struggle for liberation together with the Communist Party and the Eighth

Route and New Fourth armies, a few may be careerists who are only with us temporarily, but the overwhelming majority are working energetically for the common cause. By relying on these comrades, we have achieved a great deal in our literature, drama, music, and fine arts. Many of these writers and artists have begun their work since the outbreak of the War of Resistance; many others did much revolutionary work before the war, endured many hardships, and influenced broad masses of the people by their activities and works. Why do we say, then, that even among these comrades there are some who have not reached a clear solution of the problem of whom literature and art are for? Is it conceivable that there are still some who maintain that revolutionary literature and art are not for the masses of the people but for the exploiters and oppressors?

Indeed, literature and art exist that are for the exploiters and oppressors. Literature and art for the landlord class are feudal literature and art. Such were the literature and art of the ruling class in China's feudal era. To this day such literature and art still have considerable influence in China. Literature and art for the bourgeoisie are bourgeois literature and art. People like Liang Shiqiu, whom Lu Xun criticized, talk about literature and art as transcending classes, but in fact they uphold bourgeois literature and art and oppose proletarian literature and art. Then literature and art exist that serve the imperialists—for example, the works of Zhou Zuoren, Zhang Ziping, and their like—which we call traitor literature and art. With us, literature and art are for the people, not for any of the above groups. We have said that China's new culture at the present stage is an anti-imperialist, anti-feudal culture of the masses of the people under the leadership of the proletariat. Today, anything that is truly of the masses must necessarily be led by the proletariat. Whatever is under the leadership of the bourgeoisie cannot possibly be of the masses. Naturally, the same applies to the new literature and art that are part of the new culture. We should take over the rich legacy and the good traditions in literature and art that have been handed down from past ages in China and foreign countries, but the aim must still be to serve the masses of the people. Nor do we refuse to utilize the literary and artistic forms of the past, but in our hands these old forms, remolded and infused with new content, also become something revolutionary in the service of the people. [. . .]

In the last analysis, what is the source of all literature and art? Works of literature and art, as ideological forms, are products of the reflection in the human brain of the life of a given society. Revolutionary literature and art are the products of the reflection of the life of the people in the brains of revolutionary writers and artists. The life of the people is always a mine of the raw materials for literature and art, materials in their natural form, materials that are crude, but most vital, rich, and fundamental; they make all literature and art seem pallid by comparison; they provide literature and art with an inexhaustible source, their only source. They are the only source, for there can be no other. Some may ask, is there not another source in books, in the literature and art of ancient times and of foreign countries? In fact, the literary and artistic works of the past are not a source but a stream; they were created by our predecessors and the foreigners out of the literary and artistic raw materials they found in the life of the people of their time and place. We must take over all the fine things in our literary and artistic heritage, critically assimilate whatever is beneficial, and use them as examples when we create works out of the literary and artistic raw materials in the life of the people of our own time and place. It makes a difference whether or not we have such examples, the difference between crudeness and refinement, between roughness and polish, between a low and a high level, and between slower and faster work. Therefore, we must on no account reject the legacies of the ancients and the foreigners or refuse to learn from them, even though they are the works of the feudal or bourgeois classes. But taking over legacies and using them as examples must never replace our own creative work; nothing can do that. Uncritical transplantation or copying from the ancients and the foreigners is the most sterile and harmful dogmatism in literature and art. China's revolutionary writers and artists, writers and artists of promise, must go among the masses; they must for a long period of time unreservedly and wholeheartedly go among the masses of workers, peasants, and soldiers, go into the heat of the struggle, go to the only source, the broadest and richest source, in order to observe, experience, study, and analyze all the different kinds of people, all the classes, all the masses, all the vivid patterns of life and struggle, all the raw materials of literature and art. Only then can they proceed to creative work. Otherwise, you will have nothing to work with, and you will be nothing but a phony writer or artist, the kind that Lu Xun in his will so earnestly cautioned his son never to become.

# Eileen Chang (Zhang Ailing)

*(1920–1995)*

Eileen Chang was born into a distinguished family in Shanghai, but her childhood was difficult. Her father gave her training in classical Chinese poetry and prose, but he was an opium addict. After her parents divorced, he beat her after she got into an argument with her stepmother. Eileen was confined to a room for almost half a year, until she managed to escape and join her mother. Her mother introduced her to Western literature, art, and music. In 1939, after a period of intense studies, she received a scholarship to the University of London but could not attend due to the war. Instead, she attended the University of Hong Kong, where she studied English literature. In 1941, after the Japanese attacked Pearl Harbor and invaded Hong Kong, she decided to return to occupied Shanghai. There, in the wartime era, she wrote stories and essays that received acclaim. Many of her stories were collected in *Romances* (1944), while her essays were published in *Written on Water* (1945). In 1944 she married Hu Lancheng, but they divorced three years later. In 1952 Chang moved to Hong Kong and worked as a translator for the United States Information Service. In the fall of 1955 she left for the United States and never returned to China. At the MacDowell Colony, she met Ferdinand Reyher, a scriptwriter, and they married in 1956. She continued to write fiction, essays, and film scripts. After her husband's death in 1967, she held jobs at Radcliffe College (1967) and the University of California at Berkeley (1969–72). In 1972 she moved to Los Angeles and became a recluse.

Eileen Chang's fiction is remarkable for its sensuous and rich imagery and for its depictions of the psychological complexities between women and men. C.T. Hsia called her "a writer of tragic insight." Her major works available in English include *Love in a Fallen City; The Golden Cangue; Lust, Caution; The Rice Sprout Song;* and *Written on Water.* In 1944 Chang began publishing a novella, *Chained Links*, in serial form. As articulated more fully in the footnote below, a prominent critic wrote an essay that praised her earlier fiction but then criticized her latest work. Chang wrote "Writing of One's Own" in response.

## Writing of One's Own

Although I write fiction and essays, I usually pay very little heed to theory. Recently, though, I suddenly feel as if I have a little something to say, so I have written it down here.[1]

I have always thought that literary theory comes after literary works. That is how it has been in the past, that is how it is in the present, and in the future I'm afraid it will remain the same. If we desire to enhance

1. Chang initially wrote this essay in response to the prominent literary critic Fu Lei's criticisms of her serialized novella *Lianhuan tao* (Chained links). Fu Lei, a well-respected scholar and prolific translator of French literature, professed himself to be amazed by Chang's youthful talent. Writing under a pseudonym (Xun Yu) in an essay called "Lun Zhang Ailing de xiaoshuo" (On Eileen Chang's fiction), Fu first praises Chang's impeccable narrative techniques in stories such as "The Golden Cangue" and "Love in a Fallen City" and then moves on to criticize *Lianhuan tao* as trivial and "lacking in substance." Implicit in Fu's critique was a sense that Chang, in focusing on the "petty" and "passive" domestic lives and loves of largely female urbanites, was betraying the nationalistic and politically engaged ideals of earlier realist literature of the May Fourth Movement. Fu Lei's critique appeared in the same journal, *Wanxiang* (Phenomena), in which *Lianhuan tao* began its serialization in 1944. After producing this response to defend her work, Chang abruptly ended the serialization. The novella itself, about a lower-class woman named Nixi who travels from one man to another and maintains her vitality and optimism against all odds, went unfinished.

writers' awareness of their own craft, it would naturally be of some help to extrapolate theory from literary works themselves in order to use this knowledge as a gauge for further creation. But as we go about this process of gauging our creations, we must also remember that, in the process of literary development, work and theory are like two horses sharing the same yoke, jockeying back and forth as they drive each other forward. Theory is not a driver seated on high, brandishing a whip.

These days, it seems that literary works are impoverished, and so literary theory is impoverished as well. I have discovered that people who like to write literature usually concentrate on the uplifting and dynamic aspects of life and neglect those that are placid and static, though the latter is the ground of the former. That is, they concentrate for the most part on struggle and neglect the harmonious aspects of life. In reality, people only engage in struggle in order to attain harmony.

An emphasis on the uplifting and dynamic smacks more or less of the superman. Supermen are born of specific epochs. But the placid and static aspects of life have eternal significance: even if this sort of stability is often precarious and subject at regular intervals to destruction, it remains eternal. It exists in every epoch. It is the numinous essence of humanity, and one might also say it is the essence of femininity.

Very few works in the history of literature plainly sing in praise of the placid, while many emphasize the dynamic and uplifting aspects of human life. But in the best of these works, the uplifting aspects of human life are still portrayed against the background of its inherent placidity. Without this grounding, uplift is like so much froth. Many works are forceful enough to provide excitement but unable to offer any real revelation, and this failure results from not having grasped this notion of grounding.

Struggle is stirring because it is powerful and grand and yet at the same time bitterly distressing. Those who struggle have lost their harmony and are in search of a new harmony. Struggle for the sake of struggle lacks resonance and, when transformed into writing, will never produce great literary works.

I find that, in many works, strength predominates over beauty. Strength is jubilant and beauty is mournful, and neither can exist without the other. "Life and death are so far apart / I make my vow to you / and take your hand / to grow old together."[2] This is a mournful poem, but how very affirmative is its posture toward human life. I do not like heroics. I like tragedy and, even better, desolation. Heroism has strength but no beauty and thus seems to lack humanity. Tragedy, however, resembles the matching of bright red with deep green: an intense and unequivocal contrast. And yet it is more exciting than truly revelatory. The reason desolation resonates far more profoundly is that it resembles the conjunction of scallion green with peach red, creating an equivocal contrast.

I like writing by way of equivocal contrast because it is relatively true to life. In "Love in a Fallen City," Liusu escapes from her corrupt traditional family, but the baptism of the Battle of Hong Kong does not transform her into a revolutionary. The Battle of Hong Kong does affect Fan Liuyuan in the sense that it steers him toward a more settled existence and finally marriage, but marriage does not make him a saint or compel him to abandon completely his old habits and ingrained tendencies. Thus, although Liusu and Liuyuan's marriage is healthy in some ways, it remains prosaic, earthbound, and, given their situation, it could be nothing more.

There are very few people, after all, who are either extremely perverse or extremely enlightened. Times as weighty as these do not allow for easy enlightenment. In the past few years, people have gone on living their lives, and even their madness seems measured. So my fiction, with the exception of Cao Qiqiao in "The Golden Cangue," is populated with equivocal characters. They are not heroes, but they are of the majority who actually bear the weight of the times. As equivocal as they may be, they are also in earnest about their lives. They lack tragedy; all they have is desolation. Tragedy is a kind of closure, while desolation is a form of revelation.

I know that people are urgent in their demand for closure and, if they cannot have it, will only be satisfied by further excitement. They seem to be impatient with revelation in its own right. But I cannot write in any other way. I think that writing in this manner is more true to life. I know that my works lack strength, but since I am a writer of fiction, the only

2. The line is from a poem titled "Beat the Drum" ("Jigu"), from *Shijing* (The classic of poetry), the earliest and most influential poetic anthology in the Chinese literary tradition. The same line is cited by the male protagonist Fan Liuyuan in Chang's novella "Love in a Fallen City" ("Qingcheng zhi lian").

authority I have is to give expression to the inherent strength of my characters and not to fabricate strength on their behalf. Moreover, I believe that although they are merely weak and ordinary people and cannot aspire to heroic feats of strength, it is precisely these ordinary people who can serve more accurately than heroes as a measure of the times.

In this era, the old things are being swept away and the new things are still being born. But until this historical era reaches its culmination, all certainty will remain an exception. People sense that everything about their everyday lives is a little out of order, out of order to a terrifying degree. All of us must live within a certain historical era, but this era sinks away from us like a shadow, and we feel we have been abandoned. In order to confirm our own existence, we need to take hold of something real, of something most fundamental, and to that end we seek the help of an ancient memory, the memory of a humanity that has lived through every era, a memory clearer and closer to our hearts than anything we might see gazing far into the future. And this gives rise to a strange apprehension about the reality surrounding us. We begin to suspect that this is an absurd and antiquated world, dark and bright at the same time. Between memory and reality there are awkward discrepancies, producing a solemn but subtle agitation, an intense but as yet indefinable struggle.

There is an unfinished sculpture by Michelangelo, called *Dawn*, in which the human figure is only very roughly hewn and even the facial features are indistinct. But its expansive spirit symbolizes the imminent advent of a new era. If such works were to be produced today, one would be entranced, but none exist, nor indeed can they exist, because we are still unable to struggle free of the nightmare of the era.

And it is this era that constitutes my artistic material, one for which I believe the technique of equivocal contrast is appropriate. I use this method to portray the kinds of memories left behind by humanity as it has lived through each and every historical epoch. And by these means, I provide to the reality that surrounds me a revelation. This is my intention, although I do not know if I have accomplished it. I am incapable of writing the kind of work that people usually refer to as a "monument to an era" and I do not plan to try, because it seems that the concentration of objective material needed for such a project has yet to become available. And, in fact, all I really write about are some of the trivial things that happen between men and women. There is no war and no revolution in my works. I think that people are more straightforward and unguarded in love than they are in war or revolution. War and revolution, by their very nature, make more urgent demands of rationality than sensibility. Works that portray war and revolution often fail precisely because their technical prowess outstrips their artistry. In contrast with the unguarded freedom of love, war is inexorably imposed on us from the outside, whereas revolution often forces the individual to drive forward by dint of will alone. A real revolution or a revolutionary war, I believe, should be as emotionally unguarded and as able to penetrate into every aspect of one's life as romantic love. And it should bring one back into a state of harmony.

I like forthright simplicity, but I must portray the rich duplicity and elaborate designs of modern people in order to set them off against the ground of life's simplicity. This is why my writing is too easily seen by some readers as overly lush or even decadent. But I do not think it possible to use the elemental approach of a book like the Old Testament. This is the altar on which Tolstoy was sacrificed in his waning years. Nor do I approve of the aesthetes who advocate Beauty above all else. I think that their problem lies not in their beauty but in their failure to provide the figure of Beauty with a ground. The water in a mountain stream is merely light and frolicsome, but seawater, though it may seem to ripple in much the same way, also contains within it the prospect of vast oceanic swells. Beautiful things are not necessarily grand, but grand things are always beautiful. And yet I do not place truthfulness and hypocrisy in direct and unequivocal contrast; instead, I utilize equivocal contrast as a means of writing the truth beneath the hypocrisy of modern people and the simplicity underneath the frivolity, and this is why I have all too easily been seen as overly indulgent and criticized for lingering over these beguiling surfaces. Even so, I continue to write in my own style and can only feel ashamed that I have yet to perfect my art. I am, after all, just a neophyte when it comes to literature.

When readers of the old school read my works, they find them rather diverting but also more unsettling than they should be. New-style people find them reasonably absorbing but not quite as serious as they might be.

But that is the best I can do, and I am confident that my art is not compromised. I only demand of myself that I should strive for an even greater degree of realism.

Further, because I rely on a particular conception of equivocal contrast in my writing, I do not like to adopt the classicist manner in which good and evil, spirit and flesh, are always posed against each other in stark conflict, and thus the theme of my works may sometimes seem vague and unsatisfactory. I think the theory that a literary work needs a main theme could do with some revision. In writing fiction, one ought to have a story. It is better to let that story speak for itself than fabricating a plot in order to fit a certain theme. Readers often pay very little heed to the original themes of the great works that have come down to us through the ages, because times have changed, and those concerns no longer have the power to engage us. Yet readers of these works may at any time extract new revelations from the stories themselves, and it is only thus that the eternal life of any given work is assured. Take *War and Peace*, for instance. Originally, Tolstoy intended his story to revolve around the religious and collectivist philosophies of life that were popular at the time, but, as it turned out, the unfolding of the story itself eventually vanquished his predetermined theme. This is a work that was rewritten seven times, and with each revision the predetermined theme was forfeited still further. In the end, what remained of the theme was little more than an aside, becoming in fact the most awkward section of the novel, and there was no new main theme to replace it. This is why Tolstoy felt himself somewhat at a loss after having finished the novel. In comparison with *Resurrection*, the main theme of *War and Peace* does seem rather indistinct, but it remains much the greater work. Even now, every inch of the text comes alive as we read. The difference between modern literary works and those that came before also seems to rest on this distinction. No more does the emphasis lie principally on a main theme; instead, the story is allowed to give what it can and readers to take what they are able.

This is how I have and will continue to write *Chained Links*. In that work, the absence of a main theme is conspicuous, but I hope that people will like it for the story alone. My original idea was very simple: I would describe these sorts of things because they exist. Modern people for the most part are exhausted, and the modern marriage system is irrational as well. Thus silence reigns between husbands and wives. There are those who look for relief by engaging in sophisticated flirtation, so as to avoid having to take responsibility for their actions, and those who revert to animal desires by patronizing prostitutes (but these are only beastly men and not beasts and are thus all the more horrifying). Then there is cohabitation, which is not as serious a bond as marriage, involves more responsibility than sophisticated flirtation, and is not so lacking in humanity as whoring. People who go to extremes are, in the final analysis, the minority, and so living together out of wedlock has become a very common phenomenon in recent years.

The social status of the men who support these kinds of arrangements is roughly middle class or below; they work hard and live thriftily. They can't afford to let themselves go but aren't so reserved that they are willing to let themselves sink into boredom, either. They need vibrant, down-to-earth relationships with women, relationships that are just as vibrant and down-to-earth as the other aspects of their lives. They need women to look after their homes and are consequently less perverse in their dealings with them. In *Chained Links*, Yaheya is the proprietor of a midsized silk shop who still must work the counter himself. If Nixi could get along with him in peace, peace would continue to reign in their relationship for years to come and nothing would prevent the two from growing old and gray together. The failure of their life together out of wedlock arises from Nixi's own character flaws. Her second lover, Dou Yaofang, is the relatively prosperous owner of an herbal medicine shop, but he lacks the swanky air of a big-time capitalist. The petty official with whom Nixi lives has no more than a touch of the bureaucrat about him. Neither man is especially perverse when it comes to Nixi. What transpires between her and them is very human. And thus it should come as no surprise that these relationships are full of genuine affection.

As for women who live with men out of wedlock, their social position necessarily starts out somewhat lower than that of men, but most of them possess a fiery will to live. Still, the seductive power they have over their lovers is no more and no less than the charm of a healthy woman. If they were really as perverse as they are often imagined to be, they would not satisfy the needs of these men. Such women can work for attention, can be jealous, show off, and fight; they can be quite savage but never hysterical. They have only one problem: that their status remains forever in doubt. And because of this gnawing insecurity, they become grasping and selfish as time goes on.

This sort of cohabitation is more prevalent in China than it is in the West, but no one has yet attempted to write about it. The Mandarin Ducks and Butterflies writers find these types of people lacking in the sentimentality traditionally evoked by "talented scholar and beautiful maiden" romances.[3] The new-style writers, on the other hand, dislike that these relationships seem to resemble neither love nor prostitution and are thus neither healthy enough nor sufficiently perverse to lend themselves to the articulation of an unmistakably clear main theme.

What moves me about Nixi's story is her unalloyed passion for material life, a material life that she must struggle with all her might to retain. She wants the love of men but also desires security, cannot have both simultaneously, and ends up in possession of neither. She feels she can depend on nothing and invests everything in her children, hoping thereby to reap the bounty of their labor: a most inhuman sort of reward.

It is not that Nixi lacks feeling. She wants to love this world but never finds an opening. Nor is it the case that she is unloved, but the love she receives is merely the leftover stew and cold table scraps from someone else's meal, as in Du Fu's poem: "Leftover stew and cold scraps / everywhere bitterness concealed."[4] But she is above all a vital, healthy woman and never resorts to beggarliness. She resembles instead someone who chews greedily on soybean meal: even though she has a very strong constitution and the meal has a modicum of nutritional value, she'll still end up with an upset stomach. That a human being is made to eat fodder intended for beasts is ultimately the real tragedy.

As for the fact that I have adopted phrases and diction from traditional fiction in writing *Chained Links*—where Cantonese and foreigners of fifty

3. A Chinese narrative tradition based in part on the thirteenth-century vernacular drama *Xixiang ji* (The story of the western wing).

4. Chang is misquoting from the Tang poet Du Fu's 719 c.e. poem "Respectfully Presented to Venerable Mr. Wei: Twenty Couplets" ("Fengzeng Wei zuo chengzhang ershi yun").

years ago speak like characters from *The Golden Lotus* or when the Chinese people in Pearl Buck's fiction sound just like characters from old English literature when they open their mouths to speak—all these borrowings were for the sake of expedience and less than ideal as such. My original intention was this: the romantic ambience of Hong Kong as envisioned by Shanghai people would set up one sort of distance, and the temporal divide between the present and the Hong Kong of fifty years ago would create another. So I adopted an already antiquated sort of diction in order to represent better these two kinds of distance. There are times when it may seem contrived and overdone. I think I will be able to make some corrections in the future.

*Translated by Andrew F. Jones*

# Ji Xian

*(b. 1913)*

Ji Xian was born in Hebei but grew up in Yangzhou. He graduated from the Suzhou Institute of Art and was influenced by French symbolism. In the 1930s he edited a poetry journal, *New Poetry*, with Dai Wangshu. In Shanghai in 1944 and then in 1948, he edited two short-lived journals, *Poetic Boundary* and *Heresy*. In 1948 he moved to Taiwan and taught at a high school in Taipei. Beginning in 1953, he started *Modern Poetry Quarterly* and became a pioneer of Chinese modernism. About eighty poets joined the Modernist School, and, on February 1, 1956, in the thirteenth issue of *Modern Poetry*, he issued the famous six tenets listed below. With its emphasis on finding new forms and content, the second tenet became particularly important. In arguing for "horizontal transplantation" over "vertical inheritance," he advocated that modern Chinese poetry could borrow and draw strength and vision from Western poetries and that these Western sources were more important than the heritage of classical Chinese. As part of his poetics, he asserted the primacy of the imagination and asserted that a poem contained a universe. Although the Modernist School was dissolved in 1962, its influence continues to be felt today.

Ji Xian has published twelve volumes of poetry, including: *The Star-Plucking Youth* (1942), *Drinker* (1948), *The Betel-nut Tree* (1965), *Song of the*

*Peninsula* (1993), and *Cosmos Poems* (2001). The latest volume, *Only Ninety Years Old,* was published in June 2008, at the age of ninety-five. His three-volume *Memoirs* were published in 2001. In Taiwan he is called "the ever-green tree in the field of poetry." Since 1976, he has lived in California.

## Six Tenets

1. The society wished to promulgate the "spirit" and "basic elements of all new schools of Western poetry since Baudelaire."
2. The group believed that writing new poetry meant "horizontal transplantation" rather than "vertical inheritance."
3. The group emphasized "newness"—"to explore new continents and new virgin lands of poetry, to express new contents and create new forms, to discover new tools and invent new techniques."
4. They also underscored "rationality": one of the key features of modernism, they believed, was, its "anti-romanticism, its emphasis on rationality, and its rejection of emotional confessionalism."
5. They would like to seek "the purity of poetry": to cleanse poetry of all "non-poetic dregs, to purify, distil, and refine poetry."
6. They were "patriotic, anticommunist, and supporters of freedom and democracy—this needs no explanation."

*Translated by Leo Ou-fan Lee*

# Bian Zhilin

*(1910–2000)*

Bian Zhilin was born in Jiangsu province and developed a keen interest in classical Chinese poetry from his father, a primary school teacher. He attended high school in Shanghai, where classes were taught in English. At Beijing University, he majored in English and wrote poetry. He published his collection *Poems of Ten Years: 1930–1939* with a dedication to Xu Zhimo, but he was also influenced by Wen Yiduo's ideas about poetic form. In the early 1930s, the French symbolist poets exerted a strong influence, and, in 1934, he translated T. S. Eliot's essay "Tradition and the Individual Talent" into Chinese. He once remarked that although he employed European methods in his poetry, he also drew on the spirit of classical Chinese poetry. His remarkable poetry showed a confluence of both traditions, and he experimented with poetic forms throughout his life. In 1938 he left his position as a lecturer at the University of Sichuan to join the communists in Yan'an. He traveled with the Eighth Route Army for six months, and his poetic style shifted away from the intimacy and suggestion of his earlier poems to writing of "real people and real events." In these more public poems, Bian chose a more lucid and plainer style, but he continued to experiment with the prosody of his lines. After the 1930s, Bian wrote poetry sporadically, and he became more of a novelist, translator, and scholar. He taught at Beijing University and translated Shakespeare. In 1978, when China reopened to the West, he started publishing his writings and translations and, two years later, visited the United States.

In 1978 Bian Zhilin wrote an introduction to his collected poems, "Preface to *A Historical Record of Carved Critters*." He describes the stages of his evolution as a poet and articulates, in great detail, his ideas about prosody. In the excerpts included here, Bian articulates some key ideas about form and prosody and also addresses larger issues of literature, including "the ancient for modern use, the foreign for Chinese use."

## Excerpts from Preface to *A Historical Record of Carved Critters*

"Men prize the clarity of self-knowledge." Perhaps I still have some self-knowledge: if they say that writing poetry is "carved critters and doodads," then, used to describe my circumstances, it should be all the more fitting.

"The ability of a man can be great or small," and naturally the magnanimity of a man's spirit can be great or small as well. Looking back over my intellectual life, it could be said that it has crossed great seas, weather-weary, and yet remained unworthy of mention. Men are not wood or stone, and those who write poems may best be called "emotional animals." I write poems, and have always written lyric poems, and while I cannot stop myself, I tend toward restraint, as if in an attempt to be "a cold-blooded animal." The specifications are not great, and I enjoy rinsing, refining, in expectation of crystallization, in expectation of a blossoming, but in the end of course it is just the output of a few trinkets. Decades later, these things, even if some have gotten pleasure out of them, might in reality only temporarily occupy a small corner in some kind of history museum or warehouse of archives.

For the production of these trinkets, the creator must be conscious of coldness and warmth, and also be clear of the sweet and the bitter. Now that I have arranged them, I think I also might offer a bit of an explanation.

They comprise, whether in terms of content of thought or of artistic form, a rather long and largely tortuous journey, a journey of exploration. [. . .]

For the next several years, I wrote a little bit in periods of storm amid calm, not stopping until the end of spring in 1937.

For the poems I had written in this period, my content followed my form, and my thought tended to be shaped by artistic style, in endless change, either crisscrossing change or tortuous change, but without any real alterations.

People live in a social reality, and literature reflects reality; regardless of whether it reflects its depths or its shallows, it will always want to change reality, with some changing it this way, some changing it that way, with the only difference being in idealism or illusion. The poems that I wrote in the thirties, beyond what I put into them, have been stamped with the seal of thirties society.

In the thirties in our country the League of Left-Wing Writers formed a torrent. In Western European and in Anglo-American literature was simultaneously what people coming after would call, with praise or reproach, "the Pink Decade." Although, given the distinctions in subjective and objective circumstances, there are substantial differences, differences in development, between the two, with the latter a quick bloom and wilt, and the former already forming the mainstream of our country's literature by the time of the Anti-Japanese War, going to show only that the tide of the times did not discriminate between East and West. My own growth in thought and feeling was rather slow, and when I first read about Western "Modernist" literature in the twenties, it was like truth at first sight, as I resonated with all of its writing, and only until the War of Resistance started up in 1937 did this initial phase of my poetic creativity end.

The poems I wrote from beginning to end of this phase have many common characteristics.

Because of an unclear direction at that time, with sensitivity toward the trivial and ignorance toward the significant, in the face of the incidents of history and the storms of the era, I never knew what I wanted to express or in what manner to express my responses to these vicissitudes. Writing poetry in this period, I always seemed to be located in the depths of the valley, even though my heart would be at the mountaintop.

To start with revisiting that time, the poems I wrote were always rich in tones that would embrace the past and the faraway.

All in all I only wrote a few lyrical, short poems. But I was always afraid to stick out my neck, more at ease being silent and unheard in the crowd, the more afraid of publicizing my personal emotions. At this time I would mostly lyricize scenery, lyricize objects, lyricize people, lyricize things. With no sense of true feelings, I never really knew how to write poetry, but at this time I wrote even less about real people or real events. I tend to like to express what our nation used to call "evocation," or what in the West is called "dramatic tension," or what could also be said to tend toward the fictionalized, the typified, the impersonal, even occasionally employing the *parody*. Therefore, the "I" in the vast majority of poems in this period could also be traded for "you" or "he" (or "she"), so long of course as it were traded according to the scope of the whole poem, and were traded in accordance with logic.

At the same time, I always prioritized the vernacular, suitably absorbing Europeanized syntax and classical Chinese extraction (which is to say more with less, for concision). In poetic form then both free-verse and form poems, mainly immature attempts at writing form poems at first, were mainly using free verse for a time, finally almost completely using forms in which I considered myself proficient all the way until the new period beginning after Liberation.

This period could also be split into three stages.

The first stage (1930–32) was in those few days before I had graduated from college.

For the most part, the poems written in this stage express superficialities of social reality, with most giving expression to union with the commoners and little people at the lower levels of a declining society. This (in terms of the moderns in China) may be more or less the result of my edification by my teacher Wen Yiduo after he had written *Dead Water*. I mainly used the vernacular, and used formal styles, so as to embody deeply the Beijing streets and outlying areas, and the interiors and courtyard corners, that I had touched, which so totally were the desolate realm of north country imagery ("A Monk" and "A Piece of a Wrecked Ship" are exceptions). Maybe my ink was a bit faint, my tune a bit heavy. I began to utilize things that in the past "were not to enter poetry," such as teahouses, a pair of almonds crushed in an idle hand, iced sugar gourd, sour plum soup, yokes, and so on. I also would often use the impassioned to cover the intimate (such as "Continuous Rain") or joke about bitter hardships (such as "Crying One's Wares"). [. . .]

One of my explorations on the question of form and the question of "the ancient for modern use, the foreign for Chinese use," is still a prominent question to this day.

Here I would like to discuss my thoughts today.

When we write new poetry in the vernacular, free verse is obviously the easiest, but in fact for these to resemble poems is actually the least easy, because there is no track to follow. Form then necessarily emerges from praxis, from un-self-conscious to self-conscious, with everybody gradually growing aware, growing accustomed and, as they say, "becoming accustomed through general usage," "acquiring the taste."

Through my own praxis, I have consulted the standard creative and theoretical examples from antiquity, modernity, China, and abroad, and for the views acquired on form in new-style vernacular poetry, I am thus far in large agreement, with small differentiation, with the views that a small portion of people have raised.

When we say that poetry should be generally even (which necessitates proportionality), we could also say that a poem when read aloud can reveal an *interior* musical meter and rhythm. When we speak in Chinese, in most occasions we pronounce two or three syllables as a "beat," at the least with one syllable (a one-syllable "beat" can adhere between two two-syllable "beats" either before or after it and merge into one three-syllable "beat"), at most with four syllables (four-syllable "beats" then necessarily have a final particle such as *de*, *le*, or *ma*, otherwise they will naturally divide into two "beats," as in two-two or one-three or three-one). This is the basic *interior* pattern, the *objective* pattern, of Chinese. A sentence could vary by person, vary by time, be pronounced slowly or quickly, stretched long or shrunk short, which are subjective applications, as even a few sentences from an editorial can, at the hands of a musician, be set to music and sung, which is *exterior* processing. So to write poems in vernacular Chinese, the *basic* formal element, like our nation's old-style poetry or folk songs, similar to the majority of formal poetics in foreign languages, is not *primarily* located in the arrangement of end-rhymes but in the handling of "beats" or "sound-clusters." [. . .]

If what I advocate seems complex, in fact it is simple, and very liberating when put to use. The question that still emerges thus far is from the simplicity of this basic formal element of the "beat" or "sound-cluster." I think that we can neither modify level and oblique tones, nor can we delineate heavy and light stresses, but we might be able to use two-syllable "beats" and three-syllable "beats" as a backbone, proceeding toward a *mutually* appropriate arrangement, so that the mending of the *interior* unevenness of the "beat" or "sound-cluster" may be unobvious (and yet free), is this not sufficient?

Ultimately, this is all: we neither "chant" or "grunt" at a whim, nor "sing" along to sheet music, but that when we "read" or "recite" vernacular new-style poetry according to the way we speak, the poetry *itself* won't appear to be without the *internal* element or *objective* rule contained within an art of time and acoustics, but rather, like lines in a drama or a rousing speech, leaving the speaker with no foundation other than to rely on his own talents, freely creating, and thereby express a meter and rhythm like music, even a melody.

My views on the question of form in vernacular new-style poetry are thus. This likewise brings in my personal experience on the question of "the ancient for modern use, the foreign for Chinese use."

I remember, at a conference on the question of poetry in 1959, our theorist Hu Qiaomu said in a speech that starting to write new-style poetry after "May Fourth," in terms of characteristics, there had been three generations overall: the first generation knew a lot about Chinese old poetry, the second generation knew a lot about foreign poetry, and the third knew a little about both (this was the main point, though some large discrepancies may exist). Considering my age, and considering the period in which I began writing poetry, it seems that I should belong to what is here called the third generation. In terms of characteristics, my poems may demonstrate this. My knowledge of poetry is definitely not a polymath's expertise of all, ancient and foreign, but rather a following of my interests, with only unsystematic branching out.

In the age when I was in grammar school I could only read a few poems for pleasure in old books I'd find at home, while toward the end of high school I began to encounter some English poems in the original language, but when I began university and could understand only a little French I started occasionally and superficially to read French poetry. Because of differences surrounding my individual circumstances, the old foreign poems that I admired or delighted in may not have been that influential when I began writing. Generally speaking, not to have, here and there, consciously or unconsciously, lessons to draw from, or to absorb, would have been hard to avoid indeed.

In the vernacular new-style poems I write, just as they can be said to be "Europeanized" (as a matter of fact, to write poems with line-breaks is what Lu Xun called "grabbism" from the West), they may also be called "antiquitized." The one is mainly in exterior form, where influence is easy to spot, while the other is completely in content, where influence does not leave much of a trace. On the one hand, only when literature has a national style can it have global significance. On the other hand, European literature after the Middle Ages has already become World Literature, and by now this "world" has of course long since included China. As for myself, the question is to see whether my writing poetry can "*ize* antiquity," or can "*ize* Europe."

In the ideas and writing that I express in my own vernacular new-style poetry, the ancient, modern, Chinese, and foreign all have not a few similarities.

For example, when I write lyric poems, like the majority of our nation's old poems, I stress "evocation," and then often compose a "dramatic monologue" through Western "dramatic tension."

And again, poetry must be concise. I stress the implicit in writing poems, so with the Western poems of the strain that favors suggestiveness, it is naturally easy to keep in time.

And again, language must be rich. When I write new-style poems, I basically employ the colloquial, but I often draw from classical vocabulary and classical syntax (in the initial period this happened most at one stage); after Liberation in the new period for a time I tried to bring in various dialects, while at the same time often using a Europeanized syntax that everyone had already gotten used to.

From a negative point of view, in a phase of my initial period, for example, if there appeared the dynastic swan song of the poetry of the Late Tang and the Southern Song, there was also at the same time an approach toward the Western sentiments of the "fin-de-siècle."

The jargon of "Realism" and "Romanticism" were also "grabbed" from the West. In the poems I write I believe that there are elements of both a Realism *broadly defined* and a Romanticism *broadly defined*, only, whether they blend or conflict, I couldn't rightly say, and it should not be a matter for me to settle.

For the great poets from China and abroad, of course their influence has been great. But their effects on my new-style poems are limited by my own individual ability and temperament, so while they cannot have had no influence, it is not necessarily obvious. Meanwhile, certain works by a number of secondary poets or poets hardly worth mentioning often seemed to be exactly what I could "use."

For example, in my pieces in my initial phase I seem to have attempted to follow the motions of Li Shangyin and Jiang Kui and even the lyrics of *Amidst the Flowers*.

And again, writing the gray scenery of the Beijing streets in the earliest phase of my initial period, I could point out Baudelaire's writing of the impoverished streets of Paris and his inspiration at the sight of old men and blind men. The T. S. Eliot who wrote *The Waste Land* and other early short pieces was not unrelated to my writing in the middle phase of my initial period; a similar situation occurred in the third phase of my initial period, with the likes of W. B. Yeats, R. M. Rilke, and the short pieces of Paul Valéry's later style; in my later period through to the post-Liberation period, I am most indebted to some poems of W. H. Auden's middle period, as well as some poems from Aragon's participation in the Resistance.

For some of them I purposefully employed their style to express my own differences of sentiment.

For instance, "Long Road," a poem about the suburbs of Beijing, was consciously written in imitation of each stanzaic arrangement of an untitled Paul Verlaine poem. Within it, "Faint threads of persistent cicada chirps" more unconsciously recalls the famous line of Valéry's "Le cimetière marin" about cicada chirps. Rhyme and alliteration can still be used in vernacular new-style poetry. Common in Western poems, they are even more so in our nation's old poetry, such as the famous line from Jiang Baishi's "Moon over the Xiang," "*yī yè yí yóu chéng xīng*" [a single leaf lingering in delight], used to paint the sounds and the scenery of a boat rowed on the river.

More particular were the deliberate parodies. In "A Monk," from the poems of my prior period, was a deliberate parodying of the second- or third-rate *fin du dix-neuvième siècle* French symbolist sonnet, repeating only two end rhymes, mostly rhyming on *-ong* (*-eng*), imitating the monotony of a clock, with the content not quite Western material, obliquely reflecting the weary tones expressed in the poetry of that period.

The sonnet, which in the West still has some life force left in it, I believe to be the closest to our nation's seven-character Regulated Verse, and when the *rise, hold, turn, fold* structure is used well, it can also be applied. I have also thought about mocking the seven-character Regulated Verse in vernacular new-style poetry, removing the two parallel couplets from the middle, and creating an eight-lined genre, but I never attempted it, trying only a similar seven-character quatrain.

In the poetry of my initial and later periods, I have tried to use many Western forms, such as "The White Seashell" with its application of the most complicated end rhyme setup that Valéry used, just as I have applied a mutant short-line sonnet form of his creation to write "To Air Force Fighters."

In fact the entirety of what I wrote through my latter period and the new period post-Liberation is not much, with deliberate use of the sonnet form comprising a few, only they weren't labeled as sonnets, and readers seem only rarely to have noticed. This might explain why I did not achieve such effects in my Chinese, and might explain how I could use it so inconspicuously. My later experience is that for a sonnet in Chinese to sound natural, each line must be held to four "beats" or shorter; otherwise it will not succeed very easily.

Of course, if I write vernacular new-style poems, and write them poorly, *then* it is because in putting "the ancient for modern use, the foreign for Chinese use," I have used them poorly or inappropriately.

*Translated by Lucas Klein*

# Ai Qing

*(1910–1996)*

Ai Qing was born in Jinhua in Zhejiang Province. He was nine years old when the May Fourth Movement began and, in middle school, wrote an essay, "Each Age Has Its Own Literature," in which he spoke against the reading of works in classical Chinese. In 1928 he passed the entrance exam for the Painting Department of the West Lake National School of Fine Arts, but the director urged him to go abroad. In 1929 he moved to Paris and worked in a small arts and crafts factory and went to a free art studio to learn drawing and painting. He read literature and philosophy and was influenced by modern French poetry. In January 1932 he returned to China, joined the League of Left-Wing Artists, but was arrested in July by the Guomindang. In October 1935 he was finally released and worked as an editor and teacher. In 1936 he published his first collection of poems, *Dayanhe*. In 1941 he went to Yan'an, and Mao consulted with him on several occasions before convening the Yan'an Forum on Literature and Art. He joined the Communist Party in 1945 and, after 1949, served as assistant editor of the *People's Literature* journal. In 1956 his second collection of poems, *Spring*, was published by the People's Literature Press. A few years later, he was suspected of "rightism" and was sent to work in farms in Manchuria and then Xinjiang. He was also persecuted during the Cultural Revolution but was rehabilitated in 1978. His aphorisms, *On Poetry*, were published in Hong Kong in 1980, and two years later his *Selected Poems* was published by the Foreign Languages Press in Beijing. In 1985 he made a second trip to France and was awarded the title Chevalier de l'Ordre des Arts et des Lettres.

In the preface to his *Selected Poems*, Ai Qing charts his life story in five sections. In the following excerpt, turning to poetry itself, he discusses inspiration, metaphor, and the imagination.

## Excerpts from Preface to *Selected Poems*

"Inspiration," if we must call it that, is nothing more than a poet responding to something in a new way: it is a sudden passion, a flash or spark lighting up the heart if only for an instant. "Inspiration," so-called, is the happiest possible encounter of the poet's subjective world with objective reality. It should be the poet's best friend. [. . .]

One doesn't write poetry for the sake of playing around with verbal skills; on the other hand, one must have these skills in order to write poetry. Even when we talk, there is such a thing as talking to the point or not talking to the point.

The activity of the human mind, which produces the imagination and the ability to associate ideas, is nothing but a synthesis of life's experiences. In the course of synthesizing these experiences, metaphors occur. The object of metaphor is for one experience to corroborate another experience.

> The sense of touch and the sense of sight are mutually complementary, so that, after a while, we can speak of the outer form of something as something susceptible to touch.

What a clever notion, that of something being "mutually complementary." Engels's use of this phrase, "mutually complementary," although it relates to the senses, also applies to the relationships between things and to the relationships between thoughts. It grasps the interrelatedness and the connections between everything in creation.

The activity of the imagination consists of crystallizing all sorts of things that are difficult to grasp, all sorts of things that are vague and elusive, and presenting them clearly before the reader, as clearly as the print on a page.

The activity of the imagination consists of converting something abstract to concrete terms—something that will touch the emotions.

The activity of the imagination causes something heavy and leaden to sprout wings; or, the reverse, to freeze and fix something flowing and in flux.

In the realm of the imagination, one can grasp hands across ten thousand miles; or, one could cause hands that hold each other to wave goodbye.

The way of the imagination is the way that draws "mutual complementarities" from the abstract and the concrete.

The way of the imagination is poetry, and it is the basic tool in the creation of poetry as well as other literature.

*Translated by Peng Wenlan & Eugene Chen Eoyang*

# Lo Fu (Luo Fu)

*(b. 1928)*

Lo Fu was born in Hengyang, Hunan. In 1949 he moved to Taiwan and later graduated from Cadre Academy. In 1954, along with Zhang Mo and Ya Xian, he co-founded the Epoch Poetry Society and served as the editor of *Epoch Poetry Quarterly* for over a decade. He worked in Vietnam from 1965 to 1967. In 1973 he retired from the navy and graduated with a B.A. in English from Tamkang University. Lo Fu has published twelve books of poetry as well as many collections of essays, literary criticism, and translations. His first book, *River of the Soul*, appeared in 1957, but his early creative breakthrough occurred a year later. Stationed on Quemoy during the bombardment of the island, he began writing poems inside a bomb shelter as shells exploded overhead. The poems he wrote grew into *Death of a Stone Cell,* a major sequence of sixty-four poems that was published in 1965. This extended poem explores existence and fate through a rich and complex weave of personal symbols. His other collections include *River without Banks* (1970), *Wound of Time* (1981), *Wine-Brewing Stone* (1983), *Death of a Stone Cell* (reissued in 1993), *Driftwood* (2007), and *Lo Fu: Selected Poems* (2009). *Driftwood* is a book-length poem, and Lo Fu has said, "It sums up my experience of exile, my artistic explorations, and my metaphysics. I consider it a personal epic, the greatest achievement of my old age, and a landmark of my career." Lo Fu now lives in Canada.

In this essay, the introduction to *The Essential Lo Fu*, published in Beijing in 1999, Lo Fu suggests that contemporary poets can draw on elements from traditional Chinese poetry as well as Western poetry but that, ultimately, "literary tradition can only renew itself through innovation."

## Innovation and Continuity in Poetry

As a modern poet, I am frequently asked about continuity with regard to classical literature. On numerous occasions, I have publicly discussed the dialectical relationship between innovation and continuity—in other words, the modernization of classical literature. But the very complexity of the issue has led to misunderstandings. As a result, in recent years, people from poetry circles in mainland China have mistakenly classified me as a neoclassicist, a modern poet who has returned to tradition. They believe that I went astray with my early experiments with Western modernism and that I have since repented and returned to the fold. They often use me as a negative example in their discussions. In order to rectify such irresponsible judgments, and to correct this mistake, I would like to take the opportunity upon the publication of this collection to set the record straight.

First, let me say that I have very strong opinions on the issue of the continuity of literary tradition. Literary tradition can only renew itself through innovation and not by clinging or returning to the past. If "innovation" is not our guiding principle, then neoclassicism is reduced to pure formalism only. In time, everything dies, but death does not mean extinction; death is a transformation, and what exists eternally is the life force. Though a tree live for a thousand years, there will come a day when it must die, but its seeds, upon falling into the soil, will sprout with new life. But the new tree is different from its predecessor. With one life replacing another, life in the universe goes on uninterrupted. It is the same with the continuation of literature.

Another key point of this issue is that innovation is not merely reform—it is not so much a case of untying bound feet as it is a complete break with the practice. Prior to the May Fourth vernacular movement, Tan Sitong, Huang Zunxian, among others, had called for "innovation in poetry" and focused their efforts on the reform of poetic form. After the May Fourth Movement, poets such as Liu Dabai and Liu Bannong experimented with new poetic forms, but their poems died away as they did and had little impact on future generations. Poetic style must change with the times; old styles grow outmoded and pass away, never to be revived. Some things in poetry change; some things do not. Language and the rules and forms of poetic composition change; the quality of poetry—the appreciation of beauty—does not change, or changes only with great difficulty. What modern poets have chosen to discard is that which is changeable, and what they have chosen to continue or probe further is the unchangeable.

For the purpose of innovation, the early modern poets of Taiwan once threatened to discard tradition, opting instead for "horizontal transplanting rather than vertical inheritance." They rejected not only the tradition of old poetry but the May Fourth vernacular tradition as well, because the language of those early days was simplistic and unrefined, largely because the poets sought to express emotion and record events in a direct fashion without revising or the use of imagery. As a result, contemporary poets were dissatisfied with such language and the technique of modern Chinese poets, finding greater sustenance in the works of Western modernism. I personally believe that borrowing sometimes from the West is necessary, but a poet cannot be simply satisfied with doing so and not returning to his or her own culture. The poetry of a people must be grounded in and nourished by their own literary tradition. It is essential for the process of innovation. During the heyday of the fad of returning to tradition, some poets engaged in a painstaking display of echoing tradition. When writing landscape poetry, they had to include the obligatory small railed bridge; when writing object poetry, they would be sure to include wind, flowers, snow, and moonlight; when writing lyrical poetry, they couldn't avoid writing about spring fever and autumn-induced melancholy, all in a vernacular old poetry. Therefore, as we contemplate continuity and innovating for a new tradition, we must do so with a critical eye and historical awareness.

In other words, we must cast aside our parochial and conservative mindset. On the one hand, we must choose cautiously from tradition and absorb that which is beneficial for innovation; on the other hand, we must not reject outright the mirror afforded by the world's classics. We should be able to absorb the ideas and techniques of Western modernist masters.

Before reaching maturity, a modern poet must go through a long, arduous process of experimentation and learning, and to learn from and probe classical poetry is very important. What, after all, does classical poetry possess that is worth continuing? After many years of pursuit and experimentation, I would suggest the following:

1. The harmonious relationship of man and nature. Most classical poetry is colored by Daoist naturalism. As such, fields-and-gardens poetry constitutes a significant part of classical Chinese poetry. Be it lyrical or didactic, a poem finds expression through imagery from nature. Most classical poets were officials, who, after casting aside officialdom, would return to live amid nature. Their poems all present a "world" of peace and tranquility. In their poems, they clearly express a harmonious relationship between man and nature. For readers and writers alike, after experiencing this harmony for themselves, the soul will find refuge and life peace, thus affording a more profound understanding of life and thereby attaining freedom from suffering.

   But in contemporary society, people treat one another with coldness and indifference while people find themselves ever more cut off from nature because of developments in technology, higher population density, the complexity of human relations, and environmental degradation. As a result, people have fallen into a labyrinth of contradictions, worries, and confusion. The impact of Tao Yuanming's lines, "I pick chrysanthemums by my eastern fence, and catch sight of Southern mountain," comes from the fact that the power and proximity of nature allow us to discover our own existence. Although modern poetry reflects the depression and crises of people today, it offers no way out. If a modern poet can recover what we have lost from classical poetry and reestablish the harmonious relationship between man and nature, then modern poetry would become as profound as philosophy.

2. The poetic image. In terms of form, Chinese poetry went from four-character to five- and seven-character quatrains (*jueju*) and regulated verse (*lu-shi*); in terms of technique, from the superficial to the profound, from the simple and direct to the more hermetic, and from the realistic to the symbolic. These are all inevitable tendencies in the evolution of literature. However, the most notable thing was the evolution from a simple straightforward way of writing to the appearance of images. Through the use of imagery, the poet profoundly imbues objects with feeling, expressing them through fresh, lively, and concrete scenes. This form of expression is the fusion of emotion and scene, and for this reason it is synthetical, imaginative, emotive, meaning is implied, and its beauty simple yet profound. In other words, the richest and profoundest meaning is conveyed through the simplest and liveliest language. Du Fu was a master of seven-character regulated verse. His poems in this form are all exquisite image poems. I believe the reason Du Fu's poems have been widely read for centuries is due mainly to his mastery in handling imagery and his craftsmanship. Li Shangyin was a disciple of Du Fu's, from whom he learned to create images of emotion. Li Shangyin's lines, "Spring silkworms spin until they die, the candles weep tears until they burn away," are superb because intense emotion is captured in cool and outstanding images, increasing the depth of feeling.

   Although modern poetry has not reached all-around perfection, the language of imagery is a clear accomplishment. Undeniably, modern poets first learned a way of casting images from Western modernists, but of all the techniques the ancients had for handling images, the moderns cannot compete with the completeness or precision of regulated verse. It will require more time.

3. Surrealistic aspect of poetry. In handling the "empty" (*xu*) and "solid" (*shi*) facets of a poem, the poet sometimes believes the "empty" part is where he can give full reign to his imagination. This is the surrealistic aspect of a poem. The ancients emphasized the

> middle course beyond the concrete; the artistic effects of a poem were in the appropriate balance of the abstract and concrete. If a poem is too mundane, it becomes prosaic, vulgar, and uninteresting; if it is too unreal, it seems purely imaginary, becoming obscure. A good poem achieves a miraculous balance between the two.

Western surrealism once had a profound impact on modern poetry from Taiwan. Critics often see me as representative of Chinese surrealism. My early *Death of a Stone Cell* certainly possesses anti-rational and illogical tendencies. But I have been selective in my approach to surrealism. I can accept some of the techniques but cannot accept other things such as "automatic writing." Later, I discovered techniques similar to those of surrealism in classical poetry. For example, Du Fu's "Eight Autumn Meditations" and Li Shangyin's "Richly Painted Zither" are all able to achieve the surrealistic effect of "animating the inanimate and making the limited universal." This had implications for my later writing. I once wrote:

> Dawn, in the woods
> I hear the turning of the trees' annual rings

The surrealistic effect of these lines is no different from Du Fu's lines, "The Big Dipper is housed at Beihu, the sound of the Milky Way flows west." In emphasizing the contradictory and the irrational, Western surrealism did indeed turn reason on its head. It is expected that by bringing two totally unrelated things together, a new beauty will be created, but without the least concern as to the derivative meaning of the combination. But I have always believed that poetry possesses a meaningful beauty. This being the case, it would be better to say that my ideas about the surrealistic nature of poetry have been inspired by classical Chinese poetry rather than influenced by Western surrealism. The aesthetic effect that I longed for was the "irrational but marvelous" in classical poetry. This is close to Su Dongpo's view of poetry as "overturning the ordinary and hewing to the Way." Overturning the ordinary means distorting reality, superficially at any rate; but in doing so, the marvelous in the poem is created as well as its pleasurable effects. But in overturning the ordinary, one must hew to the Way, which means to correspond to our internal responses, or in other words, to go beyond what people expect while adhering to our common sense.

In Taiwan in the 1980s, I can safely say that there was no other poet like me who possessed such a well-developed classical spirit. At the time, I believed that a good poem had to transcend time and space, and a poet had to possess a sense of history. A poet could help readers acquire a more accurate perception of the true face of history only through a command of the classical spirit and by having assimilated the themes of classical poetry. More importantly, a clear view of history was essential if we were to understand the reality we faced. Based on this premise, I once sought inspiration in classical poetry, studying classical poetic expression, utilizing classical themes, and through assimilation and reworking, I was able to write a good many modern poems, such as "The Legend of Li Bai," "Drinking with Li He," and "Walking Toward Wang Wei," among others. The most notable example is probably my modern reworking of Bai Juyi's "Song of Everlasting Sorrow." I also reworked old lines by classical poets including Du Fu, Li Bai, Wang Wei, Li He, and Li Shangyin. For example, I reworked Li He's line "Stones split asunder, sky startles, autumn rains gush forth" in the following way:

> Stones shatter
> Heaven is startled
> Frightened stiff, the autumn rain freezes in mid-air

Sometimes I even took anecdotes from the *New Account of Tales of the World* or parables from *Zhuang-zi* and wrote them into poems. My poem "The Cries of Apes" is an example taken from the former, while "The Dialectic of Love" is from the latter, with the actual inspiration for the poem coming from the following lines in the "Robber Zhi" chapter of the *Zhuang-zi:* "Wei Sheng arranged to meet the girl under the bridge. She failed to appear and the water began to rise, but rather than leave, he wrapped his arms around the bridge pier and died."

I believe that the reworking of classical poems or themes is not the "modern translation of classical poetry" but rather a form of innovation. Not only is the result modern but also full of character, as it must possess the ideas of its creator as well as his or her aesthetics, otherwise he or she is nothing but a translator, and not a poet.

I was once asked why I used ancient poets as the subject in so many of my poems that deal with classical poetry. I believe that modern Chinese poetry lacks the implications of Eastern wisdom in classical Chinese poetry, a humanistic spirit, exalted worlds, as well as the unique temperament of the Chinese people.

What I have tried to do is compensate for this inherent shortcoming. Before the age of forty, I yearned for the wandering scholar spirit of Li Bai, the universal loneliness of Du Fu, and Li He's rebellion against popular and vulgar culture. But later in life, I have come to enjoy Wang Wei's indifference to fame and reclusive mindset. I have discovered that modern poetry emphasizes intellect and directly enters real life, which is significant for the times. I sometimes feel that modern poetry is too cruel to hold aloof from time and space. Can unforeseen artistic effects be achieved by writing about contemporary themes using classical techniques? This is what I have been working on for twenty years now. When I utilize classical themes to express Eastern wisdom in my poems, some mistakenly assume that I have "returned to tradition." As I stated previously, this is an erroneous judgment. Since the old tradition is not an option, there is no need to return to it. All I hope is to have recourse to China's humanistic tradition. I am after the most modern but also the most Chinese: the best way to continue the classical or carry on tradition is through innovation. Innovation is my ultimate goal, the essence of what I am striving for.

*Translated by John Balcom*

# Shang Qin

*(b. 1930)*

Shang Qin was born in Sichuan in 1930 but has lived in Taiwan since 1950. He began publishing poetry in the mid-1950s in such literary journals as *Modern Poetry Quarterly* and served in the military for many years. He was discharged in 1968 and attended the International Writing Program at the University of Iowa from 1968 to 1970. After returning to Taiwan, he worked as a gardener, bookstore clerk, street vendor, and editor, where he became associate editor in chief of the *China Times Weekly*. Shang Qin is the author of three volumes of poetry and an artist and calligrapher of note. Many of his prose poems have been translated into English, most recently by Steve Bradbury, whose *Feelings above Sea Level* (Zephyr Press, 2006) contains twenty-five of the poet's prose poems as well as a dozen of his delightfully surreal line drawings. Although surrealism has often been cited as an influence, Shang Qin writes a kind of poetry that is completely his own.

In the first selection, from the preface to the revised and expanded edition of his first volume of poetry, Shang Qin movingly narrates how he discovered the "New Literature" in China. In the prose poem that follows, "The Lock Electric," he makes the simple act of pulling out a key and turning it in a lock an *ars poetica*, and the play between darkness and light, inner and outer worlds is deft and accomplished. In the third selection, Zona Yi-Ping Tsou conducts and translates an interview in which Shang Qin asserts that "poetry isn't a frame but a frame of mind."

## Excerpt from Preface to *Dream or the Dawn and Other*

*August 1988, Yonghe, Taipei County*

*I*

Looking back over the years, I feel as though I have spent my whole life "doing time" or engineering some escape.

The year I turned fifteen, I was press-ganged by soldiers of Chiang Kai-shek's Nationalist Army in the streets of Chengdu and locked up in an old barn of a warehouse. After a week's incarceration I was pretty much broken in, but in the meantime I discovered the place was filled with books the like of which I had never seen before. This was my first exposure to what we then called the "New Literature." It was there I read Lu Xun's *Wild Grass* and Bing Xin's *Stars* [two seminal works in the genealogy of the Chinese prose poem].

A month later, I set out with the troops for Chongqing [Chiang Kai-shek's stronghold during the war against Japan], but before we got there I made the first of many escapes in my fugitive existence. Even now I can vividly recall the lights of the fishing boats on the Jialing River and the murmur of the water as it flows to the sea.

Three years later in Guangzhou Province in the south of China I engineered my greatest escape.

My intention was to return to my family home in Sichuan, but I was captured by one troop detachment after another only to escape again. In total, I must have run away at least seven or eight times and in the process tramped through at least half-a-dozen provinces without ever reaching my destination and at one point almost wound up in Indochina.

In the end, however, the Nationalist troops who caught me last were forced to engineer their own escape to Taiwan and took me with them.

After I got here I found the linguistic barriers to communication and the trivial distances between towns and cities took all the pleasure out of flight, and before long I no longer had the energy to run away and found the only escape left me was to flee from one name into another. But no matter how many times I changed my name, I could not escape from myself, and thus it is I am ever caught on the verge of "Dream or the Dawn."

To be "doing time" in your own mind is a sad thing to be sure. [. . .]

*Translated by Steve Bradbury*

## The Lock Electric

On this night, as always, the street-lamps in the district where I live went out at midnight.

As I was fishing for my keys, the kindly cabby kept his headlights trained in my direction as he backed down the drive. In the glare of the headlights the thick black shadow of a middle-aged man was ruthlessly silhouetted against the iron door until, that is, I finally found the key on the chain, aimed it just about the place my heart was, and thrust it in, whereupon the kindly cabby turned and drove away.

And so I gave the key a gentle *click*, drew out the ingenious sliver of metal, and in one fluid motion thrust the door open and boldly stepped inside.

I soon grew used to the darkness within.

*Translated by Steve Bradbury*

## Excerpts from "A Conversation with Shang Qin"

*Interview conducted on July 28, 2006, in Taipei by Zona Yi-Ping Tsou*

*So when did you start writing poetry?*

In 1949 or thereabouts. I was with the Nationalist troops when they retreated to the mountains of Yunnan and Guizhou. I was flat-footed and thus often fell behind. Sometimes I used that as an excuse to try and run away, but I was always overtaken by other troops, who usually took me in without a word. It was a chaotic time, and we were fighting a losing battle. Anyway, when I found myself alone up there in the mountains, I would get these feelings that I wanted to express in words. That was how I began to write poetry. [. . .]

*You were one of the first poets in Taiwan to write prose poems. How were these received in the beginning?*

With indifference, mainly. It's a bit painful to talk about. It was such a long time ago.

*Were they rejected because of their novelty?*

Actually, only one of my poems has ever been rejected, the prose poem "Giraffe." The editor was the poet Qin Zihao, who returned it with a note that said, "Your imagery is deep and sweeping, but the diction needs more discipline." Prose poetry was fairly novel at the time, but, from a Chinese point of view, it's not all that different from free verse. Lineation is a modern transplant from the West. Before the modern era, Chinese poetry didn't have line breaks, so you couldn't tell a poem's genre on the basis of its outer form. You could only tell from the language and the rhythm and tonal patterns and such. As my old friend the poet Ji Xian used to say, for the Chinese the modernist revolution wasn't a battle over genres but over poetic language, the abandonment of the classical literary language in favor of the modern spoken vernacular. It was basically a change of language tools. Being a poet who rails against any formal constraint, I naturally gravitated to the prose poem, which has none. For me, poetry isn't a frame but a frame of mind, one that I found as much in certain passages of classical prose as in the classical poetry, such as the *Zhuang-zi* and Tao Yuanming's preface to the "Peach Blossom Spring." No one remembers the poem Tao wrote on the same subject, only the prose preface, and for the reasons I've outlined.

*What writers have had the most influence on your prose poems?*

The first that comes to mind is the French surrealist poet Max Jacob. Many people think of me as a surrealistic, but I don't quite hold with that label for myself, although I am in sympathy with the surrealist agenda. To my way of thinking, surrealism is still a kind of realism, a super-realism, more real than real. Much of human behavior is repressed and constrained by social mores, but surrealist techniques are based on Freudian psychology and so have the power to take us under the surface of things, into the unconscious, where so much lies buried.

*Translated by Zona Yi-Ping Tsou*

# Yang Mu

*(b. 1940)*

Yang Mu was born in Hualien, Taiwan, in 1940, and he attended the local high school there. He published his first book of poetry, *By the Water's Edge*, in 1960, and in 1963 he graduated from Tunghai University in central Taiwan. He completed mandatory military service on the frontier island, Quemoy, and then, in 1964, attended the Iowa Writers' Workshop. He received an MFA from the University of Iowa in 1966 and then received a Ph.D. in comparative literature from the University of California, Berkeley. In 1971 he moved to the University of Washington, Seattle, where he taught for many years. He is a professor of comparative literature at the University of Washington and also dean of the College of Humanities and Social Sciences at National Dong Hwa University, Taiwan. He is the author, editor, and translator of over forty books of poetry and prose. *No Trace of the Gardener: Poems of Yang Mu*, translated by Lawrence Smith and Michelle Yeh, was published by Yale University Press in 1998.

As a poet, Yang Mu demonstrates a profound knowledge of the Chinese poetic tradition, but he is also one of its foremost innovators. As a prose writer, Yang Mu is an elegant stylist. "Further Reflections on the Headwaters of Poetry in Taiwan," published in 2005 as the last piece in a collection of essays, tracks the development of poetry in Taiwan. His poem "The Song of

Bishop Wort" is notable for its rhythmical spell and hearkens back to the first anthology of Chinese poetry, the *Shi-jing*, in its specific references to plants, but it also uses the image of the bishop wort as an emblem for Taiwan.

## Further Reflections on the Headwaters of Taiwanese Poetry

When reading or reflecting on the literature of Taiwan, some might step back for a moment and question whether or not it bears any signs of historical lineage, or, as we tend to see elsewhere, clear and reliable traces of literary headwaters. Whenever we look into the origins of modern poetry, we can't help but feel, and at times we might even wonder, if the history of this poetry before us is merely the result of centuries of accumulation. For it does not present itself as a forceful development, which would prove its vitality of purpose, nor does it offer us an intense focal point for further examination and analysis, which would enable us to recognize that this literature is as solid as the mountains. It is that steadiness and gravity that places you in its midst, and allows the rise to a historical consciousness as a matter of course.

Such thinking isn't entirely without basis, for there are grounds for it. And whenever one casts Taiwan's literature as marginal or subordinate to that of China, it's impossible not to fall into this trap. We're not denying that, geographically and historically, Taiwan does indeed appear to be a sort of poor relation, a marginal offshoot; but if you take a hard look at the massive upheavals of the past four centuries, the countless victories and defeats, you will see that these circumstances have fostered unique characteristics in Taiwan. Thus, to marginalize or treat Taiwan's literature as subsidiary, or as an outgrowth, is a gross distortion, which only becomes magnified over time. In other words, if we look at Taiwan's literature on its own merits, whether we are reading, reflecting, or engaged in literary creation ourselves, we soon become aware that it is different from the Chinese-language literature that has been steadily and continuously taking shape in China over the same centuries. Through changing times and political unrest, a multitude of genres and types of literature have appeared in Taiwan, more than one can count. In the past half century, it's become readily apparent that, far from being marginal, Taiwan's literature is an avant-garde of unstoppable force.

When we say that Taiwanese literature is indeed not an ancillary or marginal phenomenon vis-à-vis Chinese literature, what we are really saying is that the modern poetry of the past sixty years, especially, developed a unique artistry quite early on and took on a life of its own. It has displayed great variety and vigor in both form and content, creating its own distinct paradigm—particularly in comparison with traditional Chinese literature. Formally, Taiwan's modern poetry is firmly rooted in free verse, stressing the organic quality of form, and favoring freedom and a restrained sense of order in its music. This allows the language to be organized in a natural and colloquial way, and to integrate essential grammar without entirely casting aside effective classical or foreign usage. It promotes freedom, but not at the expense of artistic discipline. In its content, this modern poetry delves deep, treating a range of topics far broader than traditional poetry. It goes much further, probing the sunlight and shadows of the human mind and spirit, exploring existential angst, ridicule, and frustration—in other words, the light and darkness that combine to make up the reality of human existence. The poet cannot hide his or her personality if he or she is to be able to confront reality; nor can the poet avoid the trivial or presume to judge if he or she is to reflect human life. Because modern poetic form is determined by its content, and that content is taken from the actualities of life, this art has a goodness and beauty that is far from commonplace. In addition, modern poets are seeking to achieve a certain level of abstraction, for they believe that harmony of sound and image can also express the purpose of poetry. They present in their works an abstract universe and, in their quest for the ideal of "pure poetry," they attempt to achieve for the art of language a purity akin to that of music and painting.

Thus far, we have attempted a discussion of the headwaters of modern poetry in Taiwan, using the salient and contrasting elements of form and content to explain key points, going on to elucidate the distinguishing characteristics of its style, thus encapsulating an era. When we take another look at what has and hasn't changed over this period, holding the so-called Taiwanese style of the past sixty years alongside that of traditional China, we discover that, especially in terms of the way it has freely chosen among stylistic elements and incorporated a multitude of subjects, Taiwan's modern poetry has not only inherited and absorbed elements of China's tradition, it has also been able to extricate itself from China's turmoil, bypassing old customs, exercising choice, and affirming the positive. Whenever local culture guides our thinking and artistic creation, isn't that worth writing home about? Local culture, broadly defined, strengthens itself through its inclusiveness, for blood is thicker than water, and we can't deny it. All of this is connected to Taiwan's geography and history, as it has been for nearly four hundred years.

So-called local culture, when investigated as a literary source, may be narrow in scope, but when we focus on its wellsprings, accumulation, and transformations, we find we are able to follow the river back to its sources, to the time of Shen Guangwen. This was precisely the point at which poetic creation in the medium of Chinese language made its appearance in Taiwan. In the mid-seventeenth century, Shen, a native of Yin County in Zhejiang Province, was blown off course during a typhoon and discovered he'd made landfall on the shores of Taiwan. He spent the rest of his days practicing medicine and teaching, and he wrote poetry about both his longing for his home in Zhejiang and the delights of the island where he now lived. When he died, he was buried at Zhuluo. His poetry was profound, subtle, and condensed, and a collection of his work has been handed down to this time. In 1680 Taiwan came under the control of the Manchu Qing dynasty, and for over two hundred years officials posted to Taiwan composed a great deal of poetry. These poems expressed the sense of disappointment and failure experienced by demoted and exiled officials, and it was characteristic of them to make fun of the landscape and insult local customs. It was only after the time of the reign of the Qianlong emperor that one finally saw candidates for the imperial examinations from Taiwan traveling back and forth across the straits. It was they who, gradually and over time, came to write poetry in praise of Taiwan, which they saw as their home. Take, for example, the lines from this poem, "Mooring at Lu'ermen at Night," by a *student* from Taiwan county, Chen Hui: "Wavering, wavering a traveler's thoughts, / In dreams of return he recalls his home." During the period of Japanese rule, the study of poetry in Taiwan flourished. There were a total of sixty-six poetry societies scattered all over the island, as far as Penghu, whose members could chant poems together and encourage one another. At the same time there also appeared some talented and passionate young idealists who began writing New Poetry, and who voiced their resistance and criticism in colloquial Chinese (*baihua*) free verse. Freely expressing what was in their hearts and laying bare their consciousness, they became a threat to the colonial authorities, who repeatedly took sanctions against them under a strict system of censorship. After the 1937 invasion of northern China by Japanese forces, the governor general in Taipei barred all Taiwanese from publishing in the Chinese language, forcing them to begin writing in Japanese or else stop writing altogether. In the following decade, young Taiwanese published some outstanding avant-garde new-style poems, some of which succeeded in using language to seek the beauty and wonder of the new zeitgeist. These poets were in no way inferior either to their European, American, or Japanese contemporaries, or to writers of their generation in the Chinese interior.

Following this thread, we can see that this historical legacy is one of the sources of modern poetry in Taiwan, and we are thus better able to grasp the various theories that developed out of that period and to explain why it was that, within the first ten years after the war, the poetic voice of the Taiwanese suddenly fell silent. We can further understand why subsequent generations witnessed its rebirth, in a much livelier and more forceful form. New generations of poets have applied themselves unflaggingly to this latent artistic spirit, opening it up further, wholeheartedly declaiming to the world, and imbibing the ideas and techniques of Western modernism while also integrating the essence of traditional poetry. For the past half-century we've seen the way poets have created a place for themselves in the space between what is chosen and what is left behind. What they have embraced and what they have rejected is all in plain view. The features of traditional Chinese poetry and the style of Western literature have been transformed in our modern environment, and yet, throughout, the spirit and feeling of these works have cleaved to their portrayal of everyday truths.

These nearly four hundred years of development in Taiwan have given birth to this new poetry of ours, distinctly different from that found in other cultural locales, and always fresh and vital because its surroundings are in constant flux. Holding fast to a modernity that can't be rubbed away, it refuses to let itself become mired in set responses. It is humanistic, cosmopolitan in a way that transcends nationalism, and while it embraces nature, it also yearns for the epitome of abstract beauty. At times our modern poetry displays a fondness for tumultuous images of the old and new Taiwan. Yet it isn't afraid to make traditional China its cultural referent. Acknowledging its enduring love and admiration, it uses traditional China as a foundation for literary creation, a foundation that has contributed its written language, imagery, and allusions, and thus presides over and guides the imagination.

We use the Chinese written language, precisely, to create Taiwanese literature.

*Translated by Andrea Lingenfelter*

## The Song of Bishop Wort

*1998*

such astonishment my bishop wort
at high noon beneath the phoenix tree inclining and intense
sunlight and shade, my purple
bishop wort sings softly an aria, how
she has revealed the seeds of life
while sailing against the commercial winds of the western hemisphere
falling into the embrace and under the spell of the humid spirit
        medium
nurturing a will like the new shoots and blossoms that grow in such
        abundance
across the land in distant Formosa

I stand near the foot of a half-ruined flight of steps
feeling the summer heat make love and desire seep in and evaporate
the waters of the spring have flowed by the low wall since ancient
        times—

the meetings and tears and farewells of the past, my
bishop's wort with this half-vanished melody
voice raised high in song to pour out its identity and other
mongrel memories in which the Tropic of Cancer
leads us back north, beneath slender leaves
known by the sheen of sweat, Formosa

such astonishing features and red sun-kissed
cheeks, in early summer the wind still idles in out-of-the-way
corners of forgotten valleys, even
shuttling back and forth through bishop's wort and the clamor
of songs not understood, chanting them over on deck and floating
    near to
exploding hope—the day will come!
when the sun will turn its head as promised, stubbornly
choosing to pause where the purple-flowered bishop's wort
grows everywhere in the heat, Formosa

*Translated by Andrea Lingenfelter*

# Jia Pingwa

*(b. 1953)*

Jia Pingwa was born in Danfeng, in eastern Shaanxi province. During the Cultural Revolution, he worked for many years in the countryside, and then studied Chinese literature at Northwest University, where he began writing fiction. In 1975 he worked as an editor at the Shaanxi People's Publishing House and received several literary awards. He then transferred to the literary journal *Chang'an* and continued to write short stories, novellas, and novels. He became one of the most important writers in the "root-seeking" school of fiction. His novel *Turbulence* received the 1988 Pegasus Prize for Literature, but he is perhaps best known for his novel *The Abandoned Capital* (1993), which dealt frankly with sexuality. Between 1993 and 2000, he published four additional novels: *White Nights*, *Earth Gate*, *Old Gao Village*, and *Remembering Wolves*. He has now written over twenty-five books and, in 2003, was given the title Chevalier de l'Ordre des Arts et des Lettres by the French Culture and Communication Ministry.

In his writing, Jia Pingwa often draws on Shangzhou, near Xian, but he does not make it part of an idyllic past. Instead, he makes rural life an essential part of China's modernization. In a 2004 interview, Jia lamented that "The native place has become purely a longing." On June 9, 1984, Jia published an essay, "Life Is Changing, Even in Hilly Shangzhou," as an afterword to *The Turn of the New Year.* In this selection, Jia writes about his return, and his realization that "Chinese literature today can be said to be a Chinese and Western hybrid." More recently, Jia has turned his attention to Xian, where he lives. His recent novel *Happy* (2005) follows a junk collector there.

## Excerpts from "Life Is Changing: Even in Hilly Shangzhou"

How am I going to write this afterword? At the moment, I'm revising a piece called *Shang Prefecture* (*Shangzhou*) and my head is filled with the people and events of Shangzhou, so why not write about that? But this smacks of "Old Wang selling melons" [praising one's own wares]. Yes, the Chinese have a proverb that says: "Everybody claims that his hometown is the best." I am no exception. Probably an outsider couldn't care less about the place. Even in Shaanxi there are people who turn up their noses at the mention of Shangzhou. It is small, isolated, and poor. If you look for it on a map of Shaanxi, you will see that it is triangular in shape and located in the southeastern corner of the province. It is the gateway to the eight hundred miles of Qinchuan [Shaanxi and Gansu, China's ancient Northwest], but it is not part of the central Shaanxi plain; nor does it have the Qinchuan breed of cattle. It borders on Hubei Province in the south and Henan in the east, yet it is not really part of southern Shaanxi proper. It does not have the warm, wet climate of Ankang or Hanzhong. The Dan River is its main waterway, and the Changping Highway its longest official road. [. . .]

Last year, I finally decided to return to Shangzhou. At the time I was not actually set on writing anything in particular. I just brought along a map of Shangzhou and visited each county in it. Only after the trip did I realize how little I knew about the place, and that my earlier pieces about the mountain districts were very superficial. Actual experience changed my worldview. I hadn't expected that this "purposeless" [*wuwei*, a word with classical Daoist overtones] trip would become so "purposeful" [*youwei*] for my writing. Every place I visited provided an educational experience and stimulated me. At night I hastily wrote down my impressions. They were real and vivid. My recording of these events came naturally; I did not ponder my words or try to be fancy. After a few changes, this became my very first piece of writing about Shangzhou, called "First Impressions of Shangzhou" (*Shangzhou chulu*). I had it published in [the Nanjing literary journal] *Zhongshan*.

The reaction to the piece went beyond my expectations. Many readers and writers wrote to congratulate me, saying that I had "found a new, Chinese-style path for literature." They encouraged me to keep on writing in that style. I was really intimidated, but at the same time I gained self-confidence. I realized that I could spend a lifetime writing about Shangzhou, and it seemed that new things were surging into my mind every day, every moment. Thereupon, I returned to Shangzhou a second time, a third time, and a fourth, always visiting the various districts and feeling at one with [the Tang poet] Wen Tingyun, who once lived there and said:

> The cocks crow as the moon rises above the rustic inn,
> only footprints are left on the frost-covered bridge

Each trip was more fruitful than the last, and in quick succession I wrote "Before the 29-Day Month" (*Xiaoyue qianben*), "The People of Chicken Nest Hollow" (*Jiwowa de renjia*), "The Turn of the New Year" (*Layue, Zhengyue*), and the piece that I am finishing now, called *Shang Prefecture*.

It is true that Shangzhou is poor, but as time progresses and society moves ahead, Shangzhou, like all other places in the country, is changing. What is unusual is that Shangzhou's changes differ from those elsewhere. They bear Shangzhou's special characteristics and local color. This preposterous thought then occurred to me: Take Shangzhou as a point of reference; carefully investigate and study it, and gain from it an understanding of the historical development of Chinese village life, of the evolution of society, and of the course of change in the life, feelings, and psychological makeup of mankind in this great world of ours.

Chinese literature today can be said to be a Chinese and Western hybrid. Under these circumstances, how does one tread a path that is properly one's own? I believed that I should approach the question by investigating the geography, history, customs, and habits of Shangzhou, proceeding from the perspectives of ethnography and folklore studies. [. . .]

The profundity of a work does not depend on the writer's boldness, literary talent, or loudness. However different their styles, the major writers in China's several thousand years of literature, such as Tao Yuanming, Sima Qian, Bo Juyi, Su Shi, Liu Zongyuan, Cao Xueqin, and Pu Songling, have inherited a tradition of expressing the openness and spirituality of nature, society, life, and the mind. Openness and spirituality are treasures of Chinese literature.

How should we revitalize Chinese literature? Many writers are now pursuing this question. As I mentioned above, if we want our literature to develop, we must cross-fertilize Chinese literature with Western literature. Some writers have adopted Western literature in toto but have not digested it or harmonized with it. Therefore, they have either ignored or forgotten the merits of the Chinese spirit. This is a case of trying to achieve too much too fast. Other writers have totally rejected anything foreign. Thus, our people are either too haughty or too humble; too quick or too slow.

In recent years, we have been making great efforts to compare China with the West, beginning with philosophy, aesthetics, painting, and drama, in the hope of finding similarities and differences, and thus the direction that our own writings ought to take. We have expended much effort but achieved little. In using the traditional Chinese ways of expressing beauty to depict life and emotions in China today, I often wonder whether a work can have a kind of "distant goal" (*zhiyuan*). Can this "distant goal," built on the foundation of "starting from something close at hand" (*zijin*), give our works a sense of openness and spirituality rather than emptiness and triviality? Can it give them added depth?

At the same time, I often ponder another problem, that of magnanimity (*dadu*), which can also be considered a question of strength or power (*li*). Many of the Chinese writers famous now can be considered thinkers, or people of profound thought. Of course, "thought" should not be a narrow concept, or it might lead to the error of "making thought greater than events." Instead, it should express the power of magnanimity. The ancients said that there is melody even in a hammer, and toughness in a flower. This pertains not merely to the surface of a literary work, but to something internal. It is because of this that I earlier spoke of promoting the spirit of the Great Han dynasty. As I look at the stone sculptures in front of the tomb of [the great Han general] Huo Qubing, I feel that the art of the Han dynasty is the greatest in history. With a few finely sculpted lines, the artist made the image of his object stand out. Now that is the pinnacle of art. Therefore, as we revitalize our national literature in the course of revitalizing our whole nation, I admire the spirit of the great Han dynasty and despise the precious cloisonné objects from the end of the Qing dynasty [in the late nineteenth century]. When I read Latin American literature, I feel the same way. I can identify with it. I suddenly understand many things.

*Translated by Peter Li*

# Li Ang

*(b. 1952)*

Li Ang was born in Lugang, Taiwan, and published her first short story, "Flower Season," when she was sixteen. She graduated from the College of Chinese Culture with a degree in philosophy and then, in 1975, came to the United States for graduate study. In 1977 she received a master's degree in drama from Oregon State University. She has written many short stories, novellas, and novels, but *The Butcher's Wife*, published in 1983, was greeted with controversy. The publication of this novel was a pivotal moment in the women's movement in Taiwan. Three years later, the novel's subsequent publication in English translation received widespread attention and acclaim. In this novel, the heroine is married off to a brutal butcher who dominates her. Knowing how she abhors to see living things killed, he deliberately takes her to a slaughterhouse. She subsequently murders and dismembers him with his own butcher's knife. In her writing, Li Ang has made feminism and sexuality her intense focus: she is critical of traditional Chinese patriarchy and has explored the clash of modern Western and traditional Chinese ethics. Many of her works are still not available in English. She teaches in the theater department at the College of Chinese Culture in Taiwan.

In December 1984, tired of countless interviews in which women are asked the same stereotypical questions, Li Ang decided to "interview herself." The selection here includes her opinions about being "a female writer," about the audience for literature, and, ultimately, the vindication of her writing over time.

## Excerpt from "Protest of a Woman Author against Reckless Accusations: Another Self-Interview, This Time from Taipei"

*[. . .] Do you consciously feel you are a "woman writer"?*

I didn't when I first started. Gender simply wasn't so important at that stage. I had great ambitions then—I looked forward to winning a Nobel Prize in literature. I seldom thought about myself as a woman. And what did femaleness have to do with my writing? My works of that period were collected in *Mixed Chorus* (*Hun sheng he chang*, 1975). You couldn't tell whether the writer was male or female. Some people jokingly told me they had first thought Li Ang was a man of forty or fifty. Not until I went to college, in Taipei, did I consciously see myself as a woman. Owing to my youth, and my awakening to love, I began to write love stories. It was then that my style displayed what they call feminine "delicacy" and "sentimentalism." Representative is the series of stories in my collection *The Mundane World* (*Ren jian shi*, 1976). You can still see the experimental ambitions of my early works there, but the tone is very feminine. My life changed tremendously when I went to the United States to study. My "eyes were opened" for the first time, and I was able to rid myself of fatal female traits like small-mindedness, cattiness, back-stabbing, and sentimentalism. I began to feel that the only way I could broaden my range was to write like male writers. Unfortunately, I'm still entrapped in my own femaleness, so I've never been able to write like a man. I didn't realize this until I wrote *The Butcher's Wife*. I saw that however much I imitated male writers, I couldn't write like them, and I didn't need to. I was writing a column called "Women's Opinion" then, and I realized that historically, women have always been subordinate to men. Women have always lacked self-confidence and the courage to truly develop their own specifically female potential. Therefore, in history, the universally recognized "female characteristics" have been limited to virtues like tenderness, sensitivity, and consideration. I think women's potential is greater than that. As long as we are confident, I believe there should be a way to write something great as well as female. Women's literature will then no longer be considered the realm of proper ladies and their personal essays.

*What made you keep on writing for the past eighteen years?*

Love. I did it for love. I started, when I was young, only because I was excited inside and felt I could express myself best in writing. Now, I do it because of the power of writing itself. Creative writing is a lover one can never conquer. You think you are in control, and then in a flash he appears in another guise that you have never seen before. All love fades in time, and all lovers become boring; only writing can be an eternal lover.

*In other words, you're willing to make many sacrifices for your writing? Is that why you're still single?*

I don't think I have sacrificed anything for writing. I love this work, so how can I speak of sacrifice? The reason I'm still single may be that I can't find a husband who's as good as writing! I'm also very disappointed with most men's selfishness and chauvinism. . . .

*How do you evaluate your own work?*

I hope I will write some really good stories someday. I am not there yet. I always believe and hope that my next work will be better, and I am working hard toward that goal. On the other hand, I know I can never be one of the world's great writers, like García Márquez, Hemingway, or Tolstoy, as I once dreamed. Given my limitations, I'll have to work very hard to be just a second- or third-class writer in world literature. . . .

*Do you mind other people's attacks on you?*

I don't really care about them. Time will prove that they are just the clowns of our time. Those who attacked Flaubert and D. H. Lawrence only made themselves ridiculous in our eyes today.

*You just mentioned limitations that prevent you from becoming a great writer. What are they?*

First of all, my talent. I don't think of myself as a genius, and to be a great writer you have to be one. My background is another limitation.

Being the daughter of a successful self-made businessman, I grew up well-to-do and well protected. This caused me to like delicate and beautiful things, and also to be completely isolated from life at the lower end of the scale. If I hadn't worked at it, I would have found it hard to enter real life. I drive my own car, teach college, then return to my beautiful home. Most of my friends are intellectuals. Such a life naturally is very limiting. There was a time when I participated rather actively in social service work, to be in touch with real life and enlarge my own circle of experience, but I still found it difficult to enter into it completely. I started to write *The Butcher's Wife* at that time. When I begged my mother to take me to see pigs slaughtered at the Lugang slaughterhouse, so I could write about what went on there, she gladly accepted (though she thought it strange that I wanted to write about such a horrible thing). We stayed there over an hour. I thought my description of butchering in that novel was rather successful. That gave me a lot of confidence in writing, because I discovered and do believe that writing requires something more than just real life. I admit that I have limitations, but I want to overcome them. . . .

*Let's hear your writer's view of creative writing.*

My fundamental belief about writing has always been that it expresses truth, especially in a society and culture full of white lies like ours. I think that telling the truth is the writer's most fundamental moral obligation. So, when I think something should be written about, I don't give much consideration to whether or not this violates custom (note that I say custom, not morality) or taboos. The result, of course, has been more than ten years of uninterrupted attacks on my character. Ask me if I still keep to my ideal, though, and I will affirm it absolutely. There are still many problems that, for one reason or another, I am not able to come to grips with or write about, but I must keep on struggling with them.

*About this truth you want to express—is it possible that it is not really "truth," but something that comes from each person's own opinions and biases?*

I don't think so. We are now living in an information age. This is not a time when people debate whether the earth is round, or when theological disputes rage. It is very easy to obtain information from other countries or from different theories to correct our own views. I agree there is probably no absolute truth, but truth does exist, because it is concrete and can be verified with statistics and actual materials.

*Have you considered whether the truth you write about is so ugly and cruel, and so lacking in brighter long-term prospects, that it could be harmful to society?*

I think you overestimate the power of a writer in the twentieth century. I only refer to serious works here, not literature for passing the time, like best-sellers and martial-arts novels. Tell me now, how many people read Tolstoy or Saul Bellow? The percentage is pitifully small. And who are these readers? Teenagers, smoking pot and listening to rock and roll? The lower classes that we're continually being told to care about? (I don't say this to put them down.) We have to admit that when art reaches a certain level of sophistication, it belongs only to a tiny minority that are able to appreciate it. It's sad, but it's true. It is every artist's ideal to be appreciated by all classes, but it rarely happens. Serious works can be accepted only by educated minorities. Need one worry about shocking *them* with squalor and cruelty? Ugly and distasteful truth will at least awaken their social conscience and perhaps cause them to do a little more for society. This, too, is what I consider the influence of art—not to influence the majority, but the minority (intellectuals, in the broad sense). Naturally, when I say this, some people think I don't care about poor people, that I look down on the proletariat. But I think an honest artist should admit that art belongs only to those who are able to appreciate it. . . .

*Do you agree, then, that society should promote appreciation of "high art"?*

No. For one thing, I don't consider art to be the most important thing in life. Society ought first to provide more equal opportunity for education and participation. After the vast majority have their share of education, some people may like art and pursue it. Naturally, it would be good if one day they came to appreciate serious art. For those who aren't interested, there is no point encouraging them to use art as decoration or a means of climbing up the social ladder. I don't think that people who like only football or soap opera miss anything as long as they enjoy themselves. After all, art is not food. You won't starve without it. . . .

I believe that a society should be pluralistic, having different kinds of ideas, culture, and art, not all cast in one mold. So society can have both high art and soap operas. They serve different needs. . . .

*You've in effect been discussing the "popularization" of art among the masses. Could you also discuss "cosmopolitanism" and "nativism" in art?*

Just as the spread of art among the populace creates the opportunity for appreciation, with art necessarily spreading upward from below, instead of high art being imposed from above, I think that art must be native before it takes on cosmopolitan characteristics. I have met many overseas Chinese scholars who like to criticize Taiwan as being a hermetic society, because its intellectuals seldom concern themselves with things from beyond Taiwan. What they say is true, but I don't regard it as a serious shortcoming. Take me, for example. I didn't even know that there were great Taiwanese writers during the Japanese occupation, such as Yang Kui and Zhang Wenhuan, until I went to study in the United States after college. That really stopped me cold. A few days before, I'd been talking with some foreign friends and been terribly embarrassed to learn, again for the first time, how Taiwan's economy was taken over by five big families after the retrocession [to China in 1945]. With me still so ignorant about Taiwan, I didn't feel I had to know what problems American writers of the 1980s were exploring. Now, of course, it's best if you do know about the things outside, but if my energy is limited, I'd first like to use it to understand Taiwan—to understand what my education left out, and what things the books don't cover. . . . I don't think a writer should completely ignore cosmopolitanism. A writer in our country should have the ideal to achieve world success—not because we write like Westerners, but because our works are so great that the West will look at us from a new perspective. It's idealistic, but not impossible—look at Kawabata and García Márquez. As for me, I constantly remind myself to avoid emotional arguments and dogmatic beliefs when giving rein to nativism, so that I don't stagnate.

*Have your beliefs made you strange?*

Yes, I sometimes feel like a stranger in my native land. It seems that I'm always behind the current fashion. When, early on, I wrote a lot of "modern" fiction under the influence of existentialism and psychoanalysis, modernism was at its end. Then, when I started to write stories about my hometown of Lugang, the *xiangtu* [nativist] literary tendency had not yet started; by the time I wrote what I considered to be a very "nativist" novel, *The Butcher's Wife*, the *xiangtu* trend was over. I am not really sorry that I was out of step, but sometimes I feel just a little helpless that for one reason or another, I seem always to be out of the mainstream. Another thing that makes me look strange is that I am always the target of some criticism. Twelve years ago, after I wrote *The Mundane World*, about the sexual problems of college students, I was called every bad name in the dictionary. Six years later, after I had come back from the United States, all the problems reflected in *The Mundane World* were openly discussed, and I became like a prophet. After the publication of *The Butcher's Wife* last year, I was called all sorts of dirty names again. Will *those* crimes still be crimes in another six years, I wonder? Sometimes I feel very lonely. It's the loneliness of being misunderstood. . . .

*What do you think about being called "the most controversial" writer [in Taiwan]?*

I think I should be called the writer most often cursed at, not the most controversial writer. Being controversial means there are opposite opinions about you. All I ever got were detractions. No one ever defended me. (I think the only justice I can count on will be time.)

*Translated by Pu-mei Leng*

# Gao Xingjian

*(b. 1940)*

Gao Xingjian is a novelist, playwright, artist, critic, and the director of a number of his own plays. Born in Ganzhou, Jiangxi province, in southeastern China, he majored in French at the Beijing Foreign Languages Institute and, after graduating in 1962, worked as a translator and editor at the Foreign Languages Press in Beijing. At the beginning of the Cultural Revolution, he burned a suitcase full of poems, short fiction, plays, and essays, and it was not until after the Cultural Revolution that he was able to publish his writings. He traveled to Europe in 1979 and in the following year became a playwright for the People's Arts Theater in Beijing. His first two plays, *Signal Alarm* (1982) and *Bus Stop* (1983), were controversial successes. From 1981 to 1987, his major publications included *A Preliminary Discussion on the Art of Modern Fiction* (1981), *Collected Plays* (1985), and *In Search of a Modern Form of Dramatic Representation* (1987). In 1985 his play *Wild Man* was performed, but the following year his next play, *The Other Shore*, was closed down at rehearsal. He traveled to Europe in late 1987 and, while there, decided to remain in Paris. His landmark novel *Soul Mountain* (1990) and his new plays were first published in Taipei, and a number of his plays were staged throughout Europe. He received the Chevalier de l'Ordre des Arts et des Lettres in 1992 and became a French citizen in 1997. In 2000 he received the Nobel Prize in Literature. His other English-language publications include *The Other Shore* (plays, 1999), *One Man's Bible* (novel, 2002), *Buying a Fishing Rod for My Grandfather* (short stories, 2004), and *The Case for Literature* (essays, 2006).

*Soul Mountain* is a soul journey that is formally innovative. The protagonist is refracted through a "you," a "she," and a "he" so that the shifting pronouns provide varying perspectives on the inner state of a single character. In chapter 72, included here, the narrative is disrupted with the opening sentence, "This isn't a novel!" Gao Xingjian's essay specifically addresses his use of pronouns in fiction, and it is his assertion that "pronouns transcend ethnicity and language group and reflect a deep structure of human consciousness."

## The Art of Fiction

*Paris, August 30, 2007*

Fiction is generally regarded as a genre that cannot be without a story and characters, and indeed these are prerequisites for traditional fiction. But rather than discussing the writing methods or techniques of traditional fiction, I intend to use this opportunity to consider how fiction can be written other than by telling a story.

Fiction underwent an evolutionary process from the telling of a story to the creation of characters, so it is worthwhile surveying the history of fiction. From *Journey to the West* and *Water Margin*, to *One Thousand and One Nights*, to Rabelais's *Gargantua and Pantagruel*, and even to Dickens and Gogol and Hugo, fiction fell within the framework of telling a story, and while these works contained some vivid characters, it was in plot that they excelled. Then a shift of emphasis away from the intrigue and variation of plots to the portrayal of characters made the plot secondary, and the creation of characters with striking personalities came to be pivotal in the art of fiction. In Cao Xueqin's *Dream of Red Mansions* in Asia, and from Balzac to Tolstoy in Europe, fiction sought to reproduce real society's multitude of vibrant denizens, so the plot weakened to make way for depictions of the environment and the context of life. Such realist fiction provided broad vistas of social life and created lively images of numerous characters with unique personalities. The depiction of social life also became less important, as in Dostoevsky's writing, where the personalities of the characters became more complex, schizophrenic, and depressive, or as in Flaubert's *Madame Bovary*, where the characters' inner worlds with their secret contradictions were reflected through a multi-angled lens. Yet unable to make a break from the plot, these works continued to be traditional fiction: there had only been a shift of emphasis from the plot to the creation and portrayal of characters.

In twentieth-century fiction there was an important change in the narrative language of what is generally known as "modernist fiction," but what I prefer to call "modern fiction" because of its greater inclusiveness. Prior to that the author was an omnipotent narrator who was hidden yet knew everything about the external world and the inner minds of the characters and who spoke in the measured and leisurely manner of a storyteller. Fiction writers of the twentieth century raised a new question, namely: Who is the narrator? The question about the narrator immediately led to another question: From which angle does the narration occur? The dominance of questions about the narrator and the narrative angle marked the emergence of modern fiction.

Fiction writers abandoned the widely used practice of omnipotent narration and chose a specific narrative angle: the narrator could be a certain character in the book, and the narration in the book would be through the eyes of that character. The author was further concealed, not allowed to make random comments or criticisms, and thus made a complete withdrawal from the book. Only the characters in the book were allowed to speak for themselves, and this was a major change. Of course there were many ways of writing to achieve this change. Proust, Joyce, and Faulkner each used different methods, but they shared the common characteristic of adopting a particular subjective narrative angle, usually the narrative angle of a character, and observing through the eyes of the character to experience the character's feelings. So the conventional story and plot of fiction became even less important, and how the narrator narrated became the new issue in the writing of modern fiction.

The creation of fiction first required selecting a narrator, so what eventually emerged was narrative language, and the art of fiction lay in how an appropriate narrative language could be found, thereby relegating conventional plot and character to secondary positions. Nonetheless, there had to be at least one character, and it was how this character spoke that was the key to fiction creation.

The French *nouveau roman* appeared in the 1950s, and critics subsequently designated these as postmodernist. Some later-generation *nouveau roman* writers went further and turned fiction into intellectual discussions, and by overturning story, plot, and characters and deconstructing the narrator and narrative language, they turned fictional creation into an intellectual game. Fiction thus was transformed into a text about concepts.

Roland Barthes's notion of "the death of the author" was extremely popular for a time, and his method of explaining literary texts became a compass for the writing of fiction. However, the emergence of this sort of metafiction in fact subverted fiction. Since any text could be called fiction, the art of fiction was transformed into the conceptual analysis of fiction. That fiction had been reduced to this, of course, was related to the ideology behind so-called modernity. The introduction of social revolution and historical evolutionary theory—with its continuing revolution and perpetual overturning into the domain of literature and the arts—did not lead to creation but instead to the withering and annihilation of art and literature. Once fiction turned into an intellectual game that could be written in any manner, it lost its social and human consciousness, and could not leave behind anything worth a second reading. Instead, there was only a widespread proliferation of vacuous deconstructionist literary theories everywhere.

A baseline exists for innovations in the art of fiction, and that is the narrative language. If narrative language is removed and fiction becomes an intellectual game or the actualization of concepts devoid of living human feelings, then the impulse to create fiction as well as interest in reading it is lost, and this can only be the end of the road for fiction.

Fiction can evolve, and the possibilities for artistic expression can continually be explored, although there is the indispensable precondition, and that is the narration of fiction. Whether it was the traditional omnipotent narrator or a specific character narrating, as soon as the narrative language is activated, there must be a subject. An interesting phenomenon is that in any language of the world there are three basic pronouns—*I*, *you*, and *he*—so, in other words, is the narrator "I" or "you" or "he"? And there is no other option. These three pronouns do indeed have the plural forms *we*, *you*, *they*. However, these are public words or a form of political speech within a collective, and the fiction writer does not assume the role of public spokesperson and does not have to speak on behalf of a certain collective, political party, class, race, or nation. The writer of fiction must return to the voice of the individual, so both plural pronouns and the absence of pronouns are of no practical use. For example, what is the subject in the sentence "xiayu le"? Clearly, it is the sky that is raining, but in Chinese the subject is dispensed with, and in English or French the subject becomes a neuter general word. Furthermore, "dou shuo" such and such means everyone says such and such, so naturally it is impossible for unspecified persons and general words to undertake the narration. In fiction there must be a choice between the pronouns I, you, he, even if the narration is from the perspective of a specific character. This is an additional limitation in the narration of fiction.

For the first-person pronoun "I" to be used in narration is a common narrative method. Fiction is not autobiography, although autobiographical fiction today is fairly popular. However, generally the first-person pronoun in fiction is not the author himself speaking but a fictional character.

In the 1950s the French *nouveau roman* writer Michel Butor wrote a novel in the second-person pronoun you, and at the time it was a pioneering work. The second-person pronoun you could be either the protagonist or the reader. By placing the reader in the situation of the character, the reader perceives from the angle of the character during the process of reading: it will be as if he is the character. This is the magic of the second-person pronoun.

The second-person pronoun can also be the external projection of the narrator's ego—in other words, act as adversary when the narrator engages in interior monologue to talk to himself. The second-person pronoun facilitates this sort of interior monologue that is commonly found in plays, and is also appearing as a narrative method in fiction.

The third-person narrating subject he—although not the omnipotent narrator who appears in traditional fiction—can also become the viewpoint of the protagonist, but this involves a hierarchical change in which the subjective narration changes to the third person. This subtle change must have a definite reference; in other words, it requires first that a base be established. If initially the subject I is used as the narrator, when the narration changes to the third-person he, while still referring to the same character, he then becomes the object of focus of I, or becomes the projection of I. So I as well as he represent the same character, yet can engage in dialogue: he becomes the object of my consideration, and the thoughts of the character do not require the intervention of an omnipotent narrator.

From this it can be seen that once a certain narrative angle has been established, the narrator of the work of fiction, usually the protagonist, can also assume three different designations as the subject—I, you, he—and constitute different levels of narration. Following on from this, it is found that different levels of narration lead to different psychological levels. Human consciousness is actualized through language, and cognition of the self cannot be divorced from language. It is through the three persons of the subject—three different positions—that the so-called self is confirmed.

By establishing the subject as I, the adversarial projection of I becomes you, and the externalized projection of I becomes he, so the narrative language of fiction introduces three different pronouns to designate the one character and leads to a new and multifaceted understanding of man's self. What is interesting is that these three levels of cognition are present in all human languages, indicating that these three pronouns transcend ethnicity and language group and reflect a deep structure of human consciousness.

If three different pronouns are introduced into the narration of the one character, the character fragments into the different pronouns, and I, you, and he become the structure of the novel, replacing the usual story and plot. This also allows for the introduction of the character's thoughts, so discussion, reflection, contemplation, memory, dream, and hallucination can all intermingle, and the literary form, too, can change freely because the flexibility of the structure allows the blending of prose and poetry into the narration.

My novel *Soul Mountain* was precisely such an experiment. It broke through conventional patterns and molds for fiction yet tenaciously defended the narration and retained a firm control on the narrative viewpoint of the characters simply by fragmenting the protagonist into three different pronouns. However, the different females in the book are all denoted as she, thereby constructing a composite female image or what may be called multiple variations of the female. And this too is derived from the viewpoint of the male protagonist in the book. It is difficult for a man to fathom women and a woman's inner world, so this multiple-identity, she, intermingled with the male imagination, fluctuates between reality and nonreality and becomes even more indefinite.

Man's cognition of the external world and other people can never be divorced from a subjective viewpoint. The world and human events inherently lack meaning: meaning is conferred by human cognition. The difference between the narration of the novelist and the commentaries of the philosopher lies in the latter's direct reliance on thought, whereas the novelist's cognition of persons and events cannot bypass the characters he creates, and it is through the eyes of the characters that he must bring forth the characters' real perceptions. The thoughts embedded in the novel must be revealed through the experiences of the characters, otherwise they will be nothing more than propaganda or preaching. And what is even more interesting is that the thoughts articulated in the novel must, through a character's experiences, transform feelings into a thought process that is tinged with the protagonist's sentiments, and it is in this way that the novelist presents the thinking of living people and not abstract theories.

*Soul Mountain* deals with the animal and human elements concealed in exorcist masks, the psychological basis for curses and shaman art, the internal dynamics of storytelling and the formation of linguistic consciousness, all of which transcend the general boundaries of fiction. With the help of this understanding of narrative language, however, it was possible to introduce and accommodate them in the book.

In my other novel, *One Man's Bible*, the he chapters and you chapters alternate, weaving together the memories of the same character and his situation at present, and dispensing with the subject I. This was not just due to the special structure of the novel but also because when it came to writing about the red terror of Mao Zedong's Cultural Revolution in China, the individual's self had been strangled by the totalitarian dictatorship. In this dialogue between you who had luckily survived and he of the past, time sequence is not a concern, and fragmented memories could come and go in an instant, giving great flexibility to the writing. The pronoun-based structure made it possible to avoid lengthy narration of the protagonist's complicated experiences in China's grotesque social situation, and immediately allowed you of the present and he of the past to engage in dialogue. Poetic chapters and prose chapters are placed alongside one another, enabling readers to emerge for a respite occasionally from those suffocating times.

On the other hand, in my short story "Buying a Fishing Rod for My Grandfather," the first-person narrator, I, sinks from the present into memories, evoking all sorts of associations that are undifferentiated from dream, and inducing the inner mind to talk in dream. I becomes two, bringing you into being, so you and I are able to engage in dialogue. All this occurs in the flow of the narration.

Finding a narrative language to express the ephemeral changes of a character's inner mind was a problem. When traditional fiction wrote about a character's psychological activities, the omnipotent narrator intervened and commented, but this interrupted the progress of the story. In writings such as Stendhal's, psychological analysis was introduced into the narration. However, this sort of analysis meant retaining the omnipotent narrative angle, and it could not be too long, otherwise the writing was cumbersome and reading it was tedious. In writing that tracks a character's mental activities without disrupting the narrative, cognition of the external world and the feelings of the inner world are integrated into the narrative language, so that even reflections on the external world constitute a simultaneous act of subjective cognition. A special narrative method was needed, and modern fiction's stream of consciousness was an artistic search for this. Such writing brought together in a unified flow of language the perceived external world and psychological activities.

Fiction from Proust to Joyce and Faulkner had the same thrust of trying to capture the rich and subtle perceptions of a character's inner mind, and searching for a narrative language that closely approximated psychological truth to accurately reveal the process of psychological activities.

Unachievable by intricate wording or meticulous description, prior to these writers the extent of artfulness in language had never existed for precisely expressing man's large range of complex and ephemeral perceptions of sight, hearing, touch, smell, and taste as well as accommodating memory, imagination, hallucination, and dream all in the process of narration.

A language that actualized the flow of consciousness had to be found. But in the process of writing fiction, it was soon discovered that language could not capture these ephemeral and complex sensory perceptions. Speech and writing are linear, whereas perceptions can have multiple sites, arise simultaneously, multiply and spread, and are totally random. However, narration in language must be brought into the flow of linear time, one sentence must follow another, and each sentence must be organized according to grammatical rules in a fixed word order, so the narration of fiction must also accept these restrictions. Language must be actualized in a linear flow, and this is also true for speaking, writing, and reading.

That language can convey meaning, and allow humans to communicate with one another, is because it possesses a public aspect when it takes shape: information that cannot be conveyed is filtered out. If the signs issued by persons within a certain social collective come into widespread use, the language patterns resulting from this filtering process—that is, the vocabulary and grammar—become that society's shared accumulated culture. As an artist in language, the writer can strive for fresh expressions, but he cannot overturn morphology and syntax. And even if he creates new words, it must be on the basis of vocabulary in common use and within the limits of what others will understand. The writer cannot rebel against language rules built over the history of human society, otherwise he will not be understood or else it will be a secret language not intended for others to understand. To write sentences that are not sentences is of course possible, but the meaning of the sentences is understood only by the writer himself, and this sort of secret language or code has nothing to do with literature, and needs no further discussion.

The communication of language meaning relies initially on words—a vocabulary established through the experience of repeated confirmation—constructed into sentences according to a generally recognized morphology and syntax. The actualization of an individual's thoughts must also agree with grammatical rules, otherwise there is chaos. Language must be within the flow of time and must follow grammatical rules in order to convey meaning. If expressions of the subconscious or preconscious are not organized into sentences, and are simply words or groups of words, or strings of utterances not structured into some sort of meaning, naturally these cannot be conveyed to others, and can only constitute muddled ravings. The writer must revert to lucid consciousness when seeking to grasp and manifest the psychological activities of the subconscious. Therefore this sort of raving is of limited use, and while fragments may be selected, it cannot replace the narration of fiction.

Stream of consciousness is indeterminate and vague, and in creating fiction the writer needs to find his own method for using it in his narrative language, and what is actualized can only be a linear flow of language that cannot contravene established grammatical structures. Even if it is the manifestation of psychological activities from the subjective angle of the protagonist in fiction, the narration must nonetheless revert to lucid thinking. The articulation of dream, hallucination, and the dim impulses of the inner mind, or even ephemeral feelings and images, must all be contained in sequential sentences. Linguistic tracking of psychological activities must pass through a grammatical filter, then a time-sequence funnel, and the string of sentences obtained would more accurately be denoted as a stream of language.

This stream of language used for tracking psychological activities clearly cannot be achieved through conventional methods of narration, description, or rhetoric, because they are too regulated, and certainly not through old sayings and allusions. To capture these perceptions requires avoiding old sayings and allusions, avoiding existing patterns of writing, and searching for fresh narrative methods and a more vibrant language. This requires returning to the source of language—that is, when constructing a sentence, to listen intently to the language of the inner mind, even if it is not spoken aloud, because this sound of the language is linked to the words and sentences, and is the starting point of language. The basic substance of language is sound. At this point, it is necessary to draw attention to the common misconception that the written language is the same as the spoken language. Spoken language precedes written language. Written language constitutes the written traces left by language sounds: language is always with sound. The birth and evolution of language are always linked to human sounds, what is of interest is first the sound of language, and it only becomes language when this human sound is endowed with meaning. If the written characters and words—the symbols of language—are severed from the sound of language, then the language will perish.

The narration of fiction must revert to language with sound; in other words, the narrator must begin with a language with sound, one that is alive and can be spoken, and this cannot be achieved just with rhetoric and literary form. Quite the opposite, literary form and rhetoric often lead to specific prose styles. Only when writing an ancient tale is it acceptable to occasionally borrow a literary form with an established style. It is important for the creator of fiction to search for fresh and vibrant language, and it is the spoken language of everyday life that is the basis of fiction creation. Of course, the spoken language is not the language of literature, but the creation of the fiction writer is precisely to penetrate real life experiences via the spoken language, and to make use of living language material to communicate his unique and fresh perceptions.

The musical feel of language, that is, its musicality, refers not only to the sound of the language—for example the four tones and the level or oblique tones of Chinese words—but also to the language mood and rhythm linked to specific psychological feelings. The art of narrative language is also manifested in language mood; this is audible, and, moreover, not endowed with only one rhythm. Language moods and rhythms keep changing with the emotions. And this is the living language that is much sought after by fiction writers.

Every writer must have his own language, and each work of fiction will have different language moods and rhythms that can be heard by both the writer and the reader. In searching for this sort of language, it is important first to concentrate, and then to listen intently. This does not mean only describing the character's lovely face and smiling countenance, but also focusing one's gaze inward and listening intently to what is uttered by the inner mind. Otherwise, it is impossible to enter the deep consciousness of the character, and only a commonplace description will result.

When the fiction writer starts looking for a tone of language, he will have an attitude toward the object of narration, even if the narration is from the perspective of the character and relies on the perceptions of the character. The writer must have a definite attitude toward the narrator in order to maintain control of a certain tone of language in the narration. The character's tone of language is manifested through the author's attitude to him, and if the writer fails to capture an appropriate attitude, the writing will not go smoothly and could even end as a mess. In other words, he has failed to get a good grasp of his character. The more intricate work of the fiction writer involves finding a suitable attitude to his character, and this attitude will continually evolve in tandem with the narration; at times ridicule, at times sympathy, humor, or pity will be infused into the writing.

The author's attitude to his character does not derive solely from a certain sentiment. At the same time, it is aesthetic, and all sorts of aesthetic values—tragic or comic, absurd or funny, beautiful or ugly, noble or poetic—stem from the author's attitude. This attitude also allows the author to keep the necessary distance from his character, otherwise he can easily slip into sentimentalism or emotionalism. Fiction differs from poetry in that the latter derives from subjective expressions of the poet, but if fiction were also to give vent to the emotions, people would find it intolerable and impossible to read. Through listening intently and observation, the fiction writer creates a distance from his characters, and thus gets rid of the author's unnecessary narcissism and self-pity.

When a person listens attentively, the omniscient self begins to purify itself. The outpouring of emotion must be abolished from fictional narration. Especially in modern fiction, even if the narrative language begins from a specific subjective perspective, even that of the first-person pronoun, the author must maintain a distance from the character and not be emotionally involved. The less the fiction writer expresses of the self, the more he distances himself from the self, and, including when writing about his own experiences, he must create a distance so that he will be able to listen intently and observe. In other words, the author must purify himself and extricate himself from the total chaos of his self to allow for lucid thinking. And, using a pair of wise eyes, or what might be called a pair of neutral eyes, he will be able to concentrate and listen, as he immerses himself in the character's inner mind and grasps the right tone of language to manifest the feelings of the character.

To listen or to look are mere actions that have no other implications, but in highly concentrated observation and intense listening, the attention of the observer endows meaning to the object. This form of observation brings with it aesthetic judgments. The poetic sense in fiction is not due to the expression of feelings but derives from these observations of the author. Under this form of concentrated gaze, even a marsh can have aesthetic implications.

Language is not simply a tool for conveying meaning. At the same time, language is also purposeful activity, and is permeated with the intent of the speaker. The narrative language of fiction likewise must have concealed but strong intent, and that is the author prompting the reader to arouse his sympathy, thereby conveying the author's feelings about his character.

The function of language is to suggest, not describe, and, strictly speaking, descriptions are merely rough approximations. Overly detailed descriptions cause the object depicted to become less clear, and this is due to the inherent nature of language. Language, unlike painting, cannot reproduce detailed images of still objects or persons. In language we can say only this is a tea cup, or add a few qualifications by saying that it is a white porcelain cup, but to go on to describe the shape, luster, and texture will make the writing clumsy, and people will not want to read it. It is impossible for language to accurately paint an object or a person's face, because words are the basic units of language, and words are concepts. Words are already abstractions of things. The word "cup" is an abstraction of the function of this container, and making all sorts of qualifications does not constitute an actual cup. It is through concepts that language evokes people's existing perceptual experiences, so to explain the difference between purple-red and bright red to someone who has been blind since birth is impossible. However, if the person became blind after having had visual experiences of colors, it is completely different.

Language evokes experiences via words and sentences, and the fiction writer in his narration suggests past perceptions experienced by the reader. While the author is listening intently and observing, what is important is not description but finding a means of speaking—that is, the right narration that will evoke people's experiences and produce associations.

Consider, for example, describing the dream world, whose intangible mental images are inherently ambiguous. The once popular method known as automatic writing attempted to record the dream world and obtained nothing more than some fragments of words and sentences. However, when it comes to describing dreams, it is usually just a very brief outline of the dream. Psychoanalysts have obtained accounts of their patients' dreams, but it goes without saying that these accounts were doctor-induced, so that the patients' accounts were shortened a great deal. It is virtually impossible to give an accurate account in language of the dream world, and this is because the boundless chaos of the conscious and subconscious of the dream world cannot be accommodated in sequential sentences. What can be narrated must, after waking, consciously be ordered and placed into grammatically acceptable linear word order. If the fiction writer wants to relate as precisely as possible the dream world of his characters, he must find a narrative mode, and stream of language is the narration most closely approximating dream. What is important is not description but the process of the telling, so it is best to resort to speech when dealing with the inner mind that eludes description.

With memories, finding an accurate narrative mode is difficult too. When people look back on the past, it inevitably bears sentiments of the present and could be grief-tinged with homesickness, frustration, or anxiety, and these psychological elements will color and change the images in memory. The fiction writer must separate the telling of events and the narrating of the character's memories: these are different levels. The latter will have retreated to the psychological level, and in fact is a re-creation of past circumstances that are colored by sentiment. Especially when memories are derived from the narrator's perspective, the thoughts produced by both memory and wish are often chaotically interwoven.

It is the same with impressions. Indeterminate by nature, these are furthermore contaminated by psychological elements, and so a direct mode of narration is clearly inappropriate. Instead, it would be best to borrow the help of narrative sequences and to add coloring during the process of forming the sentences. Such sentence structures differ from normal descriptions, and they are nonjudgmental.

Even observation is a process, because concentration and focus are continually shifting. So relating an observation with accuracy is not simply a matter of providing what is seen, but similarly must rely on a stream of language that is actualized in sequential sentences. Furthermore, narration is a form of purposeful behavior that is actualized within time, and this determines that the language of fiction is not the same as scientific language. The latter is established on the basis of categories and concepts; uses logic and rationality as the basis for analysis, evaluation, explanation, and deduction; and is language demanding that time be discarded. On the other hand, the language of fiction is every instant inextricably bound to the perceptions and psychological activities of the characters and is constantly actualized during the process of narration. The art of fiction, finally, is actualized in the narrative language. Through revisiting narration and further study, a new realm for the creation of fiction will open up.

Although the narration of fiction is founded on perception, thought is not discarded. Yet this sort of thought is not purely rational. The thoughts expressed in fiction must be via the personal experiences of the characters, because to relate it directly would end up as preaching. Fiction avoids sentimentalism, and the preaching of thought is taboo. When the art of fiction turned from story and plot to the inner world of characters, the thinking of characters became more and more important, and many pages and whole chapters could be devoted to interior monologue. However, fiction cannot be written up as a work of thought. When revealing a character's thoughts, the fiction writer who is bound to the circumstances of the character must find a suitable mode of narration that will make the thoughts emerge as the inner experiences of the character. The changing of pronouns in this sort of interior monologue possesses special meaning and is not simply a narrative technique.

Fiction is different from drama, and in plays monologues can be made very lively by the performance of the actor. However, fiction relies only on narration, and if there are interior monologues they must be converted into false dialogues, for example between the first-person pronoun, I, and the second-person pronoun, you. Once the two levels of the inner mind are separated, thinking will have a basis on which to develop. With these two types of introspection turning into a dialogue, the reflections of the self become lively, and with layer upon layer of breakthroughs and progressive deepening, the process of thinking is also precisely manifested.

If one proceeds further and uses the second-person you to narrate and externalizes the character's ego as he, then you and he will be distanced. This focus will make the train of thinking clearer, and this form of distanced observation will simultaneously possess aesthetic significance. In manifesting thought, the fiction writer differs from the philosopher, because what is related is not strictly rational and at the same time is infused with aesthetics.

As far as the fiction writer is concerned, deliberation does not rely on the assertion of maxims and aphorisms. Philosophical deliberations are abstract, without persons, and the person deliberating is not confirmed. The fiction writer is exactly the opposite, because both deliberation and thought must be induced in a character at a certain time, in a certain place, and when the character is in a particular frame of mind, and this narration constitutes the present action of the character. In other words, the articulation of thought in fiction is not divorced from perception, and must constitute a link in the character's life that unifies perception and thought in the character's experiences.

Fictional narration of sensed perceptions and past experiences goes further to expand into an interactive dynamic between a person's inner consciousness and subconscious. When an appropriate mode is found for articulating the character's thoughts without loss to the infectious power of fiction, the process of deliberation and the formation of thought can be introduced into the literary genre of fiction.

In *Soul Mountain,* there are chapters concerning the birth of myths, legends, and folksongs, explanations of allegories, lamentations on history, definitions of fiction, the implications of pronouns, and analysis of the self. Once this plethora of deliberations on the deep structure of human culture had been connected with the protagonist's circumstances, only a suitable narrative mode was needed for inserting the thoughts evoked into the novel.

Such deliberations, of course, are not the same as a scientific treatise and do not require logic and verification; on the contrary, these must be eliminated, because what the fiction writer must ascertain is how to enter into the process of deliberations and thought production. The understanding arrived at in fiction travels a path going in the opposite direction to the philosopher's.

The art of fiction must be linked with aesthetics and not just provide an understanding of it. When the author becomes aware of this certain person and what is happening, he cannot restrain himself from making aesthetic judgments. Initially, these stem from emotions such as liking or disliking, liking yet disliking, being amused or sad, feeling pity and yet more so sympathy or hate, but at the same time there can also be entry into the higher aesthetic levels of comedy, pure theater or tragedy, the noble or the absurd, the funny or the humorous. When the author focuses and listens to his characters, he will give such aesthetic judgments, and moreover these will be realized in the narrative language of the fiction. Hence fiction is also a unity of perception and aesthetics.

The aesthetics of fiction can also gain entry to the spiritual realm via the perceptual level. The realms attained in poetry can likewise be attained in fiction. The frog appearing in the snow in *Soul Mountain* constructs an image, and this sort of enlightenment is similar to a Chan Buddhist realm. Perception can transform into enlightenment, thought can sublimate into the spiritual, and conscious observation and contemplation of existence does not lead only to religion but can also lead to aesthetics.

If the writer of fiction fully immerses himself in discovering the functions of language from the subconscious and the preconscious to the conscious, from the mental to the spiritual, from nonlanguage information to supralanguage spiritual enlightenment, it seems he will find the language for expression. It is in this respect that the linguistic art of fiction is far from exhausted, and it is in this that its magic lies.

Indeed, the writer of fiction cannot reform this perplexing world, nor can he change people or their innate nature. He merely provides perceptions that mock or contemplate those in the predicament while presenting an aesthetic judgment. In doing so, he gains pleasure and spiritual release and gives readers something interesting to read.

This understanding can come only from the individual and is actualized in the unique language of the author, a language that the author has worked hard to create. A fiction writer provides a rich world that is actualized through language. Historicist analysis often claims that certain societies, eras, or political and economic conditions determine the kind of writer that is produced. However, the fiction writer does not emerge as a necessity for any era. Instead, each writer has his own specific circumstances, his own innate abilities, and his own perspectives and modes for dealing with the world. How he deals with language and his unique perception of the world are linked, and these are infused into a work along with his aesthetic perceptions. Fiction is the creation of the individual fiction writer, and its significance does not lie in commonality or identification—for example, race or national identity, cultural or even political identity. Rather, its significance lies in its uniqueness: the creations of fiction writers are each distinctly separate, and the more outstanding the writer, the more unique his work. This is the quest of the fiction writer, and all fiction writers seek to find their own unique form of narration. A history of literature is written like this, and so is the history of fiction.

Writers of fiction leave individual footprints in history, and it is meaningless to call them progressive or reactionary, and historicist judgments as to whether they are modern are also meaningless. Postmodern is not necessarily more progressive than modern, and it is not the case that revolution is certain to bring progress, or that the realism of the nineteenth century is superior to the romanticism of the eighteenth century. Historicist judgments of fiction writers are inevitably bound to politics and ideology, and the fiction writer must slough off such externally imposed burdens and, returning to the art of fiction, search for his own unique language that will enable him, as accurately as possible, to relate his perceptions of the world. This boundless search has no direct links with the methodologies of science; instead, it is manifested simultaneously as aesthetic interest.

*Translated by Mabel Lee*

## Chapter 72 from *Soul Mountain*

"This isn't a novel!"

"Then what is it?" he asks.

"A novel must have a complete story."

He says he has told many stories, some with endings and others without.

"They're all fragments without any sequence, the author doesn't know how to organize connected episodes."

"Then may I ask how a novel is supposed to be organized?"

"You must first foreshadow, build to a climax, then have a conclusion. That's basic common knowledge for writing fiction."

He asks if fiction can be written without conforming to the method which is common knowledge. It would just be like a story, with parts told from beginning to end and parts from end to beginning, parts with a beginning and no ending and others which are only conclusions or fragments which aren't followed up, parts which are developed but aren't completed or which can't be completed or which can be left out or which don't need to be told any further or about which there's nothing more to say. And all of these would also be considered stories.

"No matter how you tell a story, there must be a protagonist. In a long work of fiction there must be several important characters, but this work of yours . . . ?"

"But surely the I, you, she, and he in the book are characters?" he asks.

"These are just different pronouns to change the point of view of the narrative. This can't replace the portrayal of characters. These pronouns of yours, even if they are characters, don't have clear images they're hardly described at all."

He says he isn't painting portraits.

"Right, fiction isn't painting, it is art in language. Do you really think the petulant exchanges between these pronouns can replace the creation of the personalities of the characters?"

He says he doesn't want to create the personalities of the characters, and what's more he doesn't know if he himself has a personality.

"Why are you writing fiction if you don't even understand what fiction is?"

He then asks politely for a definition of fiction.

The critic is cowed and snarls, "This is modernist, it's imitating the West but falling short."

He says then it's Eastern.

"Yours is much worse than Eastern! You've slapped together travel notes, moralistic ramblings, feelings, notes, jottings, untheoretical discussions, unfable-like fables, copied out some folk songs, added some legend-like nonsense of your own invention, and are calling it fiction!"

He says the gazetteers of the Warring States period, the records of humans and strange events of the Former and Later Han, the Wei and Jin, and the Southern and Northern Dynasties, the *chuanqi* romances of the Tang dynasty, the prompt books of the Song dynasty, the episodic novels and belles-lettres of the Ming and Qing dynasties, as well as the writings through the ages on geography and the natural sciences, street talk, morality tales, and miscellaneous records of strange events, are all acknowledged as fiction. But none of these have ever had any fixed models.

"Are you from the searching-for-roots school?"

He hastens to say you sir have stuck such labels on him. However, the fiction he writes is simply because he can't bear the loneliness, he writes to amuse himself. He didn't expect to fall into the quagmire of the literary world and at present he is trying to pull himself out. He didn't write these books in order to eat, fiction for him is a luxury beyond earning money and making a livelihood.

"You're a nihilist!"

He says he actually has no ideology but does have a small amount of nihilism in him, however nihilism isn't the equivalent of absolute nothingness. It's just like in the book where you is the reflection of I and he is the back of you, the shadow of a shadow. Although there's no face it still counts as a pronoun.

The critic shrugs his shoulders and departs.

He feels confused and uncertain about what it is that is critical in fiction. Is it the narrative? Or is it the mode of narration? Or is it not the mode of narration but the attitude of the narration? Or is it not the attitude but the affirmation of an attitude? Or is it not the affirmation of an attitude but the affirmation of the starting point of an attitude? Or is it not the starting point but the self which is the starting point? Or is it not the self but perception and awareness of the self? Or is it not the perception and awareness of the self but the process of that perception and awareness? Or is it not the process but the action itself? Or is it not the action itself but the possibility of the action? Or is it not the possibility but the choice of action? Or is it not whether there is a choice but whether there is the necessity of a choice? Or is it not in the necessity but in the language? Or is it not in the language but whether the language is interesting? Nevertheless he is intrigued with using language to talk about women about men about love about sex about life about death about the ecstasy and agony of the soul and flesh about people's solicitousness for people and politics about people evading politics about the inability to evade reality about unreal imagination about what is more real about the denial of utilitarian goals is not the same as an affirmation of it about the illogicality of logic about rational reflection greatly surpassing science in the dispute between content and form about meaningful images and meaningless content about the definition of meaning about everyone wanting to be God about the worship of idols by atheists about self worship being dubbed philosophy about self love about indifference to sex transforming into megalomania about schizophrenia about sitting in Chan contemplation about sitting not in Chan contemplation about meditation about the Way of nurturing the body is not the Way about effability or ineffability but the absolute necessity for the effability of the Way about fashion about revolt against vulgarity is a mighty smash with a racquet about a fatal blow with a club and Buddhist enlightenment about children must not be taught about those who teach first being taught about drinking a bellyful of ink about going black from being close to ink about what is bad about being black about good people about bad people about bad people are not people about humans by nature are more ferocious than wolves about the most wicked are other people and Hell in fact is in one's own mind about bringing anxieties upon oneself about Nirvana about completion about completion is nothing completed about what is right about what is wrong about the creation of grammatical structures about not yet saying something is not the same as not saying anything about talk is useless in functional discourse about no-one is the winner in battles between men and women about moving pieces backwards and forwards in a game of chess curbs the emotions which are the basis of human nature about human beings need to eat about starving to death is a trifling affair whereas loss of integrity is a major event but that it is impossible to arbitrate this as truth about the fallibility of experience which is only a crutch about falling if one has to fall about revolutionary fiction which smashes superstitious belief in literature about a revolution in fiction about revolutionizing fiction.

Reading this chapter is optional but as you've read it you've read it.

*Translated by Mabel Lee*

# Bei Dao

*(b. 1949)*

Bei Dao was born in Beijing, attended the Fourth Middle School, and was briefly a Red Guard. From 1969 to 1980, he was "re-educated" as a construction worker. In 1976 Bei Dao's poetry gained recognition as part of the Democracy Movement. In 1978 he and Mang Ke founded the literary journal *Today,* which, from 1978 to 1980, published a new generation of poets. In the early 1980s, he worked at the Foreign Languages Press and, when the political climate changed in the mid-1980s, Bei Dao traveled to Europe and the United States. Since 1987, he has lived in England, Germany, Norway, Denmark, Sweden, the Netherlands, France, and the United States. He has published many books of poetry in English as well as a collection of short stories and two collections of essays. These works include *The August Sleepwalker* (1988), *Old Snow* (1991), *Forms of Distance* (1994), *Landscape over Zero* (1995), *At the Sky's Edge: Poems 1991–1996* (1996), *Unlock* (2000), *Blue House* (2000), and *Midnight's Gate* (2005). He is the recipient of the Aragana Poetry Prize from the International Festival of Poetry in Casablanca, the Tucholsky Prize from Swedish PEN, the PEN / Barbara Goldsmith Freedom to Write Award, and a Guggenheim Fellowship, and he is an honorary member of the American Academy of Arts and Letters. He was named a presidential lecturer at Stanford University and has taught at the University of California at Davis, the University of Notre Dame, the University of Alabama, and Beloit College. In August 2007 he moved with his family to Hong Kong and is a Professor of Humanities at the Chinese University of Hong Kong. He was named the fellow of the 2008 Puterbaugh Conference on World Literature, sponsored by *World Literature Today* and the University of Oklahoma.

The prose selections included here foreground observations about poetry. As a writer who has lived in many countries, his observations about reading with Palestinian poets at Ramallah's Al-Kasaba Theater, where "for at least one night, poetry broke the siege of the language of hate," and his description of Gu Cheng meeting with Wolfgang Kubin are insightful and moving. Bei Dao has written a short, new piece to precede the selections from his previously published essays.

## Drifting

For as long as I have written poetry, people have looked at me a bit askew. It was only after I started writing essays that these same people began to consider my work worthwhile. My cousin even declared: "Enough with the poetry already, when your next collection of essays comes out, I'll read that." Because of poetry's inherent heterodoxy, poets are viewed as being not quite right in the head; essayists, on the other hand, are part of a literary world in which they can lead open and public lives.

Modern China is a powerful wellspring for essays with an innumerable number of specialized newspaper columns, leisure magazines, and cultural websites penned by essayists. You could say that essays are more in line with our current national condition, and with the vast, densely populated world of information exchange, our national character, and commercialization. Sichuan's essays are the teahouse, in Beijing it's the taxis; the well-informed opinion of a scholar at an institution of higher learning is an essay, Miss Bai Ling's text message can also be an essay.

My writing assignments in elementary school often earned praise from my teacher Dong Jingbo, who would ask me to recite them aloud. I can remember my heart beating wildly. This was the initial phase of my "public" career. You could even say that Teacher Dong was my first editor and publisher. Half a century later, I went to see her. She was generally in good health, though now confined to bed because of her legs. I took out my collection of essays that had been published in Taiwan. Behind her glasses grew the same tender smile from years past. I was a child at sunset—both fearful and warm.

Essays have the ability to reflect the middle-aged realities of hormones, blood pressure, heart rate, and other factors. Like someone coming down a mountain, you must adjust your rate of breathing, slow the pace; stop to "pick chrysanthemums from the east hedge, and gaze at leisure on South Mountain" [from Tao Yuanming's "Drinking Wine"]. Nostalgia is difficult to avoid, like growing lost in one's breathing when hiking up the mountain, unaware of just how high and dangerous things have become until you finally take a moment to stop and look around.

Essay writing and a life of drifting enjoy a symbiotic relationship: essays are the drifting of language, and drifting is the geographical and social aspect of writing. Between 1989 and 1993, I lived in seven countries and moved fifteen times. This type of continuously shifting state lends itself to the essay form. Where did you go? What did you do? These are things that my poetry is not equipped to explain clearly.

I float amid languages
the brasses in death's music
full of ice
[from "February," in *Landscape over Zero*,
trans. David Hinton & Yanbing Chen, p. 19]

the background needs revising
you can return to your hometown
[from "Background," in *Landscape over Zero*,
trans. David Hinton & Yanbing Chen, p. 13]

At its best, poetry dots the pupil in the dragon's eye. To actually draw the dragon requires scales, claws, and other fragments of detail that must be outlined and woven together.

Allen Ginsberg died in 1997. The commemorative essay that I wrote was the beginning of this stage of my writing career. Ginsberg was an eccentric character who behaved unscrupulously and persisted in his own ways regardless of what anyone else thought. He was not constrained by the political correctness of the American mainstream consciousness and ideology. We first met in 1984—a chance meeting—and if I had not been exiled, we probably would not have become friends. On the anniversary of his passing, I wrote "Death of a Poet."

> The death of a poet does not add or subtract anything from this earth: however unsightly his gravestone might be, however much his books might pollute, however much his gritty spirit may secretly impede the normal operation of the vast mechanism itself. [from *Blue House*, trans. Ted Huters & Feng-ying Ming, p. 22]

From drifting around the world I have gotten to know Gary Snyder, Octavio Paz, Tomas Tranströmer, Breyten Breytenbach, and other notable international writers. I have also become acquainted with nonliterary characters such as Mustard and Yuyong, less visible figures who follow the tides.

I should be thankful for all these years of drifting, which have placed me far from any center, have kept me from becoming too impetuous, as life washes around me.

During the long slow nights of northern Europe, I'd sometimes fall into despair, silently praying for the future to overcome my heart's inherent weakness. I once said in an interview, "Exile is an endless journey through emptiness." When you have experienced this emptiness you gain a new understanding of what is a limited existence. [quote and the sentence following are variations on a conversation with Gabi Gleichmann, "An Interview with Bei Dao," *Modern Chinese Literature* 9 (1996): 387–93]

Though she doesn't show up in my writing often, my daughter Tiantian plays an important role. She is the anchor for my drifting boat and the latent reader that pushes me to write. Sometimes I will read her a few passages, but her Chinese is not that fluent and she only comprehends a fraction of the work. But I believe that someday she truly will understand. I want to tell her my life stories, including the tears on history's mask, the shattered myths and enemies; and we will travel beyond all this, reaching a way beyond countries; I am there, she is there, along with countless others.

*Translated by Jody Beenk*

## Excerpts from *Blue House*

### *Reciting*

When I was in primary school I was known for my ability at comic dialogue, but I later switched to dramatic reading, reciting Gao Shiqi's poem "The Song of the Times." I can remember the athletic field enveloped in dust, with the entire student body gathered around and the teachers supervising. I stood on the brick platform, raising my voice: *Oh time*—time, which sweeps by.

The Cultural Revolution can be thought of as a mass recitation led by Mao Zedong. Those at the back inevitably lost track of what was being said and ended up chanting counterrevolutionary slogans.

Moreover, there was an obvious problem with the pronunciation used on the Central Broadcasting Network: it made it seem as if the whole country was correcting the old man's high-pitched Hunan accent word by word. I did odd jobs for our school's propaganda team. It was more interesting working backstage; almost metaphoric. And as metaphors are always slippery, and can be neither touched nor seen directly, they provide the ultimate interpretation. When the performance was concluded, and the recitations were finished, it was time for the metaphors to come along and confer meaning. [. . .]

On April 8, 1979, the editorial board of *Today* organized a poetry reading at Yuyuantan Park. We applied for permission to the police and received no response, which we took as tacit approval. I went with Mang Ke and Lao E to survey the terrain. There was a little clearing in the woods and a hill that could serve as our stage. Huang Rui painted an abstract pattern on a bedsheet and hung it between two trees as our curtain. Lao E went out to round up some storage batteries so we could have an amplifier and some speakers. He looked a bit as if he were planning to make a homemade bomb. It was, in fact, an explosive device, which blew open a sizable breach:

this was the first such privately organized poetry reading since 1949. It was very windy that day, which held the crowd down to four or five hundred, fewer than we'd expected. An aerial view would have revealed three distinct rings of color: the audience at the center dressed in gray and blue and khaki; then the foreigners in their garish clothes; finally the ring of police, all in white.

*Translated by Ted Huters & Feng-ying Ming*

## Excerpts from *Midnight's Gate*

An artist or intellectual who has inherited one ancient tradition has a difficult time living in another. Even more serious than practical pressures is the sort of internal conflict that it produces—the two traditions are incompatible with each other. [. . .]

At eight that night, at Ramallah's Al-Kasaba Theater, we gave a reading with a group of Palestinian poets. The house was packed. One person told me there hadn't been this kind of cultural event for a long time due to the siege. [Mahmoud] Darwish read first. From the sound of the appreciative sighs in the audience, one could sense he was the pride of Palestine. His poems made me think of the late Israeli poet Yehuda Amichai, whom I had met twelve years earlier at the International Poetry Festival in Jerusalem. There was, to my surprise, a certain similarity of tone in their poetry: the lonely quality of their words, their impotence and alienation regarding the state of things, their fear of the clamorous crowd, their attempt to maintain a last bit of dignity by mocking themselves. I don't know if they've read each other's work, and maybe this isn't important. What is important is that people of both cultures really listen to their poets. As Octavio Paz said, poetry is a third voice apart from religion and revolution. This voice cannot truly eliminate hatred, but perhaps can alleviate it to some degree.

For at least one night, poetry broke the siege of the language of hate. [. . .]

Around that time, [Wolfgang] Kubin had recently finished his professorial qualifying thesis, *Empty Mountain*. His university studies touched on a wide range of subjects, including philosophy, Germanic studies, and sinology, but his major was divinity, and according to the original logical progression of things, he should have gone on to become Pastor Kubin. I recently read a Chinese translation of *Empty Mountain*, re-titled *The Chinese Literati's View of Nature*. In the preface to this book, the hitherto laconic Kubin finally dropped a clue: At the end of 1967 Li Bo's poem "On Yellow-Crane Tower, Farewell to Meng Hao-Jan Who's Leaving for Yang-chou" convinced him to bid farewell to Protestantism and the Gospels. If a person changes his entire life because of a poem, it must be because of a mysterious calling rooted in the blood of his core. [. . .]

To this day I still cannot understand how that simple poem by Li Bo could have caused him to go down a completely different road:

> From Yellow-Crane Tower, my old friend leaves the west.
> Downstream to Yang-chou, late spring a haze of blossoms,
>
> distant glints of lone sail vanish into emerald-green air:
> nothing left but a river flowing on the borders of heaven. [. . .]

I am still surprised by the power of Kubin's memory. He was like a shaman who can supernaturally summon a mass of details from a deep night long ago. We were living west of Chongwen Gate, on Xi Damochang Street, very close to Tiananmen. Why did we choose to meet under the flag? Most likely because it was the most obvious landmark in Beijing. It got dark early that day, and the air was icy. With a drinker's sharp eye, I noticed the half-dozen bottles of Danish Carlsberg beer (no doubt bought at the Friendship Store) in the plastic bag hanging from the handle of his bicycle. Taking advantage of the remaining daylight, I hurriedly led him through the five courtyards that led to my house, the air filled with the mildewy smell of cabbages that had been stored away for the winter. We propped our bicycles by the door. I pushed the door open and bright light poured out. Our house didn't have a sofa, so Kubin and Gu Cheng sat facing each other on two cushioned armchairs upholstered in red cloth. At first Gu Cheng was like a timid animal, nervous and afraid, but Kubin's fluent Chinese put him at ease, and he began to speak about the Cultural Revolution, about [J. H.] Fabre's *Souvenirs entomologiques*—a fluid torrent of words, unstoppable once begun. [. . .]

At the time of the Tiananmen Square massacre, I was in Berlin. Whenever [King] Martin wrote or phoned, he would express his condolences and then ask endless questions about the fate of the Chinese writers who were being persecuted. He said that he and his colleagues were exerting all their influence to get poets around the world to help their Chinese comrades. At the 1990 festival, the annual prize in the imprisoned poets category was given to the Chinese poet Song Lin and accepted on his behalf by a Romanian poet. The awards ceremony was grave and dignified, handled more like a memorial service. Martin put aside his smile, like a minister praying for a departed soul. Actually, due to communication difficulties, the poet himself had already slipped out of the coffin, and at that very moment was riding his bicycle beneath laundry hanging in the back alleys of Shanghai.

Emphasizing the close tie between poetry and politics was the basis of King Martin's national strategy. For a Dutch person, this was doubtlessly the correct policy: following the premises of Western humanism, he treasured the human voice and struggled against the powers that tried to silence it. Sadly, there is no so-called "universal truth." And from the point of view of many who have been rescued, true resistance lies in allowing poetry to separate itself from politics, leaving behind the language of states and thus freeing itself from the vicious circle of history. These misunderstandings between East and West sometimes exist in tacit accord, and are sometimes a cruel joke, embarrassing both sides.

*Translated by Matthew Fryslie*

# Gu Cheng

*(1956–1993)*

Gu Cheng was born in Beijing, and his father was a well-known writer and party member. In 1968 his family was sent to Shandong province for "re-education," and they lived in the countryside and bred pigs. He read widely but, in his own words, learned more about poetry from nature. In 1974 he and his family returned to Beijing, and he worked as a carpenter, house painter, and editor. In 1976 he participated in the Tiananmen demonstrations and became friends with many of the poets associated with *Today.* Although he knew American poetry well through translation—he often mentioned Whitman and Dickinson—he was also knowledgeable about Chinese classics and often cited the *Zhuang-zi* as an inspiration. Gu Cheng traveled with his wife, Xie Ye, to Europe and the United States, and, in 1987, relocated to New Zealand. He taught Chinese at the University of Auckland, and, in 1988, he and Xie Ye bought a small house on an island off the coast of Auckland. Their son, Samuel, was born the following year. In 1992 they moved to Germany; but he suffered from severe depression, and they returned to New Zealand. In October 1993, he killed his wife and hanged himself.

Gu Cheng wrote many essays about nature, language, and poetry, and the selections included here are instances of his lyrical insight. "Poetry Lessons" was first published in 1980, and, a year later, his interview on Misty poetry followed. "A Brief Self-Introduction" appeared in 1983, and his selection ends with his memory of awakening to poetry at Tiananmen Square on April 5, 1976.

## Poetry Lessons

*1*

It was a raindrop that first introduced me to poetry.

On the way to my primary school there was a spire-like pine tree, but whenever I passed by, it never spoke.

Then one day, after a rain shower, when the world was fresh and clean, that pine tree suddenly was all aglitter, with crystalline raindrops hanging from every needle; at that moment I completely lost touch with my own being. Inside each single drop I saw a rainbow floating; each drop was full of the clear blue sky; each drop held a new world for me. . . .

I knew then that a single small drop of rain was able to contain everything, and to distill everything within it. The world that sparkled in the raindrop was purer and more beautiful than the world in which we live our lives.

Thus, a poem is just that: a raindrop glittering on some tree of the imagination.

*2*

I grew up on a stretch of barren, alkaline land.

The earth and sky there were of a perfect beauty, they formed a perfect sphere. There were no hills, no trees; not even the angular lines of a building to disturb the view.

When I walked along my imaginary road, there was only me between the earth and sky: me, along with a type of pale purple plant.

These plants grew tall in that salty soil, so slender and dense; they stood beneath the sky, under dark clouds and blazing sun, accepting all that befell them. No one knew that they were there, no butterflies, no bees, there were no startled sighs or praises sung about them. Nonetheless, they grew, putting forth their small flowers, proudly holding their heads high. . . .

They taught me about springtime, poetry, and poetry's duty.

*3*

Between the outcropping of coral headlands, there was a small sandy beach.

There in the sand, over many years, the tides had left behind shells, forever beautiful and undisturbed.

But when I stopped, what drew my attention were not those brightly colored shells, but rather a very plain spiral shell, one that scuttled there alone through the shallows. When I grabbed hold of it, I then realized that there was a crab hiding inside, alive.

I want to thank that crab for teaching me about poetic language.

One spirited spoken phrase, unique in its construction, is far better than dozens of antiquated and elegant expressions.

*4*

Because of my deep needs, I often travel the far edges of society.

There, in front of me are plants, clouds, and the sea—nature cast in green, white, and blue. The purity of these colors wipes away the dust of the everyday world, letting my mind recover its senses.

Is this something I am learning for the first time? No, it seems to be a recollection of an earlier time, as if before I was born I was one of them. I once was curved like the tusk of a mammoth, once as innocent as a leaf, once as minute and happy as floating plankton, that free . . .

I want to thank nature for letting me discover myself, discover the story of all things of the world, living and not. I want to thank it for giving me an endless supply of poems and songs.

This is why in the midst of the battle with reality, in the midst of the howl of the grinding machines, I still can still say in a sweet, quiet voice:

I'm yours.

*5*

All things, material or alive, including people, have their dreams.

Each of these dreams is of its own world.

The desert dreams of the cloud's dark shadow, flowers dream of the butterfly's kiss; and dew dreams of the sea . . .

I too have a dream. Distant but distinct, it is not just of its own world, it is of a paradise beyond the world.

It is beautiful and pristine. When I opened the book of fairy tales by Hans Christian Andersen, my young mind flooded with light.

I travel toward it, gradually becoming transparent, casting away the shadow behind me. There is only the road, the open road.

The value of my life is in this moving on.

I want to use the pure metal of my mind to forge a key to open the gates of this paradise for people to see. If possible, I will then have the good fortune to sink into the darkness.

## Misty Poetry: An Interview

*Recently we have been reading about different interpretations of the much discussed "misty poetry" (menglongshi). We were hoping you might answer some questions about this from your own point of view.*

I'd be glad to do so.

*First, could you discuss what has been called "misty poetry," particularly what these poems may have in common?*

This name "misty poetry" has a strong sense of Chineseness to it, and it's a term that came about in a quite conventional way. The name was actually first used several years ago, but at that time the type of poetry that the term now "represents" had just come into being and hadn't yet gone through its formal christening. Later, when people began to take notice of this new poetry, it had already suffered through a rough childhood and had become a rapidly growing teenager. But the question was, What would it be called? Different people working from different perspectives came up with different names for it: new modern poetry, misty poetry, peculiar poetry, etc. Later, when the controversy erupted, we needed some commonly accepted terminology. What could we do? Our traditional way is to compromise; so "misty poetry" became the common expression.

My fellow poets and I have always thought that term "misty poetry" was a little misty itself. What does this word "misty" mean? According to its classical usage, it suggests a feeling something akin to "flowers viewed through the fog" or "losing sight of the ford crossing in the moonlight." According to the new theories, the term refers to poetry that is symbolic and suggestive, with deep conceptions, layered impressions, and a consciousness of the subconscious, etc. There's certainly some sense to this, but if you limit yourself to these ideas, I don't feel you'll really grasp the defining characteristic of this new sort of poetry. The defining characteristic of this new type of poetry is its realism—it begins with objective realism, but veers toward a subjective realism; it moves from a passive reaction toward active creation.

Basically, this poetry is not misty at all, but rather involves the awakening of a new type of aesthetic consciousness, whose field of concern is gradually becoming more clearly distinguished.

*You have said that "the defining characteristic" of "this new type of poetry" is that it "veers toward a subjective realism and moves toward active creation . . . whose field of concern is gradually becoming more clearly distinguished." But there are others who claim that the defining characteristic of these poems is that they are difficult to understand. What do you think of this "difficulty in understanding" the poetry?*

In slightly more scholarly terms, "to understand" means "to comprehend." I don't believe that it has ever been a simple matter to comprehend poetry or humanity. Comprehension always depends on two points of view, that of the writer and that of the reader. These two points of view are determined by many factors; among the most important are: (1) the stage of one's aesthetic development, (2) one's lived experience, (3) one's personality, and (4) the success of the writer to capture the moment.

Let's first talk about stages of aesthetic development. Anyone who has even a rudimentary understanding of critical theory knows that aesthetic judgments are not cast in stone, but rather are constantly evolving with broad social change and one's individual development. If we speak of social change, then this is like the flow of a river; if we speak of the individual development, it is like the growth of a tree.

Back when I was reading only comic books, I once flipped through something by Walt Whitman. I was shocked. Was he some sort of nut? His language was completely goofy; how could this ever get published? Was the publisher nuts too? Didn't his mom know how to bring him up right? It was all so scary. But there were lots of scary things back then: for example, there were also Lu Xun and Qu Yuan! Luckily they were all a lot older than me and it wasn't anything for me to worry about, so I went back to my comic books.

Of course, later I gradually came to comprehend such literature: from the children's tale "The Song of the Stream" by Yan Wenjing (1956) to the short story "Long Flowing Water" by Liu Zhen (1960s), from O. Henry to Jack London, to Hugo, to Romain Rolland, to Tagore, etc. And when I reread Qu Yuan's "Encountering Sorrow" or Whitman's *Leaves of Grass* I was shocked, but shocked in a very different way than when I was young. This was a shock of being overwhelmed by the work.

When I asked my fellow poets about this, it turned out it was the same for them. At any given moment of their lives, in each stage of their aesthetic development, every one of them had works of which they were especially fond. This fondness was something that evolved, however, and the final objects of their attention were always those works most widely appreciated by humanity. Moreover, these works (except for children's literature) could not be comprehended by someone in primary school. This is a normal phenomenon.

In addition to "not understanding" because of one's stage of aesthetic development, a lack of comprehension can also be caused by different artistic styles and different conceptions of art. Some of these disparities normally co-occur, but sometimes distortions result from the sense of practicality that is the legacy of our "time of turmoil." If we weigh these distorted ideas against our traditional Chinese aesthetics, we cannot say they are normal.

During the time of the "Gang of Four" people became used to viewing the literary arts as mere explications of government policy printed in an attractive format, as if literature were a "multiform system" for fighting illiteracy. And poetry? It became merely a competition of rhyming editorials. Later, things got somewhat better; starting with the "April Fifth Demonstrations" in 1976, poetry began to speak truthfully and show some hope of revival and development. Very quickly, as it began to reflect contemporary issues, this new poetry established some independent social value; this was very exciting for us. But was that all there was to be? Humankind needs other intellectual and emotional fields of interest. It is in these fields that our ancestors planted and harvested their art, and the fruits of their labors have become the stars that eternally shine in the sky of humanity. In recent years, however, these have largely become desolate lands filled with weeds. The fields of interest that are important to humankind include the life of the mind, the wonder of nature, and those mysterious realms of which men can have no clear conception.

Such interests must be rediscovered and expanded; the vitality of the Chinese people must find expression, only then will there be those who go forth to explore new lands. These explorers will revere the master poets of ancient times, but they will not try to repeat the literary methods of the past; to repeat the old is not what art is about. These explorers will use their creative powers to express the needs and ideals of the new generation. (The so-called "misty poetry" is just one of these methods of expression.)

The conceptual reach of poetry finds so many forms and is so fecund that no one can encompass it with just one idea. Poetry's inherently dreamlike quality determines that it will forever be opening new fields of interest, constructing new spiritual worlds. The philosophy of an unchanging response to the myriad changes will in the end become history.

In addition to the conceptual issues discussed above, there are also some things that pertain directly to the individual that should be considered since these have a clear role in the way poetry will resonate with someone. These are an individual's personality and life experience. These two factors determine, to a great degree, a person's specific connection to poetry. Since personality is a very difficult thing to assess, I will skip that and speak only of the role of one's life experience.

We have received many letters from young readers that raise such issues. Why is it that it is mostly young people who like "misty poetry"? How is it that the hearts of these really not very well-read young people can find a way to beat together in the distant world of "misty poetry"? Is this some purely surrealistic condition? No, it is not! What is important is that this younger generation has shared a journey together, has faced a shared reality, and has searched for ideals together.

Of course, those who seek the truth must pay the price; when you try to cut a new path through the wilds, you will encounter more thorns than flowers. Life is like that, and so is the creative learning process of the writer—more thorns than flowers. Both age and things unknown will mean that there will always be failures, going the long way around, running aground, hitting snags, maybe even sinking forever into oblivion. There is no glory to speak of in this. Ordinary people will think these artists are silly, and relatives and friends will be distressed for them. Yet a nation needs people who will first sacrifice themselves, because among them there will be some who are able to learn from the failures of their companions and find a new direction, in the end discovering new lands and new horizons.

*Your analysis above regarding the issue of "understanding" literature has given us some insight into the controversy surrounding "misty poetry." Since you do not agree with "this sort of narrow function of poetry and the literary arts," what do you think the social function of poetry and the literary arts should be?*

I have said that poetry with its conceptual reach finds many forms, and thus I think social function also has many forms. I appreciate politically engaged poetry that directly exposes social problems, and I like even more lyrical poetry that gives creative expression to the beauty of the spiritual and natural worlds. I believe all truly beautiful poetry has some positive social value. The sword and the rose do not stand opposed, to fight is not our purpose, the fight is just a means by which we can improve the world. From this point of view, the sword is there for the rose.

Having paid such a great price, we now know that neither politics nor material objects can be all there is to life. If a people are to move forward, they need more than technology and science, they also need higher spiritual cultivation, including a new form of aesthetic consciousness. Beauty cannot be held prisoner or enslaved any longer. It must be like the sun and the moon, filled with light, rising high into the sky, chasing away the shadows of evil; it will then fall through the windows of art and poetry to shine on souls of people both awakened and sound asleep.

For the next generation to rise above us, we now need more, cleaner, and larger windows.

*Translated by Joseph R. Allen*

## Excerpts from "A Brief Self-Introduction"

10. At eleven or twelve I started using some sentence fragments to record the feelings and inspirations the natural world was giving me. Were they my first artistic language? I certainly don't think so. Because at that time all of my affections and spirit were fastened on the wings of insects.

One afternoon, as the book confiscators from the workers' Propaganda Squad were dragging off a heavy canvas sack, I sat alone in front of our empty bookcases, not knowing what to think. As the light faded, my hand touched something under an old newspaper. I turned on the light: it was a famous book of popular science—Fabre's *Souvenirs entomologiques.*

The happy existence of this *Souvenirs entomologiques* turned me into a passionate lover of insects overnight. Over a million kinds of insects made up an endlessly mystical world—the golden sheen of the scarab beetle, the black-pottery luster of the cicada's back, the strange markings of the ladybug and vanessa, all floated through my dreams at night. . . .

I was rich. I gathered so many specimens—a poetic language given to me by nature.

11. Language wasn't enough. What life needed was a world.

Vaguely I felt its call.

Trudging down a gray Beijing street, pulling a brick on a thick power cord, my body was constructing an "underground Great Wall." My eyes were raised to the sky.

I was thinking of Fabre's words:

"My greatest dream was to have an outdoor laboratory—a little piece of land fenced in on all four sides, deserted and uncultivated. At last I got such a playground. In a secluded corner of the village there were plentiful weeds: couch grass, centauries, oyster plants . . . communities of Mason bees and wasps in piles of sand . . . woods full of singing birds, green orioles . . . a pond surrounded by frogs. In May they formed a deafening orchestra. . . .

"With so many dear little companions, I gave up the city for the countryside. . . ."

Yes, my whole family was moving to the countryside.

12. I am dreaming. / My dream is shattering. / Dreams always forgive their destruction, / but destruction never lets go of dreams.

*—on the eve of leaving Beijing, 1969*

Sometimes, a poem needs to be a little smarter than its writer.

As a rocking truck carried our family and belongings into a village built out of grass and mud, I believed this much.

Our first night in the countryside was miserable: things scattered in the courtyard, on the road; the whole family stretched out on a mud-brick bed;

everything completely still, black. It seemed like the world would never come back into being. We started learning to consider the earliest words invented by humanity—water, fire, light. . . .

Goodbye, J. H. Fabre. [. . .]

15. My father and I used to trade poems in the pig pen. He wrote one called "Fish in a Swamp"; I wrote one called "The Shot Goose." When we finished writing, we were happy for a while, then we stuffed the poems into the stove along with the rice straw. The stewing pig feed on the stovetop steamed. . . .

Father said: "The flames are our only readers."

I wrote this sentence on the stovetop with a piece of charcoal and wiped it away bit by bit with my finger. [. . .]

23. It was Tiananmen Square, on April 5, 1976.

Dusk. Gold flames and blue ribbons of smoke rose. Amid the shouting, the most fervent dream of my civic-minded life was reaching its climax—I clapped. I yelled. I wanted to cut the fire hoses. I wanted to join the people in burning up this blackest of moments. . . .

The loudspeakers blared. I was knocked to the ground by a crowd of strapping soldiers. As I hit the pavement, I suddenly understood my life's mission. [. . .]

31. After tireless mailings, some of the poems from *Water Country* and *Daylight Moon* were published in *Poetry, Stars, Chang'an*, and other journals.

The unexpected response to them terrified me. Almost a hundred periodicals published critical essays and a debate unfolded around two very short, sketch-like poems. Both express a particular state of mind.

A GENERATION

the black night gave me black eyes
still I use them to seek the light

FAR AND NEAR

you
look at me
then look at the clouds

I feel
when you look at me you're far away
when you look at the clouds you're near

The former received some praise. The latter received some criticism.

Both the criticism and the praise drove me to delve more deeply into the study of theory. I began to read book after book of philosophy, aesthetics, and psychology. My beliefs slowly started to coalesce. . . .

*Translated by Aaron Crippen*

# Zhai Yongming

*(b. 1955)*

Zhai Yongming was born in Chengdu. She graduated from high school in 1974 and, during the last two years of the Cultural Revolution, did manual labor in the countryside. She returned to Chengdu, studied in the Laser Technology Department of the Chengdu Institute for Telecommunications and Engineering, and earned a degree in 1981. That same year, she published her first poems in literary journals. Three years later, she rose to prominence with the publication of her twenty-poem cycle "Woman," a work that articulated a female point of view in China's largely patriarchal society. She became one of the leading post-Misty poets and is the author of many collections of poetry, including *Woman* (1986), *Above All the Roses* (1989), *Collected Poems of Zhai Yongming* (1994), *Plain Songs in the Dark Night* (1997), *In the End I'm Brought Up Short* (2002), and *The Finest Euphemisms* (2008). From 1990 to 1992, Zhai lived in the United States, and she has read her poetry at many international poetry festivals, including ones in England, the Netherlands, France, and Italy. In 2007 she received the first Zongkun International Poetry Prize in Beijing. In addition to being a poet, she is also a prolific essayist and installation artist. She owns a bar in Chengdu, where she hosts poetry readings and other cultural events.

Zhai's essay "Black Night Consciousness," written in 1985 and translated here for the first time into English, is an important statement on feminist poetics. As a poet, she has continually shifted her poetic concerns from book to book. Although her poem reprinted here, "The chrysanthemum lantern is floating over me," does not explicitly refer to writing, I have included it because its sensuous imagery and mysterious tone make it an excellent example of drawing on the classical tradition yet also transforming it.

## Black Night Consciousness

*Chengdu; January 24, 1985; revised April 17, 1985*

Now is the moment when at last I've become powerful. Or perhaps I should say that now I've finally become aware of the world around me and of the implications of my place in it. An individual and universal inner consciousness—I call this Black Night consciousness—has ordained that I be the bearer of female [*nüxing*] consciousness, beliefs, and feelings, and that I directly take that charge upon myself, and put it into what I see as the best work I can do on behalf of that consciousness. Namely, poetry.

As one half of humanity, from the moment of her birth, a female faces a completely different world. Her first glimpse of this world is of course colored by her individual spirit and sensibility, and possibly even by a psychology of private resistance. Will she muster all of her strength and energy to engage in life by creating a Black Night—to the extent that she reshapes the world into an immense spirit? In fact, every woman faces her own abyss—her most private pain and experience perpetually annihilated and affirmed—and very few are able to resist being ground down to destruction by these equal forces.

This is the very first Black Night, and as it ascends, it brings us to an altogether new and unique position and point of view, which only the females of this world possess. This isn't a process of redemption, but rather a process of complete awakening. Ever in flux, the female soul can accommodate anything that this ever-changing world might offer up, while also displaying its own spirit at its most fascinating and most difficult to realize. Thus, a woman's [*nüxing*] real power lies in her ability to confront the cruelty and perversity of her own fate, while at the same time being guided by the truth called forth by her innermost being, so that she creates a Black Night consciousness between these two conflicting forces.

In the end, consciousness is a sort of raw material. From birth, the interior of the female body conceals a premonition of destruction. It is precisely this premonition that, charged by a reality full of infinite possibilities, brings us into a condition of predestination from which we can never return. And for precisely this reason, when a woman poet lays claim to her mythological world, that world is not only linked with the moment of birth, but it is also connected to the kingdom of death. In the increasingly blurred boundary between the two, you have to see yourself clearly in order to maintain the reality of the Black Night in your own heart. Only when you're permeated by a Black Night consciousness that you've unearthed through the revelation of the pain that lies inherently within you, can you truly annihilate your own fear. This is why some people have said to me: "A woman poet's most powerful opponent is herself." I believe this is true.

For a woman, there exists an uncanny intuition between the self and the Black Night. From the moment of our births, we are bound to the Black Night by a mysterious relationship, a kind of hidden language that encompasses both what we can and cannot sense, extending from our bodies to our spirits and threading them together. For us, it is darkness, a silently burning desire, the original as well as the ultimate nature of humanity. It is precisely this, the feminine beauty found everywhere in the world and manifested in each woman's body, that ultimately becomes a symbol of her life as a whole. It transcends her self-knowledge and connects with a higher plane. This truest and most direct of impulses embodies the power that lies in poetry. In order to grapple with herself, she must not only discover this power but create the process. Moreover, through this power, she can reach the growing lucidity of the terrifying light that lies in the midst of the Black Night.

To my mind, women's literature is inherently composed of three levels with their own distinct tendencies. Within the freedom of this plurality, one discerns a tentative feminine lyrical pathos as well as an unvarnished feminism. The former takes the loneliness, narcissism, and lovesickness of naïve girls and assembles them into a fragmented mood, while the latter merely takes language and teases it into a hyper-rational and narrow-minded concept that unites cause and effect. While these two tendencies might appear to be strikingly at odds, nonetheless each one independently confirms its own triviality in terms of actual human nature. We need to recognize that in this context it is "women's" [*nüxing*] literature that occupies the highest level. While it participates in the shared fate of humanity, a genuine female consciousness, and the unique language and form that express that consciousness, it can also construct a durable impulse that enters into the poem's true and sacred precinct. It must be pointed out that most women poets fit one of the following descriptions: still unaware of her power; stuck in a narrowly circumscribed sphere where she magnifies her emotions; or else so steeped in other people's ideology and sentiments, without understanding or experiencing those people's situations, that she is just a simulation or reproduction of some male poet or another.

The most important thing of all is this: we must face reality—even if that reality is heartless and unforgiving. Alone in quiet contemplation, one may perceive one's own cruelty. This cruelty isn't something we imagine, but something we create. (This latter point is a truth that's hard to recognize.) Some people are capable of seizing this brilliant moment, sublimating every transcendent and mysteriously pleasurable intuition into a poetry tempered by experience and forged anew; but there are others who spend their entire lives standing on the outside of this world, content in their self-deception, ready at any moment to catch hold of fleeting and superficial epiphanies. Thus, among these three strata—femininity, women's rights, and the female sex [*nüxing*]—it's only the last of these that has true literary value. We must recognize this: that the wisdom of poetry has to be sought sincerely and diligently in experiences that are born in the individual's psyche but that transcend the poet's own time and place. Only then do we enter into the highest realm of wisdom: what the poet seeks in art must be a wisdom representative of humanity, and a mature woman cannot confront anything unless she grasps this.

I may not be a sage, nor do I see myself as a representative of the female sex, but I do represent myself, and it's my limitations that make me unique as a poet. I'm especially passionate about expanding on the simplest and subtlest feelings in my spirit, what I regard as "female temperament" [*nüxing yizhi*]—a certain stubbornness that causes me to be preoccupied with my inner feelings, and the unfathomable mystery of the Black Night, which separates me from the naked daylight and reveals the order guiding its motivations and its way of thinking. Black Night consciousness compels me to peel away many different experiences of myself, society, and humanity, until I achieve a clarity of perception. In the face of so many contradictions and conflicts, it enriches and matures my will and the power of my personality, while at the same time daring to expose the truth about itself. And thus poetry floods my body with suggestive power, making my entire spirit tremble uncontrollably, uniting me with things outside myself. Standing in the blind center of the Black Night, and following where my will leads, my poems will unearth all that has lain hidden in my body since before my birth.

This is a moment of immense significance, when we can voice anew the consciousness of humanity and the universe. As they face the troubling and tumultuous realities of our time, how will women poets, through their exhaustive efforts, be able to found their own Black Night and bring balance and order to poetry? Unless you're trapped in the status quo, you will always be able to find the most apt language and form to manifest the Black Night that unquestionably exists in everyone's body, while continuing to search for the one steady light that exists in the depths of that Black Night.

*Translated by Andrea Lingenfelter*

## The chrysanthemum lantern is floating over me

A chrysanthemum lantern is floating toward me.
In the enveloping silence of pitch darkness –
a low murmur of children on the riverbank.
The lantern is so sheer a bird's shadow shows through it.

The children's chorus floats over with the lantern.
There's no fear, no pain,
only the lantern, the lightness of chrysanthemums,
and the red glow of its candle.

A young girl also floats over –
a girl and her maids,
their hair up,
their luxurious clothes nothing but
silk, ribbons and buttons,
nothing but tinkling tassels when they walk –
tassels, earrings, phoenix hairpins.

The young girl and her wet nurse
have known death.
They are both searching for something leisurely.
They face the midnight moon.
The girl is gentle and the light soft.
They float toward me
transforming the ordinary night
into a somnambulist trance.

Every night
the lantern floats over me.
Its owner wanders to the end of heaven,
his pace sometimes fast, sometimes slow.
No one can catch up with him,
the children grow up with him.

This is the story of the changing world and of the lantern.
If I sit on the floor
the chrysanthemum's shadow, the light's shadow, and the shadows
of people
frighten me
and I sometimes slowly, sometimes quickly
make a silvery sound in my room.

If I sit on the bed
I can enjoy this sensation
while I gradually turn transparent,
gradually change color.
All night I merge into mist
then rise into the air.

*Translated by Pascale Petit*

# Zhou Zan

*(b. 1968)*

Zhou Zan is a poet, essayist, literary critic, and translator. She holds a doctoral degree from the Chinese Department of Beijing University, where she completed a dissertation on the role of the avant-garde in contemporary Chinese poetics. She began writing poetry as an undergraduate and is the author of multiple collections of poems, including *Dreaming or Self-Questioning* (1999) and *Loosen: Selected Poems 1997–2005* (2007). Her work is also featured online at *Wings: Women's Poetry Forum* as well as in numerous other Chinese literary journals. Her scholarly writings include *Through the Periscope of Poetic Writing* (2007) and *Studies on Contemporary Chinese Literature* (2001). Her translation of Margaret Atwood's *Eating Fire: Selected Poetry 1965–1995* was published in 2007. In 2007–8 she served as a visiting scholar at Columbia University. At present, she works as a research fellow at the Institute of Literature of the Chinese Academy of Social Sciences in Beijing, where she also serves as editor in chief of the influential unofficial women's poetry journal *Wings*, which she established with fellow poet Zhai Yongming in 1998.

The following essay was written in 1998 and revised in 2001.

## Musings on Poetry

### *For Whom I Write*

I both anticipate and seek out poetry. Confronting the self through writing, I've come to comprehend that exchanges formed between she and he are actually betrayals. Someone I've never met and might never meet, a particular historical figure, occasionally myself, a hypocritical mirror: for these few who get it—my literary confidants—I write down the first word.

### *Voice*

Strains of measured conversation. Biting the tongue, perplexed, perceiving the impact of my voice (poetry's eloquent sensibilities and ambitions are intertwined with my grasp of poetic prosody; the rhetoric encountered in a poem isn't really voice, but rather a precise discourse on mood and consciousness). Perhaps it constitutes the basic makeup of my best-loved poems. I loathe the drone of collective monotony (which has already disturbed one generation, the schooling of my early youth) discordantly dwelling on my body. Mine has been a different path, one grounded in individual desires—Frost's road.

### *Prosody*

From sound to prosody, I believe in the potential of receptiveness. Sound's mood, cadence, pitch, and tempo are merely stylistic elements, but only with the development and maturity of a distinct prosody is there any possibility of achieving true style. The likelihood of altering one's voice is comparatively small, while the prosody of specific words frequently changes. The lectures of a professor whose intonation and rhythm never vary are no different from hypnosis. A poem's prosody demonstrates the rhythms and melodies that the poet is able to cultivate on a particular theme.

The self splits. Despondent feelings amplify and persist. An effective poet knows his or her own limits. To prevent one's expressions from being burdened with indulgence, one must master the art of concealing and conquering. In China, when Romanticism was simplified to pertain to any articulation of passion or enthusiasm, with no regard for the context of its historical origins, modern poetry discovered its own mission. Prosody is a poetics of political stance, comprised of control and self-discipline.

### *Words*

Beautiful words are not universal; they convey the yearning for universality. Written words are animate, refusing to issue a verdict that refutes poetry's existence. Ideally, words should be positioned among the currents of creative forces. As such, their beauty anticipates the poet, a mystical natural talent in need of discovery. The pinpointing and scrutinizing of the sole significance of one specific term is indicative of the quintessential poet mindset, not some glamorous hobby.

If possible, the lexicon of a great poet should form a reciprocal relationship with culture, a mutual reflection and influence; meanwhile, the lexicon of an inferior poet accumulates into a linguistic trash heap, not unlike the cityscape of modern industrial culture. Great poetry is analogous to a city's brilliant night scene, the illusion of beauty persisting, possessing an imagined metaphysical meaning, while the trash heaps remain dormant, unable to be discerned. Poetry is Magritte hovering above the city skyline.

The beauty of words can only be achieved in their existential space, that is, by the relationships forged between voice and prosody.

### *Relationships Among Words*

Having abandoned an assiduous pursuit of famed maxims, I've come to admire the relationships among words. One characteristic of such relationships is noting the intermediary between sound and meaning in modern Chinese poetry. While a single word can stir the imagination, it can also all too easily degenerate into a cliché of rudimentary experiences.

Word associations presume a link between sound and meaning, similar to that between a lubricant and glue. The carefree pleasure of reading exceeds a one-time conscious appreciation, as the utility of appreciation distorts one's genuine impressions. Are the endless ways of interpreting poetry intimidating, poised for attack? Perhaps. Only prose is fair to the act of reading, which is why it's so well received. Poetry is alluring and relevant to merely a small group of readers who can endure the weight of its words. In prose, word relationships are ripe with symmetry, facilitating comprehension.

Patterns of words train the poet to replicate the patterns of the world. They herald the triumph of the poet's mood and thoughts, a testament to the poet's vitality. Since the May Fourth Movement, particular poets and texts in modern Chinese literature have only been sustained by the potency of reading.

## *The Memory of Words*

Poetry nests in the memory of words. Memory is the soul of a people and their language. The memory of words is a consciousness, the blood ties between history and culture. Experience reveals that history and culture are the fruits of poetry. When writing for a confidant, the power of writing is funneled into a corresponding concentrated space. The limitlessness of writing presupposes limits; possibility uses impossibility as a basis for reflection. The world is irresistible but not immune to scrutiny; it is invincible, but it can be transformed through self-transformation. Poetry consists of the world's complexities, precisions, and fidelities.

Complexities, self-aware beginnings. When the complexities of experience prod the complexities of writing, the wings of words and prosody will unfurl. Acknowledging the complexities of writing can in turn lead to contemplating the persistence and blindness of experience, to cleansing the self and self-cleansing.

Precision, when writing curbs the force of indulgent youthful vigor. It is also using compositions from one's youth to cultivate stamina and freshness.

Fidelity, rereading and revising experiments in fidelity. Fidelity demands that I use imagination and self-confidence to construct my convictions, capable of feeling and knowing. In accordance with poetry's greatest truth, fidelity is always present in writing, testing its vitality.

There is no other literary form that is more intense or directly dependent on words than poetry. Poetic language frequently adopts an unflinching pose to prevent readers from evading its profundity. As the Dutch critic J.J. Oversteegen has remarked, "Poetry's truth is precisely the tension between the linguistic world and our daily experiences. The reader confronts a new linguistic world with which he is unfamiliar." Examining the effects of reading, what poetry offers readers is not empirical experience (like a novel or prose). Instead, it challenges and introduces a new realm to the reader—it impels the reader to distrust his ability to sum up mundane experiences or his awareness of impressions of the beauty of mundane life.

*Translated by Jennifer Feeley*

# Zhang Er

*(b. 1960)*

Zhang Er was born in Beijing and moved to the United States in 1986. She is the author of three collections of poetry in Chinese: *Seen, Unseen* (*Meiren Kanjian Ni Kanjian de Jingzhi*, QingHai Publishing House of China, 1999), *Water Words* (*Shuizi*, New World Poetry Press, 2002), and *Because of Mountain* (*Shanyuan*, Tonsan, Taipei, 2005). Her poems have also appeared in English translation in many poetry journals. She has six chapbooks in translation: *Winter Garden* (Goats and Compasses), *Verses on Bird* (Jensen/Daniels), *The Autumn of Gu Yao* (Spuyten Duyvil), *Cross River. Pick Lotus* (Belladonna Books), *Carved Water* (Tinfish Press), and *Sight Progress* (Pleasure Boat Studio). Her selected poems in two bilingual collections, *So Translating Rivers and Cities* (2007) and *Verses on Bird* (2004), are from Zephyr Press. She coedited the bilingual volume *Another Kind of Nation: An Anthology of Contemporary Chinese Poetry* published by Talisman House Publishers (2007). She has read and lectured at international festivals, conferences, reading series, and universities in China, France, Portugal, Russia, Peru, Argentina, Canada, Singapore, Hong Kong, Taiwan, and in the U.S. She currently teaches at Evergreen State College in Washington.

In this new essay, Zhang Er discusses Chinese women's poetry and the rich tradition of folk poetry.

## A Female Voice from the Past: An Alternative Tradition of Chinese Poetry

*Olympia, Washington, November 11, 2008*

A few years ago, *Wings* (Yi), a Beijing poetry journal devoted solely to women's writing (edited by Zhou Zan, one of the contributors to this book), organized a debate on the tradition of Chinese women's poetry. At the time, my position was that we didn't have much of a Chinese women's poetry tradition. Yes, there were a few known women poets in the classical period. However, in the huge chorus of collected poetry, the genuine female voice was shockingly lacking. We had a decadent tradition of female-persona lyric mode employed by male poets, fully displaying the male aesthetic assumption about how the female voice should sound. The familiar voice in this tradition is one that whines. "She" longs for and complains about a powerful male figure coyly or coquettishly with an exaggerated femininity. Hardly fashioned out of empathy for an underprivileged and deprived woman, this voice often offered a soft disguise for male authors to vent their own dissatisfaction with the rulers, while engaging in narcissistic self-pity. Unfortunately, time and time again, this female-persona style had been treated as the template of female writing. Any would-be woman poet in order to be accepted had to tailor her voice to fit this aesthetic "standard" of the established genre of female-persona mode. The later surge of women poets in the Ming and Qing Dynasties rediscovered and published in several recent anthologies, although impressive in volume, adds very little to the dominant mode of writing. These poems for the most part inevitably mimic male writing, including the female-persona-style lyrics. The originality, urgency, and the clearly recognizable individual voice of earlier women masters such as Cai Yan (born between 172–78) and Li Qingzhao (1084–1155) remain unique cases.

As a contemporary Chinese woman poet, I found myself gasping for air in this pinched vocal repertoire set up by many of our brilliant male counterparts from the classical past. Until recently, that is, when I finally with some confidence came to believe that another tradition of female voice in Chinese poetry does exist.

There has been a long debate about the authorship in the first poetry collection in Chinese, *The Book of Poetry* (*Shi* or *Shi-Jing*), legendarily edited by Confucius, although the book evidently existed before Confucius's time (551–479 B.C.E.). One of the three sections in the book, *Book of Songs* (*Feng*), consisted of folk songs that were collected by the "agents" sent from the Zhou central state, as intelligence information on the mentality of people in subservient states. It seems the "heavenly son" of Zhou shared a similar view on folk songs as T. S. Eliot on poetry: to know a people is to know their poetry. The authors of the work were not recorded; the only things we know about them were hinted by the name of the state where their works were collected. In *Feng*, besides many examples of venting, lamenting, and expressing dissatisfaction with the rulers and other aspects of life in peace and in war, there were songs for courtship and celebrations, work songs and songs for day-to-day mundane themes. These verses (we no longer have a record of their melodies) possess all the typical features of folk song depicted by modern scholarship. Among them, notably, are songs with a distinct female voice, judged not just by their assumed persona, but also by the subject matter, such as work songs of picking and gathering fruits, vegetables, mulberry leaves for silkworms, and of weaving, typical of women's work. The songs about marriage and love affairs and family relationships also occupied a significant volume of *Feng*. Scholars debated over the authenticity of the authors' female gender, some using classical female-persona lyric tradition as a proof to discredit the hypothesis of possible female authorship. Interestingly, in the awakening of women's poetry writing since the late Ming dynasty, male scholars began seriously entertaining the idea that women had contributed to *Feng* substantially.

As a poet, I have always suspected some of the work in *Feng* must have been composed and sung by women. Who else on earth would know the difficult relationship between daughter-in-law and mother-in-law, and invest so much vindictive emotion in the bickering? Who else would be so emotionally affected by a sister's marriage procession? Who else would boast a "ripening" beauty like plums and solicit suitors to come on quickly? Who else would call out repeatedly into the thunderstorm for the beloved husband to return home? Who else would worry so much at the sight of two young sons getting into a boat, afraid they might perish for no particular reason? The narrative voices, unlike that of the female-persona style in the classical period, are self-assured, forceful, and open, with a brilliant sound quality. We can hear them wailing, gossiping, laughing, calling, swearing their eternal love, throwing things around, or even setting them on fire when their loved one turned out to be unfaithful! Their anxious steps on the dock thumped over the millennia. There was not a trace of the familiar pinched disguise or passivity.

Another piece of indirect evidence comes from the way *Feng* was brought into being. All these songs were presumed to be composed orally, sung by people orally, and collected by sent agents of both genders. The well-known Han Music Bureau (*Yue Fu*) several hundred years later, modeling its organization after Zhou, sent out, with government stipend, male collectors over age sixty and female collectors over fifty who had no child, from the capital to the provinces to collect folk songs. The scarcity of women who knew how to read and write—another argument that is often used to discredit the female authorship—is thus moot, as the authors here, male or female, were not writers: they were singers and oral reciters. Second, why would the central government send out paid female collectors if not for the purpose of having access to female voices in the women's quarters?

I believe at least two thousand years ago we indeed seem to have had a rich tradition of women's poetry in the form of folk songs. My recent thought is that perhaps in spite of the scant evidence of women's poetry in writing since the *Feng* and Han *Yue Fu* collections, this women's oral folk song tradition may have been alive and healthy, through the classical period, until the early modern era, and only faded into oblivion when women started to attend private and public schools. By then, rather than orally composing verses, women who happened to be gifted with creativity in words would choose to write poetry. Once the collecting mechanism for their work (oral verses in the form of folk songs) disappeared after the Han dynasty, the female voice in classical Chinese poetry recorded in writing diminished significantly. It doesn't mean women stopped composing after Han, only that we don't have a record of their work.

Here is an account of the recent discovery that pushed me toward this view. I have long been fond of folk songs and rhymes from different regions of China, and I am always attracted to their bold, explicit, and expressive vocabulary, straightforward grammar and line structure, without heavy-handed artistic intentions, unweighted by moral conventions, full of spirit, humor, interesting variations in rhythm, and fun. In my own writing, I would periodically break out of the meditative or rhetorical, tightly controlled verse and prose, and indulge myself in the folk-style song. It seems that I need both styles and they are complementary to each other in my work. Over the years, I keep on reading and purchasing collections of folk songs to nourish my poetry.

Two years ago, I happened to find *Old Peking Rhymes,* edited by Zhao Xiaoyang, published by the Beijing Library Press in 2004. The rhymes in the collection are selected from three earlier published collections: *Pekinese Rhymes*, by Baron Guido Vitale, 1896; *Chinese Mother Goose Rhymes*, by Isaac Taylor Headland, 1900; *Peiping Rhymes*, by Kinchen Johnson, 1932. The three original editors worked and lived in Beijing for extended periods of time during the late nineteenth and early twentieth centuries. They collected the rhymes from Beijing residents they encountered, nannies to their children, handymen working in their homes, kids in the neighborhood, etc. They all chose to publish their collected rhymes in Chinese and English translation, with notations, and, in some cases, photographs to accompany the work. There were over three hundred verses presented in Mr. Zhao's book. I was so charmed by the authenticity of the work and the richness of the selection that I went on to locate the original books. As I excitedly flipped through the pages, it dawned on me that as a native Pekinese, born and having grown up in Beijing from the 1960s till the late 1980s, I hardly knew any of these rhymes. Out of the three hundred rhymes, I could only recognize a few lines from childhood memory and not a single rhyme in its entirety. Apparently, most of these rhymes from thirty to sixty years earlier had vanished or been significantly altered by the time I came on the scene.

Urged on by the sudden realization that oral poetry could change so quickly, and that one or two generations would bring out a complete new set of authors and their creations, I started a little project of my own collecting oral rhymes from my childhood (i.e., Beijing rhymes from the 1960s). From school friends, courtyard neighbors, poets of my generation, and family members back home, I came up with one hundred or so rhymes. I compared what I had collected with Mr. Zhao's selection, as well as with another rich collection in a scholarly book on Chinese folklore (which contains rhymes of the Beijing region from the 1920s to the 1940s) by Zhu Jiefan, published by the Taipei Pure Literary Press in 1974. Rhymes in my collection tend to be much shorter, simpler, and with many nonsensical wordplays and vulgar vocabulary. Their contents are things that interest children most—food, animals, other kids to taunt, games to play, body parts, and bodily functions to laugh at. It seems somehow my little collection only consists of the children's own compositions, while Mr. Zhao and Mr. Zhu's collections indicate other authorship. Their collections contain much wider subject matter, with much better developed narrative skills and the apparent capacity to carry a theme to a fuller completion. The obvious gaps in contents are subjects of women's life, such as marriage, family relationships (especially parents and children, evil stepmothers, lazy and unruly daughters-in-law, hateful mothers-in-law, unfaithful husbands), weaving, cooking, dressing, jewelry, hairstyles, love, and courtship. Other gaps include moral teachings on fairness, on social orders, and on compassion for the misfortunate, and wisdom sharing of frugality, household economy, and cleanliness.

I now believe, through this comparison, that some of these vanishing rhymes were authored by the female voices I have been looking for. One of the major social changes in Chinese society in the recent past is women's education and their joining the workforce. Although in my grandmother's generation only a few women out of thousands knew how to read and write and almost all stayed home, most women of my mother's generation could read and write and worked outside the home. Therefore, their creative energy was channeled into other venues than composing nursery rhymes; therefore my generation of the 1960s never got to hear our mothers' rhymes when we grew up. The broader social consequences of the phenomenon perhaps deserve more studies than my little excursion. Nevertheless, I would conclude for the sake of the discussion here that the female voice or women's tradition in Chinese poetry remains in large part as folk songs and oral verses, from *Feng* till the early twentieth century. The anonymous authorship and collective or communal creation process remain part of the tradition. This oral tradition transformed into written form largely as modern poetry, with individual authors, keeping in time with the birth of contemporary Chinese poetry in the early twentieth century. As poets, when needing inspiration or guidance from the female voices of the past, we should train our ears beyond classical poetry, into folk songs (including *Feng* and Han *Yue Fu* proper), oral rhymes, and folklore. They offer an alternative tradition to classical poetry. Their lyrics have been enriched by a genuine female voice.

# Hsia Yü (Xia Yu)

*(b. 1956)*

Hsia Yü was born in Taiwan and studied drama and film at the National Taiwan Academy of the Arts, where she received a B.A. She subsequently moved to New York City and, later, lived for nearly ten years in France. She is a poet and occasional lyricist and translator from the French. She makes her living primarily from her poetry, which she designs and publishes herself. Her five volumes of poetry include *Memoranda* (1983), *Ventriloquy* (1991), *Rub: Ineffable* (1995), *Salsa* (1999), and *Pink Noise* (2006). Her poetry in English translation, *Fusion Kitsch: Poems from the Chinese of Hsia Yü*, was published by Zephyr Press (2001). Hsia Yü is a founding editor and driving force behind the Taipei-based avant-garde journal *Xianzai Shi,* or *Poetry Now*. She lives in Taipei.

Hsia Yü received widespread attention for her early poems that explored relationships between men and women, but she has also explored and enriched the possibilities of language. Her poetry often twists words out of established contexts, and she plays with multiple meanings and stretches language. In the following excerpt from an interview of the poet by her English translator Steve Bradbury, Hsia Yü discusses her latest book, *Pink Noise*. In it, she cobbled together phrases in English from a variety of sources to create poems and generated Chinese translations by running them through a computer translation program. After the interview excerpt, one poem, along with a back-translation of the Chinese version of the same poem, is included.

## Excerpt from "Hsia Yü: Interview by Steve Bradbury"

I brought something I want to show you, but first you've got to close your eyes and hold out your hand. Now squeeze. Doesn't the spine feel just like the rope of flesh on a man's hip? It's so sensual!

*What is it?*

It's a mock-up of my new volume, *Pink Noise*.

*A transparent book!*

I originally had a hard acrylic cover with a spiral binding, but a friend of mine just hated it, so I told him to find me something better, and he came up with this soft vinyl cover. He used clear silicone glue to bind the pages together. I soaked it in my tub for a couple days, then left it out in the rain, and even held it under a running tap for a while, and as you can see it's still in one piece. It sounds so nice to flip the pages I'm beginning to think the book is taking on a life of its own.

*I love the fact that you can see traces of all the poems at the same time, but how will anyone be able to read the individual poems unless they insert something opaque between the pages?*

That's part of the charm, don't you think? That everyone will have to read the poems against some other surface, some other texture. It could be anything—a piece of paper, a tabletop, a pant leg, skin.

*Where did you get the idea for this?*

I'd been listening to a lot of great acoustic art CDs—the ones where they mix the tracks from low-frequency noises—and I got to wondering if the same concept could be applied to words. Words and phrases can never become transparent, they're always freighted with referential meaning. I've found this so frustrating at times that I've long had the idea of making a completely transparent book, one in which all the referential meanings would be so intricately interwoven that they'd cancel each other out like white noise. That's what I was originally going to call the book—white noise—like in a restaurant where there are so many conversations going on at once that you can't understand a word anyone is saying who is not at your table. Anyway, it was just when I was getting into all these CDs that I stumbled on the translation program I used to make the Chinese versions in the book. I ran a bunch of stuff through the program to test it—Shakespeare, Allan Poe, Pushkin—and it translated the whole lot into the most unimaginable Chinese, so queer and uncanny that it left me speechless. I thought, "Isn't this the noise I've been looking for?" I was so hooked on this program it was like being on drugs. When I came out of it, I had the thirty-three poems in *Pink Noise*. So then I put together this mock-up to make my ideas clear to the printer I work with.

*Pink Noise—did you coin that phrase yourself?*

No, it's a real term, from acoustics. It's basically a kind of white noise but more pleasant to listen to. It's the stuff they play in the white noise machines you can get to mask traffic sounds and tinnitus symptoms. There are other color bands—brown, green, and so on—but I have a thing for pink.

*How did you compose the English poems?*

I cobbled phrases from English-language blogs, Internet archives, and personal websites. Well, most of them were in English. I have a few French poems in the book. The first poem I wrote with the program was from lines I liked in *Jacket Magazine*. But then I got to worrying about copyright infringement and switched to blogs and other websites where I didn't think the authors would be concerned about my filching a phrase or two.

*Where did you find "Jenny! If we can but weld our souls together?"*

That's from a love poem Marx wrote to his wife, before they got married. I found it in an Internet archive of his letters. A lot of the websites I raided were really bizarre ones that popped up when I clicked the hyperlinks in some of the spam I was getting. Most of the blogs were fairly boring ones for things like shopping, cooking, pornography. . . .

*I was wondering what your source was for "They're back they're sad they're talking about making a porno movie."*

Isn't that great? Actually, I culled that title from three different sources.

It's a good example of how I worked, of my patience in going about this. I wasn't interested in the topic at all, only in the phrasing, most of which is really quite ordinary. But what's funny about the Chinese version of that poem is that while the English version reads like erotica, the one produced by my cybernetic poet-translator completely deconstructs all the pornographic elements in such a clever and captivating way that I almost feel as if it were deliberate. It was intensely arousing to be at the scene of this linguistic assassination.

*I can imagine. Did you write the poems one at a time?*

No, I did several at once. That way I could see in which poem each line fit best until I had a page or two of text to run through Sherlock to see what it looked like in Chinese.

*Sherlock?*

That's the name of the software I used to generate the Chinese translations. It came with my Apple computer. It's actually a file- and web-searching program—hence the name. But it has an incredibly fast translation function. It can translate anything in two or three seconds—ten at most. And it's incredibly faithful, or perhaps I should say obedient. Sherlock takes such a straightforward approach to translating the words that it ignores the logical sense behind them, to the extent that virtually every line of the Chinese version is estranged from its source—and that's what I was really after. For me, the poetry is in the differences between the two versions, in their *différance*. You know, no one has ever written Chinese like this before. Reading these translations makes me feel like a foreigner in my own language. I love that feeling.

*Do you know if you're the first person to use this program in this way?*

I'm sure I'm not. Someone told me this software has been around for a long, long time. But I felt like I was the first when I stumbled on Sherlock. I couldn't believe my luck. I felt like I'd been chosen or something. It's important that *someone* do this now because this technology is only going to get better with each version. One day the translations are going to be so fluent, these cybernetic Sherlocks will turn into mediocre poets. In a sense, this whole experiment returns us to the old debate about whether translators should take a literal or liberal approach. Nabokov insisted on a literal approach in the conviction that any translated text should read like one—that translators should make an effort to preserve the literal meanings of the words and not polish the text to make it sound like it was originally written in the target language. The deconstructionists carried this logic even further by arguing that any good translation should result in the alienation of the source text rather than its naturalization. Sherlock's deconstruction is more radical still, albeit entirely unconscious, for he feels accountable only for providing a word-for-word equivalence without regard for any underlying meaning or significance. That's why he produces so many wonderful discrepancies. All that, and just that, is poetry to me.

*Translated by Steve Bradbury*

## Excerpt from *Pink Noise*

### BROKENHEARTED TIME AND ORDINARY DAILY MOMENT

How fucking creepy is that?
So different and sweet
A promise awaits us
At the limits of the mystical love
In the bright, shining, god-like glow
If we must die
We will need those rhyming skills
Some people are born with
Others develop them

Outside, sleet is falling
And there's a dull pain of festive hangover everywhere
If we must die
We can be comfortably ensconced at the center of an admiring crowd
We're too apathetic to stop
To hold back the feeling
That real life is happening somewhere else

[*English poem by Hsia Yü*]

### BROKENHEARTED TIME AND ORDINARY DAILY MOMENT

How is the sexual intercourse wriggles that
Very different and the sweet
Pledge waits for us
In to be bright in the mystical love
Quota, shines, resembles the god to glow
If we will have to die
We to need these rhymes the skill
Certain people will be the birth develop
Them with their other people

Outside, the sleet falls
And has the happy hangover dull-witted pain everywhere
If we must die
We possibly comfortably to place we too are aloof in the admiring
crowd's core
By some method down to cannot expire
Postpone the feeling
True life to occur other places

[*back-translation from the Chinese by the*
*Macintosh web-and-search application Sherlock*]

# Haizi

*(1964–1989)*

Haizi was born and raised in Gaohe of Anhui province. At fifteen, he entered Beijing University to study law and, upon graduation, became a professor at the Chinese Politics and Law University. In the 1980s he emerged as an influential figure in Chinese poetry. With his keen interest in Western literature, combined with an intense Romantic sensibility, he created a remarkable body of work in his short lifetime. Haizi once said, "My ideal poetry is a mighty volume in China's achievements. I don't want to become a lyric poet, or a dramatic poet, or even an epic poet, I just want to fuse the achievements of China's actions into a sort of wedlock between the populace and humanity, a large poem where poetry combines with truth."

On his twenty-fifth birthday, Haizi committed suicide by lying down on railroad tracks near Jiayu gate at the western end of the Great Wall. He had traveled alone along the entire wall with nothing more than four books: the Bible, *Walden*, *Kon Tiki*, and a collection of Joseph Conrad's shorter works. Haizi's dramatic, premeditated suicide was a major jolt, but as time passes it is apparent that, like many gifted, troubled poets, the influence of the poetry will outlast the influence of the biography. His books, all posthumously published, include *Earth* (1990), *The Works of Lao Yihe and Haizi* (1991), *The Poems of Haizi* (1995), and *The Complete Works of Haizi* (1997).

In the following excerpts, written in 1988 and published posthumously, Haizi extols Hölderlin, but he is of course articulating his own aspirations and ideals for lyric poetry.

## Excerpt from "The Poet I Most Love—Hölderlin"

There are two types of lyric poets: the first kind of poet loves life, but what he loves is his own self in life; he believes that life is only the endocrine or the synaptic sensations of his self. But the second type of poet loves the vista, loves the landscape, loves the winter horizon at dawn or dusk, what he loves is the spirit in the landscape, the breath of existence in the scenery. Van Gogh and Hölderlin are precisely the latter type of poets. They shed tears to welcome the horizon at dawn. Bald-headed, they draw the stones and sky, letting the sun become baptized. They are poets that make an ancestral temple of the universe, they evolve from "love myself" into "love the landscape," making the landscape a part of "the secret of the cosmos" in order to love, thus extending beyond the limited force of the first kind of lyric poet.

Yet the landscape is not enough. [. . .] You love the taverns of the two banks, the carriage store, the empty flight of birds on the river, the ferry crossing, the wheat fields, the country-trees waiting, but all this is landscape. All this is not enough. You must learn from experience that the river is an element, like fire. [. . .] You should not merely love the two riverbanks, you should still love the river's own body while it's passing time, love death and the life of the river water. [. . .] To bear with his secrets. To bear with your suffering. Make a temple to the universe for love. Bear with your suffering until it gives rise to joy. This is precisely Hölderlin's poetry. What's the meaning of his corpus of poems? You must love life and not love one's own self; you must love the vista but not love simply one's own eyes. What's the meaning of his corpus of poetry? To become a poet that loves "the secrets of mankind." These secrets encompass the secrets between man and beast; and encompass the secrets between heaven and earth, men and gods. In response, you must love the secrets of time. To become a poet you must love the secrets of mankind, in holy night roaming from one place to the next, love the happiness and suffering of mankind, endure what must be endured, sing what must be sung.

*Translated by Gerald Maa*

# Zang Di

*(b. 1964)*

Zang Di was born in Beijing in 1964. He received his Ph.D. in literature from Beijing University and is currently an associate professor there. He worked briefly as a journalist for the Chinese News Agency and started writing poetry in 1983. He is the author of four books of poetry, including *Remembrance of Swallow Garden* (Art and Culture Publishing House, Beijing, 1998), *Wind Blows and Grass Waves* (Chinese Workers' Publisher, 2000), *Fresh Thorns* (New World, 2002), and *The Universe Is Flat as a Pancake: New and Selected Poems* (Writers' Publishing House, Beijing, 2008). He has edited many anthologies of poetry and poetics as well as unofficial poetry journals, including *The Best Chinese Poetry for 1998* (Spring Wind Press, Liaoning) and *Annual Anthology of Chinese Poetry* (Beijing University Press, 2005), and has served as editor for *Contemporary Poetry Review* (People's Literature Press) and the semi-annual *New Poetry Review* (Beijing University Press). He has also translated Gerard Manley Hopkins, R. M. Rilke, and Robert Hass into Chinese. In 1999 he was a visiting scholar at the University of California at Davis, and in 2006 he was a visiting scholar at Tokyo University.

Zang Di's influential essay, "Toward a Writerly Poetry," first published in 1993, was a review of the 1050-page two-volume *Collected Post-Misty Poetry: A Chronicle of Chinese Modern Poetry*, edited by Wan Xia and Xiao

Xiao. At that time, people mostly talked about Misty poetry, but few people discussed the writing that came later. In this excerpt, Zang Di deals with the intentions of post-Misty poets (including such poets as Haizi, Yu Jian, Zhai Yongming, and Xi Chuan) and their place in the history of modern poetry. He believes it is a major responsibility for poets to rediscover or redescribe the relationship between a human being and the world around him. His poem, "A Charm about Things," exemplifies this kind of poetry.

## Excerpt from "Toward a Writerly Poetry"

The outstanding writing of the post-Misty poets indeed represents a major paradigm shift in modern Chinese poetry. It also involves the complicated and difficult-to-delineate relationship between modern Chinese poetry and poetic tradition. In terms of the critical history of modern Chinese poetry, the concept of poetic tradition has long been in a state of confusion that is hard to distill from the praxis of writing. Using post-Misty poetry as an example, we note, on a superficial level, that post-Misty poetry is not lacking in traditional sources. It can select from, recombine, and/or integrate at will from existing classical Chinese poetry, modern Chinese poetry, Misty poetry, and Western poetry. But in the actual process of writing one discovers that classical Chinese poetry, modern Chinese poetry, and Misty poetry do not constitute an anxiety of influence among post-Misty poets when it comes to the spirit of writing, or the power and insightfulness of poetry. However, Western poetry does exert such an influence, but the form of this influence is an increasingly dubious intertextual challenge. In other words, the great nurturing impact of Western poetry on the post-Misty poets has gradually dissipated and is now challenged by each individual poet's power of poetic perception and taste. This does not imply a severing of influence or a fear of influence, but rather suggests that the influence is already widely felt among the post-Misty poets as one of their personal traditions. As Harold Bloom points out in his *Anxiety of Influence*, they discover through their creative logic that they can suppress that influence, making it a weakness that allows them to emphasize their own powers of poetic perception and uniqueness. "He who is willing to labor shall bear his father" is how Kierkegaard put it in his *Fear and Trembling*. But I prefer to cite Bloom's words with regard to this statement and say that post-Misty poets are already at the stage of "having borne their fathers."

In general, the writing of post-Misty poetry has been done entirely within a vacuum of poetic tradition. This has led to the appearance of an attitude that is a mixture of thorough knowledge and superficial acquaintance. On the subject of writing, post-Misty poets are conscious that, in all likelihood, they will never reach consensus on the issues of tradition and criticism. For this reason, they have adopted a nihilistic attitude in public, but in their writing they are in fact able to clearly delineate the tradition they face. This disparity has produced the basic post-Misty strategy, which temporarily lays aside all questions of "What should a poem be?" or "What tradition should modern Chinese poetry follow?" and all others, and gets down to the business of writing itself before anything else. This allows the poets to do their utmost to fulfill the possibilities that history has provided, that the essence of modern Chinese poetry is part and parcel of writing itself and nothing else. For the post-Misty poet, existence is to write, whereas for the traditional poet existence was to write poetry. This means, then, that writing itself is the poet's goal, and that writing is no longer the handmaiden of poetry. To use Thoreau's words as quoted by W. H. Auden: "The writer has only one goal: to speak." As to what it is he says, influencing or making demands on writing is outside our control.

The critical world's focus on "tradition" needs to be temporarily put aside. Roland Barthes, in his *Writing Degree Zero,* holds that modern poetry is language breaking its social bounds, like a cicada sloughing off its skin, and the powers of poetic perception consciously deviate from the unity of language. For this reason, modern poetry is of "a quality *sui generis* and without antecedents." Barthes seems to suggest that there is a fatalistic relationship between modern poetry and tradition, because through special perceptive powers, writing modern poetry constantly and consciously deepens the rift between itself and literary tradition and finds itself trapped in a state of "tradition without antecedents." This characteristic of the "tradition without antecedents" appeared in the writings of

Baudelaire and is still present in the writings of post-Misty poets today, more than a hundred years later. However, a number of questions must be dealt with before coming to terms with the special character of this tradition of writing modern poetry. Before examining these, three points need to be clarified: first, "tradition without antecedents" does not mean that modern poetry has no relationship with a previous literary tradition. In many instances, it bears a closer relationship to tradition than poetry that is normally viewed as descending directly from tradition. Second, it strictly means that its powers of poetic perception are independent of literary tradition. Third, it does not imply that modern poetry defies criticism because it still possesses the requisite and undiminished craftsmanship. The criteria for evaluating poetic expression—accuracy, simplicity, clarity, power, symmetry, and completeness—are equally applicable to modern poetry, including, of course, post-Misty poetry.

The act of writing a post-Misty poem, as one form of modern poetry, takes place in the critical state of the "tradition without antecedents." This, however, does not mean that the links between modern poetry and the world poetic tradition have been severed, nor does it mean writing in opposition to the world poetic tradition. With regard to the post-Misty banner of "down with tradition" at the movement's beginning, it should be understood in the following sense: first, it was intended to eliminate the pressures of traditional criticism in order to return writing to a pure, elemental state free from any anxiety or restrictions on creativity; second, it was a direct way to self-consciously awaken poetic creativity to better grasp the essence of modern poetry's "tradition without antecedents." In essence, the nebulous relationship between modern poetry and traditional poetry has been forgotten in writing. Among post-Misty poems, of course many banners against tradition are empty signs. The greater the distance between writing and tradition the better, because distance endows writing and tradition with new creative vitality. Distance provides familiarity with tradition. In general, I feel that post-Misty poetry is not only related to modern poetry since Baudelaire, but that it is also in the lineage of modern Chinese poetry from the early days through Misty poetry. Chinese and Western classical poetry are sufficiently distant. With regard to the relationship between post-Misty poetry and tradition, however, I believe such critical terms and concepts as "conservative" and "radical" are rather crude. The problem with such terms is not their inaccuracy, but rather they are not sufficiently analytical. For example, when a poet is engaged in the interior process of writing, it is impossible not to be "radical"; and when the poem is completed and circulates among readers, it is impossible for the poet not to appear "conservative." In an age where so much quibbling is about language, if the word "radical" can imply a certain intention, then so can the word "conservative." The basic issue is that the standard for evaluating good or bad poetry can never be confused by the myth of intention. In Roland Barthes's words, as cited by Todorov: outstanding poetry is "that which possesses superior expression without entering the personal. . . . It is secret while being open." Based on this criterion, two important post-Misty poets are exemplary: Bai Hua and Zhai Yongming. They display a genius in handling the relationship between the special characteristic of the tradition without antecedents of writing modern poetry and traditional poetry. Their writing is not simply a product of a consciousness of style but manifests an even greater comprehension of the essence of modern poetry.

*Translated by John Balcom*

## A Charm about Things

On a windowsill, three pine cones.
The size of each
is almost the same.
But they vary from dark to light.

Each cone is larger than my closed fist,
in fact, not less than twice as big.
But I do not feel embarrassed. Already I see
my fist is a pagoda shaped like a cone.

The darkest is the one
which fell from the tree this year –
I hesitate in deciding when the two lighter ones fell,
but I know the color of these two is not lighter than ash-gray time.

And I know that squirrels
have been inspired by such lightness
to make their own small fur coats.
The secret recipe of lightness remains unrevealed.

Each pine cone possesses its own source,
yet a small part of each origin
holds its mystery. Same thing with poetry.
Yet poetry won't be suffocated by this problem.

I am writing poetry, secretly in love
with the clear structure of the cones.
It asks me to take it to where I picked them up.
It asks to be placed on top of the Red Pine.

*Translated by Murray Edmond*

# Yu Jian

*(b. 1954)*

Yu Jian was born in Kunming and contracted pneumonia when he was two years old. He was given an overdose of streptomycin, and although it saved his life, he became partially deaf. In 1969 he became an apprentice in a factory north of Kunming and worked as a riveter and welder. He was a voracious reader and says that reading Whitman's poetry was a decisive influence. In 1974 he began writing poems in free verse, and when university education was again possible, he studied Chinese language and literature and graduated from Yunnan University. As a student, he helped to establish literary clubs and also edited several publications. His first collection, *Sixty Poems*, was published in 1989 by Yunnan People's Publishing. In 1994 he published a long poem, "File Zero." In China, the personal file or dossier serves as an official life history and exemplifies a means of surveillance. In writing his poem in the form of a file, Yu Jian drew attention to a file's inability to document the true life of an individual. He has now published ten collections of poems, essays, translations, and travel writing.

In Yu Jian's evolution as a poet, he has consciously rejected literary allusions, rich images, and startling metaphors. In the two selections here, the excerpts from "The Brown Notebook" are from an essay published in 1995 in which Yu Jian champions poetry's naming power and rejects metaphor. In

2008, however, in the excerpt included here from an interview with Simon Patton, Yu qualifies his earlier assertions and discusses his current views on poetry.

## Excerpts from "The Brown Notebook"

To name is to create. The first person who named things is the first poet. After that came the era of imagination, understanding, reading, and correcting names. . . .

We have forgotten language. Metaphor becomes a means of transportation, disguising itself as poetry.

Language games become life games. Metaphor equals mask.

Chinese culture is a "metaphor culture."

Poetry today rejects metaphor.

Rejecting metaphors means rejecting the tyranny of the mother tongue.

This restores poetry's naming power.

Real poetry rejects readers. It rejects the reading habit, not reading itself.

Poetry is not a noun but a verb.

Poetry is its own reason for being. Poetry begins from language and ends in language.

Poetry is a language game that kills metaphors. The more metaphors it cleans, the more revealing a poem becomes.

There can be no fish when the water is too clear. The fish are long gone. Let the water be clear. Let the readers see that there are no fish, and let them see the water itself as liquid, temperature, and size. "How difficult it is to see things before one's eyes!" said Wittgenstein. Poets are the ones who say there are no fish in the water.

Rejection and depth: reject "instinct," "inspiration," "passion." Reject "self." Reject "we."

Poetry doesn't express emotions. It is a process of the mind.

Don't wait for inspiration. Control language.

Poetry provides a language fact: eliminate imagination, eliminate Romanticism, eliminate metaphor.

Genuine writing is the most subjective and the most rational.

The process of writing poetry is the process of cleaning out garbage.

A poet is not a genius or a romantic prince or a martyr. A poet is a worker in a factory, a language operator.

To write real poetry is to refuse every metaphor.

A successful poem means it has successfully cleaned all metaphors, therefore liberated its readers.

Poetry is not a way of observing life. It is a way of living life.

Poetry mocks those who look for "depth" and "essence."

Poetry is naming. It's as simple as that.

Return to where the language came from. Return to the time before metaphor.

How? I can't answer. It's poetry.

*Translated by Wang Ping*

## Excerpts from "They Tattoo Their Bodies for the World": Yu Jian Interview by Simon Patton

*November 2007–February 2008*

*You grew up during the Cultural Revolution, a time that seems completely bereft of poetry. What got you interested in writing poetry?*

That's hard to answer. When I was a kid, Mao Zedong was the only poet around: he made me go looking for those poets hidden away in the dark.

Poetry is not merely the art of combining bits of language. Writing poetry is definitely connected with individual talent. Actually, Chinese is a shamanistic language [*wuyu*]. In primitive times, it was a set of pictographic signs used by the tribe to dialogue with spirits. So, in a sense, poets who write in Chinese are, to some degree, shamans of language. Language's mysterious power exists within language itself; writing only intensifies this power. In the *Dao De Jing*, Laozi says, "Know the white / But keep to the role of the black": white is what is [*you*], black is what is not [*wu*], and the poet is a shaman who uses the *you* of language to summon *wu*. The frenzied insanity of this world comes from its obsession with the white [. . .], but black alone is the root of the world. Poetry lies along that mysterious line that runs between the black and the white of the *Taiji* symbol. [. . .]

[. . .] *Your early poetry is not mysterious or imbued with the marvelous, but employs a tone that seems extremely plain and accessible.*

I try to avoid as far as possible mysteriousness or any aura of religiosity. This is perhaps where I differ most from *menglong* [Misty] poetry: I take great pains to avoid obscurity or indeterminacy [. . .]—this is not an issue in my writing; on the contrary, I strive to write clearly, steering clear of metaphors and figurative language in favor of the straightforward signifier. This is because I understand the power of language: as long as you write, you are creating symbols and metaphors—this is the fate of writing. Language possesses a force we cannot fully grasp; it is far more chaotic than we realize. One characteristic of Chinese is what Laozi refers to in the lines "Indistinct and shadowy, / Yet within it is an image." Perhaps the reason why Western poets consciously pursue mystery and indeterminacy is because of the overwhelming logicality and determinacy of alphabetic languages. As someone writing in Chinese, I am deeply aware of the importance of writing comprehensibly and clearly. In my view, it is very easy to be obscure [. . .]: Chinese is by its very nature obscure. It is rather more difficult to write clearly. In writing, brought face to face with the history of language, I believe that it is extremely important to return to non-being [*wu*] and the ahistorical, especially in Chinese, a language that is saturated with history and in which the signified has enjoyed a total dominance over the signifier. In the 1980s, I put forward the notion of "the refusal of metaphor," and I stressed that this was a manner of writing, because I knew that, fundamentally, it was impossible to refuse metaphor and obscurity. As long as you write, you are creating metaphors. To refuse metaphor was to write in a particular way, knowing that it could not be done. [. . .]

*What struck you most about* menglong *poetry?*

In my view, there was nothing unfamiliar about the rhetorical manner of *menglong* poetry despite the fact that it was written in the vernacular. This is because I had been reading classical Chinese poetry for many years.

As it happened, the rhetorical manner of classical Chinese poetry had at one time influenced Western modernist poetry. Ezra Pound is the best example of this. While *menglong* poetry's rhetorical manner was influenced by Western modernist poetry, its emotions were those of Romanticism and a certain epic heroicism—in its heart of hearts, it lacked modernism. In my opinion, the modernity of contemporary Chinese poetry does not lie in the persistent Romanticism that runs through twentieth-century literature; instead, it lies in the sober critical realism of those writers in the Lu Xun mold who "squarely confront the problems of life." This mode of critical realism could be called a form of existentialism.

*Had you read Sartre at the time?*

When I was at university, I was influenced by Sartre's thought, and I also noticed things in Daoist thought similar to existentialism. I've always been a fanatical reader of Laozi. One important phenomenon of twentieth-century Chinese knowledge was that some aspects of it were only taken seriously in China after they were picked up by the West. Western knowledge is like a mirror: reading Sartre, Popper, together with Heidegger, who was later translated to China with Berlin, Pascal, and Jaspers, gave me a more profound understanding of Daoism. [. . .]

*The critic Fred Inglis once wrote: "Writing poetry begins with the planning of one's life; it is a long discipline." In the process of becoming a poet, what sort of measures did you adopt to help you reach your objective?*

The writing of poetry is the work of a lifetime—I realized this at a very young age. When I first started writing, I had no way of publishing my work because there were no literary magazines in existence during the Cultural Revolution, and you were not allowed to write the kind of poetry I wrote. Poetry was considered to be a tool for state propaganda. All I could do was to write in secret; writing for me was a very private affair, and so for this reason it never occurred to me to earn a living as a writer. At the factory, I worked as a carpenter, a riveter, an electric welder, as well as a drilling machine operator, and I was very conscientious in my work. After ten years, I became a highly skilled worker, and I would have had no problems earning a living in that capacity. When the Cultural Revolution came to an end, the state suddenly reopened universities and it became possible for me to go and study there. In the ten years I had been at the factory, I had already completed a study of Chinese and world literature in the course of my underground reading, and I had no difficulty in passing the university entrance examinations. Later on, literary magazines were allowed to exist in China again and it was possible for me to publish some of my poems, but I was intent on earning my living from something besides writing. Indeed, I didn't believe that I could rely on earning a living by my writing, especially in China after 1949—writing became a very dangerous thing to do, and at any time could turn a writer's life completely upside down. [. . .]

*What kind of challenges are you facing in your writing now?*

From the latter part of the twentieth century, it has been extremely important for Chinese writing to uphold common sense. In the period we are currently living through, there has been a wholesale opposition to common sense, and many fundamental points of common sense have been disregarded by society. The classical Chinese philosophy expressed in the phrase "the way [models itself] on that which naturally is" has been seriously challenged throughout the course of the past hundred years.

This is perhaps the most frenzied time in the 5,000-year history of China; of course, it is, at the same time, the most dynamic. Those looking on from outside China would find it hard to imagine that the changes that used to take place over twenty years now take place in a single day, but this is a reality in China now. From the Anti-Rightist Campaign of the 1950s, the Great Leap Forward to the Cultural Revolution, to the market economy, up to the present when money is revaluing everything, China has been undergoing intense, surreal changes, and many fundamental values and many fundamental things have been obliterated.

It is extremely important for writing to uphold—with naturalness and plainness—a connection with contemporary life, to insist on a basic common sense, and to show respect for universals. I am constantly traveling, and this enables me to maintain a basic connection with nature.

*Translated by Simon Patton*

# Yan Li

*(b. 1954)*

Yan Li was born in Beijing and is a poet, editor, fiction writer, and painter. As a poet, he is identified with the Misty poets. In 1985 he moved from Beijing to New York City and, in 1987, founded *Frontline*, a quarterly journal that featured the works of contemporary Chinese poetry as well as American poetry in Chinese translation. He is the author of six books of poetry, including *Those Poems May Not Be Too Bad* (Shulin Publisher, Taipei, 1987), *Twilight Maker* (Nanjing University Press, 1989), and *Give Back to Me* (Yuanxiang Press, Sydney, 2001). He is also the author of two novels: *Bring Mother Back to Home* (*All People Magazine*, 1995, later published by Nanjing University Press) and *Meet 911* (Shanghai Art and Literature Press, 2002). He is a member of a group of artists known as the Stars and has held many exhibitions of his paintings. In 1998 he started to live seven to eight months in Shanghai and about three months of each year in New York City.

Yan Li writes, "All art and literature come out of thinking. I'm a thinker. You have to think about what kind of form to employ: some people use music, some people prefer drama or movies, but I like poetry, art, and essays. For a long time, I've believed that art and poetry are invaluable in terms of presenting one's thinking. Because I experienced two different systems, the United States and China, I feel some things are different, while other things are the same. For instance, for people who don't have power, and that's true for 70 to 80 percent of the people, they just follow the system. But poetry lets those people speak out." Yan Li's poem "Thanks for That" was written in 2001 but was not published until it was included in the *Pamirs Poetry Journey: The First Chinese-English Poetry Festival at Huangshan Mountain, China, 2007.*

## Thanks for That

The state has occupied all geographical surfaces
I can only construct my inner world downward
The government has occupied the biggest banquet table
The plate in my hands has to serve as my table
Social institutions occupy all the skeletal joints
So I pound out a romantic mood with percussion of flesh
Schools have occupied the vantage point of education
All my theories can do is fight guerilla actions
My wife has occupied the facial expression of family life
All I can do is polish the mirror a little brighter
My children have occupied the future
All I can do is help them tie their shoes
For this kind of arrangement
All I can say is thank you

*Translated by Denis Mair*

# Wang Anyi

*(b. 1954)*

Wang Anyi was born in Nanjing and grew up in Shanghai. Her parents were both well-known writers, and her father was targeted as a rightist. During the Cultural Revolution, she was sent to a rural area in Anhui to live and work with peasants. In 1972 she joined the Xuzhou Art Workers' Troupe, played the cello, and began writing short stories and essays. In 1978 she returned to Shanghai, worked for the magazine *Childhood Years*, and published her first short story, "On the Plains." In 1980 she became a member of the Writers' Association and, in the following year, published "Rustling Rain," a short story that featured a young woman in search of love. In 1983 she and her mother attended the International Writing Program at the University of Iowa, and her fiction shifted from her earlier socialist realism toward deeper, psychological exploration. From 1986 to 1987, she published her "Love Trilogy" (*Love on a Barren Mountain, Love in a Small Town,* and *Brocade Valley*), in which she explored female sexuality and marriage. Her fiction continued to evolve in the 1990s as she extended the range of her writing to include works that crossed into mythology, memoir, and fantasy. In 1995 she published her landmark novel, *Song of Everlasting Sorrow*, which received the Mao Dun Prize. Set in Shanghai, from 1946 to 1986, this novel follows a third-place beauty pageant winner through her aspirations, love affairs, and tragic death.

Wang Anyi is now the author of over thirty-six books of fiction and essays. Some of her recent works that have not been translated into English include the novels *Modern Life*, *I Love Bill*, *Age of Enlightenment*, as well as a collection of shorter fiction, *Age of Melancholy*. In 1998 she wrote "Why I Write," which describes her journey and evolution as a writer. Although she describes her process of growth—"my next action is always to return to myself to reflect, dissect what I have done, expand upon it, and improve"—she also recognizes the process mysteriously entwines art and life so that "my life is a part of my fiction, and my fiction is a part of my life."

## Why I Write

Why do I write? I sometimes ask myself this question, only to discover that there is no single answer.

It would seem that the drive to pursue literature took root quite late, and at the earliest stages my motivations were actually quite petty.

It wasn't at all the case that I grew up dreaming of one day becoming an author and writing for a living. From an early age my parents taught me to study hard so I could one day become a doctor or scientist. This hope was inspired by all the difficulties they had experienced in their own lives; working in literature and the arts, they had gone through all kinds of hardships because of their chosen profession. But I only learned that much later; at the time I had no idea about any of that—I just felt that a career in the natural sciences was a lofty profession. This was a perspective that would have an impact on me for the next thirty years, all the way up until now. Owing to the fact that I devoted myself to my studies, earning good grades, displaying keen interest in different academic fields, I assumed that further advancing my studies wouldn't be a problem. One day, the campus unveiled a program to "train us to achieve our dreams," and as a part of the program we all had to talk about our dreams in life. When it was my turn to speak I answered without hesitation, "I want to be a peasant." At the time, everyone was emulating the model educated youth known as "Swallow Xing," one of the first volunteers to go down to the rural areas. The countryside may have been filled with hardship, but it is also a mystical place brimming with hope. My response also represented a rather romantic yearning inside me. Another reason I gave that answer probably also had to do with the fact that, deep down, I never really believed that I would actually ever end up in the countryside. The countryside was like a phantom dream that would never materialize—and so I made my dream known without the slightest hesitation.

To my surprise, just as all my other dreams were being shattered, this hazy and fanciful dream of becoming a peasant actually came true. The Cultural Revolution broke out, and, as if in a daze, I somehow graduated from elementary school and made it through middle school before joining a rural production team—I went to Huaibei in Anhui province to become a peasant.

At the time I had only made it as far as basic arithmetic in my mathematics class. When it came to physics, chemistry, foreign languages, biology, and other subjects, I was completely ignorant. My dream of becoming a scientist was hopelessly distant, and there were no bridges or roads to get there. As far as my general learning went, the only area in which I knew something more than a basic elementary school level was literature. In that sense, I was the beneficiary of all the books we had at home and the habit of reading that my parents had fostered. There were books galore at home and they seemed to be the best friend to everyone in our family. Even at a very young age I had already gotten into the habit of reading myself to sleep. For some uncanny reason I felt especially close to books, and from the very beginning they were never difficult for me to understand. As I read more I began to occasionally write myself, usually in my diary. And so, along with reading, keeping a diary became another habit that would stay with me.

During those trying and lonely days in the countryside, reading books and writing in my diary became even more precious to me, becoming a real part of my life. Back when I lived in Shanghai and the countryside was still a distant place, it felt magical. But once I had entered that world, I immediately realized that I could never be a real peasant—for one thing, I would never be able to support myself working the land! I needed to find a way out. The only weapon I had in hand was this talent for writing, which back then was still rather half-baked. I began to write fiction; I knew from day one that publishing my work would be impossible, but still I wrote. I remember that one of the pieces I wrote was a coming-of-age story about an educated youth in the countryside. That piece went completely against my true feelings; as I praised the sent-down experience with laudatory words I felt that writing was nothing more than a boring homework assignment. That proved to be the first time I really thought of becoming a writer. But it was an early blossoming that would come to an early end. In the late 1970s, colleges reopened and began to accept students, but the recruitment process required local recommendations. I had been waiting for someone to recommend me, but it never came. During that long year of waiting, I began to teach myself mathematics. I got as far as higher-degree equations when I realized that my dream of getting into college would never be realized. I began to consider other possibilities.

Later, owing to my ability to play the accordion, which I learned in my spare time as a young girl, I tested into the Xuzhou Song and Dance Cultural Troupe. The first two or three years with the troupe I lived a very quiet and peaceful life, feeling that I'd finally found my home; a place where I could be at ease.

Life with the troupe was extremely relaxed and carefree, leaving my mind free for much of the time. I didn't know how to make use of all my spare time and gradually began to feel dejected. During those carefree days my books and diary became an even more fundamental part of my life. But as new books became more difficult to come by, I discovered that I had less and less to write about in my diary. At the time, I still hadn't realized that everything going on in my environment around me was all worthy subject matter to be writing about. All I paid attention to in my diary was my own life, which left very little room for what was happening around me. Day after day, month after month, everything grew dull and uneventful. I felt increasingly depressed, but my desire to read and write only increased. As this cycle of loneliness and despair played out, the desperate urge to find a way out became ever more pressing.

Years had passed, but I still had no real skills—the sole exception being my literary sense, which had slightly matured by then—and so I decided to write. I wrote a short essay about an educated youth who sacrifices the small for the many. I never expected to make it on my first try, but the piece was selected for inclusion in a collection of essays about educated youths to be published by the Shanghai Arts and Literature publishing house. Publication got held up and this book, which was slated to be in print in 1975, didn't actually get published until 1977. During those two years, China went through monumental changes so that by the time it was published many of the ideas presented in the book were already behind the times. The entire stock of books was pulped; they just gave each contributor a copy as a souvenir. But no matter what, I had already convinced myself that I had a talent for writing and began to work harder. Although I didn't really achieve anything through my writing, I felt fulfilled—I finally had an outlet for all my excess energy and emotion.

But when it comes down to it, my earliest motivation to write boils down to my search for a way out; whether it was to improve my basic material situation or a higher spiritual desire, it was a way out. I had found it and began to write nonstop. I replaced my diary with fiction, which became where I could record the happiness and sadness inside me. It was only then that I began to feel true pleasure in writing. Finally, writing was no longer another boring homework assignment. I eventually fell in love with writing. I poured all of my true feelings into my work, writing became habitual, a part of my life. I was finally delivered from all of those years of aimless wandering.

Once I started expressing my genuine emotions through writing, people would respond by telling me that I had also spoken for *their* joys and sorrows as well. I realized that I was touching people's hearts, and began to feel a responsibility toward others. With that I began to take my fiction more seriously, expanding the content and embracing a wider spectrum of people's lives. It was around that time that I first began to reflect upon myself. I became conscious of my petty and reclusive nature and tried to tear down the wall I had built up around myself and use the limited emotional range I possessed to do my best to engage with the world. I wanted to embrace and reflect the impressions I had of a larger canvas of things, revealing a broader history, society, and spectrum of lives. As I was diligently working toward this, I found my emotions opened up, I was happier and the burden of so much sadness and regret left me. Things also became more transparent to me as I tasted the boundless joys of life. If someone at that time had asked me why I write, I would have responded, "In order to make life better." But that answer is akin to a dog chasing its own tail. But just as history plays out against the ceaseless revolutions of the earth, so too the meaning of life contains endless cycles within its mysteries.

I set out intent on writing about a broad grand vision of life and encountered many examples of good and ill fortune along the way. Facing all this I feel that the range of my own emotions is so very paltry, even making me conscious of how insignificant I really am. As I again reflect upon myself, from finding where my responsibility lies amid my own personal joys and sorrows, and then finding greater responsibility from a larger canvas of joy and sorrow, I write of the good fortunes and tragedies of the world and the responsibilities that man must shoulder. Whenever I feel dissatisfied with something I wrote and feel I want to do better, my next action is always to return to myself to reflect, dissect what I have done, expand upon it, and improve; and then I lose myself again in writing, on and on it goes. As I become increasingly well-known as a writer, recognized by more people, and the subject of praise and criticism, I become helplessly conscious of the fact that I must be responsible for even more lives. I think to myself: I must make my life, my work, my joys and sorrows, happiness and pain, my self even larger, broader, and more embracing.

It is at that point that I am struck with a strange feeling, sensing that my fiction and my life have grown so very close, participating in each other. My life is a part of my fiction, and my fiction is a part of my life. And it is at that point that I find myself unable to answer that question of why I write.

*Translated by Michael Berry*

# Can Xue

*(b. 1953)*

Can Xue was born in Changsha, and her father was lead editor for the *Hunan Daily News.* At the outset of the Cultural Revolution, her parents were denounced as ultra-rightists, and she was raised, under extreme poverty, by her eccentric grandmother. Her formal education stopped after completing primary school, and, from 1966 to 1976, she worked as an iron worker. She taught herself to sew, and in the early 1980s she and her husband set up a tailor shop. As business flourished, she began to write fiction and also taught herself English. Her early controversial works include the novellas *Yellow Mud Street* (1983) and *Old Floating Cloud* (1986). They were included, along with eight short stories, in *Dialogues in Paradise* (1988). Other books in English translation include *The Embroidered Shoes* (1997) and *Blue Light in the Sky and Other Stories* (2006).

Can Xue has cited Kafka, Borges, Cervantes, Virginia Woolf, and Dante as influences on her work. She was the sole female writer to emerge among a group of avant-garde Chinese fiction writers in the mid-1980s. Instead of focusing on sociopolitical issues, she explores the irrational and draws her readers into psychologically haunted and disorienting situations. In 1992 she visited the International Writing Program at the University of Iowa and read her fiction at fifty universities across the United States. She currently lives in

Changsha. In her essay "A Particular Sort of Story," Can Xue says that when she writes, she expels all outside forces and focuses on the human soul.

## A Particular Sort of Story

The particular characteristics of my stories have now been acknowledged. Nevertheless, when someone asks me directly, "What is really going on in your stories? How do you write them?," I'm profoundly afraid of being misunderstood, so all I can say is, "I don't know." From any earthly perspective, in truth I do not know. When I write, I intentionally erase any knowledge from my mind.

I believe in the grandness of the original power. The only thing I can do is to devoutly bring it into play in a manmade, blind atmosphere. Thus, I can break loose from the fetters of platitudes and conventions, and allow the mighty logos to melt into the omnipresent suggestions that inspire and urge me to keep going ahead. I don't know what I will write tomorrow, or even in the next few minutes. Nor do I know what is most related to the "inspiration" that has produced my works in an unending stream for more than two decades. But I know one thing with certainty: no matter what hardships I face, I must preserve the spiritual quality of my life. For if I were to lose it, I would lose my entire foundation.

In this world, subsistence is like a huge rolling wheel crushing everything. If a person wants to preserve the integrity of his innermost being, he has to endlessly break his self apart, endlessly undergo "exercises" that set the opposed parts of one's soul at war with one another. In my exercises, while my self is planted in the world, at the same time my gaze—from beginning to end—is unswervingly fixed on heaven; this is forcing a division between soul and flesh. By enduring the pain from this splitting of the soul, I gain a force of tension—conquering the libido and letting it erupt anew on the rebound. Through this writing, where the self is split apart, one achieves the greatest joy in the midst of an infinitude of keen feelings. As for the world, it constantly exhibits an unprecedented godly purity.

It isn't possible for people to live in pure spirit, because we are situated in a world that is highly filtered and conglutinated. The birthplace of pure spirit is situated in our dark flesh and blood. Perhaps my stories simply return to the old haunt: while pushing forward the dark abyss, they liberate the binding desires and crystallize them into pure spirit. The impetus for this kind of writing lies with the unending desires that make up ordinary life. While the conglutination decomposes wondrously and while the wide-awake imagination receives a clear message from profound restlessness, my pen achieves its own spiritual power. If one is in pursuit of the very purest language, one has to encounter grime, filth, violence, the smell of blood. While writing, you have to endure everything, you have to give up all worldly things. If you still care about being graceful, concerned with your posture and stance, you can't write this kind of story. In this sense, I exist only after my stories exist.

Stories with this kind of unusual language open another life for me. These stories and my ordinary life pervade each other, are interdependent. Because of their intervention, all commonplace vulgarities are imbued with secret significance; human feelings become the greatest enigma of them all. Therefore, daily anguish is no longer something that can't be endured, because the unending source of inspiration lies precisely in this. Perhaps it's from the boundary which is between melting and blending that artists are able to derive truth in a split second, the result being a coagulation into a work of art.

I believe that art is instinctive in human beings. Artists are simply those who are able—via mighty restraints—to exert their instincts to the utmost. My realm is one shared with all artists. When I enter this realm, the first thing I do is to remove the stone foundation from under my feet, and suspend my body in a semi-free state. Not until then is there an acceleration of mystery. And that is only in spurts. Years of repeated practice have gradually made me aware that success benefits from the mighty logos, inside myself, that is like a murderous machine. The more rigorous the sanction of reason, the more ferocious the rebounding of flesh and blood. Only in this way can the stories have a powerful, unconstrained style and fantasy, yet also have a rigorous and profound level of logic.

I certainly did not painstakingly set out to write this kind of story. From the beginning, as I practiced, I heard the faint drumbeats of fate.

Afterward, my life naturally evolved in pursuit of that summons. From my experience, one can see how great the power of art is to transform a person's life. Whether or not a person is a writer, if he maintains the sensitivity of art, his humanity can be greatly increased. So, art very much harmonizes with human nature and humanism. Art is the most universal pursuit of what it means to be human. Its essence is love.

Some people say that my stories aren't useful: they can't change anything, nor do people understand them. As time goes by, I've become increasingly confident about this. First, the production of twenty years' worth of stories has changed me to the core. I've spoken of this above. Next, from my reading experience, this kind of story, which indeed isn't very "useful," that not all people can read—for those few very sensitive readers, there is a decisive impact. Perhaps this wasn't at all the writer's original intent. I think what this kind of story must change is the soul instead of something superficial. There will always be some readers who will respond—those readers who are especially interested in the strengthening force of art and exploring the soul. With its unusual style, this kind of story will communicate with those readers, stimulating them and calling to them, spurring them on to join in the exploration of the soul.

Self-reflection is the magic formula for creation, a particular self-reflection different from passive self-examination. This kind of self-reflection brings all one's strength to bear on entering the profound world of the soul, and makes what one has seen there appear again through a special kind of language. Thus, it opposes the scenes of the spiritual world with the exterior world we're accustomed to, so that we can deepen our understanding. So artistic self-reflection is virtually an active process: it is taking the initiative to go down into hell, to establish oppositions, to strengthen self-contradictions. And in the brutality of fighting closely with oneself, one achieves a unified, highly conscious creation. This dynamic process comes from the longing of the artist to deny his worldly, carnal existence.

To satisfy this innermost desire, I put into effect this sort of drill every day. I bring into play my energy to seek out ancient memories that faded long ago. I feel instinctively that there's no way to stop this kind of exercise. Beginning a long time ago and continuing until today, it is my purpose for living. When I face this world that is filled with material desire and immerse myself fully in the worldly roles, it is precisely what endows my worldly life with meaning. Without it, I would be ashamed to show my face, I would have no foothold. Now, every day, I put into effect artistic activity and restrict my daily life to serve my artistic calling. I feel that I am mightier than ever!

In essence, there's no way for modern art to consider its viewers. Modern art cannot "consider" who its observers are. It can only provide information and summon people, inducing them to stop in their busy lives to think and self-consciously make time for a certain kind of spiritual activity. And so we can say that modern art—approaching human instincts ever more closely—as a spiritual pursuit, can only be an adventurous activity filled with initiative. The relationship between a successful work and its readers is described by the priest in Kafka's *The Trial* when he says to K, "It receives you when you come and it dismisses you when you go."

What I try hard to reach in my stories is this realm of freedom. I believe; when writers create their uncertain imaginary world, they are restless; their eyes are blurred, their hearts startled. But only when it receives affirmation from perceptive readers does this world exist. There must be this kind of reader. I deeply believe that humankind's soul is a shared place: humans are those who can reason, who are good at self-criticism. In the process of deepening their understanding of the self, people, uninterruptedly, have developed a high level of reason, and have begun to construct a spiritual mechanism forever at odds with "jungle culture."

*Translated by Karen Gernant & Chen Zeping*

# Xi Xi

*(b. 1938)*

Xi Xi is one of the most accomplished avant-garde writers in the sinophone world. She was born in Shanghai and immigrated to Hong Kong in 1950. She attended secondary school at Heep Yunn School, where she learned Cantonese and English. In 1957 she continued her studies at the Grantham College of Education and became a teacher at a primary school. During her teaching career, she was an activist for teachers' rights. She is the author of novels, essays, fairy tales, poetry, and television screenplays. In the 1960s she wrote a fairy-tale column in *Tin Tin Daily.* In 1979 she resigned from her teaching position and devoted more time to writing. In that year, she co-founded *Plain Leaf Literature*, a literary journal, and served as editor from 1981 to 1984.

In 1982 the *United Daily News* in Taiwan republished her novella *A Lady Like Me*, and it received the *United Daily*'s first prize for fiction. Her collections of essays include *Puzzles* (2001); her novels include *My City* (1979), *Whistling Deer* (1982), *Mourning for Breasts* (1992),and *Strange Tales of the Floating City* (1992); and her poetry collections include *Stone Chime* (1984) and *Collected Poems of Xi Xi* (2000). "Goatskin Raft—In Lieu of Preface," originally written in October 1985 as a preface to *Xi Xi, Volume in Hand* (Hung Ban Bookstore, Taipei, 1988), is a marvelous testament to the writer's versatility and art.

## Goatskin Raft—In Lieu of Preface

One summer day, she rode on a goatskin raft for the first time. Before the raft touched the water, she caught a glimpse of a man—lean, young, wearing a hat—coming out of the village with the raft on his shoulder. At first she couldn't tell what it was; all she saw was a man walking in the field with a huge square frame, the way a peddler carries his goods. As he came closer, she realized, upon scrutiny, that it was a goatskin raft. The entire wooden frame was covered with pelts—fifteen of them. The goats' heads and tails were no longer there, only the legs remained. The preserved pelts no longer evoked the softness associated with goatskin. She seemed to be looking at some large, dried-out gourds. Apparently the raft was not heavy at all. The man walked briskly; with an oar running through the rope openings in the frame, he carried it easily on his shoulder. At the end of the oar handle hung three pillow-sized sacks of considerable weight.

Our ancestors observed fallen leaves floating on water. They carved a single log into a canoe to cross rivers. But sometimes they couldn't find logs, and it was hard to fell a tree; so they bundled branches and built a raft. She has seen wooden rafts—some with branches loosely tied together—float down the river till they push against the shore. Young boys run around on them and have a jolly time. These days she sees rubber rafts floating down shallow streams, made with five or six long tubes. Fishermen and fish hawks squat and perch on them. Once she saw a bamboo raft, even a man standing astride a single bamboo, crossing a wide river.

Our ancestors built rafts with wood and bamboo, and used bamboo and wood for writing material. The Han dynasty slat books from the Dunhuang caves are mostly made of birch. Ancient Chinese cut bamboo into short cylinders, broke them into narrow strips, and baked them over fire to absorb the moisture so they could write on them with pen and ink. Then they used ropes, silk cords, or leather strings to hold them together, like a row of teeth. Ancient Egyptians used papyrus to make paper; the reed-like plant growing by the Nile was also used to build boats. Originally, ancient Egyptians used palm leaves to inscribe words; others used olive leaves. We call those Buddhist scriptures written on long narrow palm leaves Pattra Sutras. It is recorded that "The ancients observed falling leaves and used them to build a boat," attesting to the fact that leaves float on water.

In the second century B.C.E., when the King of Pergamon had a hard time obtaining Egyptian papyrus, he used parchment instead. Jews wrote their law on parchment, and Persians recorded their history on it. When the Mongols ruled China, they wrote the emperor's order in Mongolian on parchment and called it the "Goatskin Imperial Decree." Ancient Tibetans wrote Buddhist scriptures on dyed goatskins. Liu Ji of the Ming dynasty was banished outside the border. Having no paper, he wrote books on parchment, which came to be known as "Leather Books." The day before she rode on the goatskin raft, she opened a book and read about monks who worked in libraries in medieval times. On every desk lay tools for scribing and embossing words: ink wells made of horn, goose quills that the monks sharpened with small knives, stones for making parchment smooth, and straight rulers for drawing lines before writing. In those days, parchment was first scraped with a stone blade, softened with lime, and flattened with a blunt knife; then the two sides of parchment were perforated with a sharp pen.

The goatskin raft entered the river and was now afloat. It was steady, with excellent buoyancy. The sacks hanging at the end of the oar served as seat cushions. She boarded the raft, carefully stepped on the wooden frame, and sat down. A raft could accommodate five or six passengers. Skimming the water, it was not wet on the surface at all. The raft-builder used only one oar and rowed on the right side then the left, propelling the raft forward. She had not witnessed the making of the raft, nor had she seen how the goatskins were treated. All she knew was that the dried goatskins were sewn tightly with thin threads to close off all the crevices so air could not go through, leaving only one leg for ventilation. A skillful raft-builder only needs to blow on the leg five times to fill a large goatskin with air; it is so stiff that when you tap it with your fingers it makes a *bong* sound like a drum. Finally, she also learned the way to keep the goatskin from leaking: add water to a catty of salt, seven ounces of clear oil, and some millet grains and salt cakes, pour it into the goatskin, and let it air dry for a few days till the white pelt turns reddish brown. Now it's ready for sailing. Once a month you need to rub it with four ounces of oil to keep it from drying and cracking.

She often longs to go to the other shore, where a fertile green land lies. But between her and the land is a river, an invisible and untouchable magical river. Sometimes the waters are calm, sometimes treacherous. She can hear black birds chirping in a distance and smell the fragrance of the roses from across the river. It reminds her of her boat. She opens a book, because a book is a goatskin raft on the river of her life.

A goatskin raft is unsinkable, in the midst of crashing waves or on rock-dotted waters. Even if only one goatskin raft is left, it can still cross the river to reach the other shore. Inevitably a wooden boat cracks; only a goatskin raft stays whole, conquering strength with gentleness. A goatskin raft is neither a boat nor a horse; it can only go one way. Afloat on the water, it goes with the current. To go against the current, it has to be transported. When the distance is short, it is easy to carry it around. When the distance is long, you can deflate it, roll it up into a bundle, and use the oar as a pole to carry it, the way the Mongols move around with their yurts. When she opens a book, she boards her goatskin raft to get to the other shore. Sometimes, she needs to return by going against the current; so she carries the book with her, across thousands of miles, never leaving it behind. The goatskin raft is hauled from the water to the shore and stood on its head. The raft-builder splashes water on it with the oar to wash off the mud, and uses the oar to help it stand up on the sand. In the sun, it dries quickly. The raft-builder picks up the oar and sticks it into the rope crevices in the frame. Carrying it on his shoulder, he walks back to the village on the path in the field.

Once, she was a guest at someone's home, where she could not see a single book. She was not surprised, for just as not every household had a goatskin raft folded up in a corner, people had different ways of ferrying the torrents of life. Some were even lucky enough to board Noah's ark to survive the flood. But she can't help but feel sad for many people. Even in this age of advanced technology, the only unsinkable mode of transportation is still the ancient goatskin raft. Suddenly she hears birds singing in a distance again. It is time for her to explore on the other shore. So, she opens a book and sails quietly on a small stool.

*Translated by Michelle Yeh*

# Zhang Dachun

*(b. 1957)*

Zhang Dachun was born in Taipei and graduated with a B.A. in Chinese literature from the Catholic Fu Jen University. He achieved fame in the early 1980s with short stories that either deconstructed the grand narratives of nationalism and history or depicted the absurd conditions of contemporary urban life. He has since become one of the most prolific and versatile writers in Taiwan, having written in many genres: political satire, martial-arts saga, juvenile bildungsroman, literary criticism, newspaper columns, and classical poetry. His popularity is not limited to literature, however. Host of television and radio shows, he is a media celebrity and cultural icon in Taiwan. Two novels, *Wild Child* and *My Kid Sister*, were translated by Michael Berry and published in one volume in English translation as *Wild Kids* by Columbia University Press in 2000.

"All Is Creative Writing" first appeared in the *China Times Evening Express* on April 7, 1991, and was also the preface to *Zhang Dachun's Literary Views* (Yuanliu Publishing, Taipei, 1992). In the essay, Zhang mentions Qiong Yao (b. 1938, née Chen Zhe), who has been the most famous writer of romance novels from Taiwan since the early 1960s. Many of her works have been made into popular films and television series.

## Excerpt from "All Is Creative Writing—News, Fiction, News Fiction"

If we choose to put it in simple terms—consider it as an either-or question—we can say: There are two kinds of people in the world. One would rather read news, while the other would rather read fiction. Of course, the one who would rather not read at all is rather lucky (who can skip even this essay), because news and fiction make the world a far more complicated place than it is without them.

If we complicate the situation even more, we can say: surely there is a third kind of reader who can respond with "would rather." He might say: "But it's not a clear-cut case. Sometimes I feel like reading news, other times I feel like reading fiction." Indeed, reading is not a test and does not require the rigidity of an either-or question. If we pose the question in a more casual way, probably quite a few people "would rather" belong to the third kind.

Compared with the second kind of reader (one who would rather read fiction), the first (one who would rather read news) seems to have more "concern for reality." But this is not clear-cut either. Some people, being extremely concerned about this messy world, would like to sneak into the messy world of fiction—the latter appearing all the more interesting exactly because its messiness poses no threat to real life.

By the same token, those who would rather read fiction may be better able to "appreciate fiction" than those who would rather read news. But again it's not a clear-cut case. A reader who deeply appreciates fiction will find the unsolved homicide in the domestic section, the movie star's scandal in the entertainment section, or the U.S.-Iraq war in the politics section more riveting than any work of fiction—whether by Tolstoy or Qiong Yao—that he happens to have at hand.

Since uncertainty applies to both kinds of reader, we have to admit: it is perhaps the third kind of reader—one who cannot be put in the box of either-or—who reminds us that when we think we are the first kind of reader, we are actually reading fiction like news, and when we think we are the second kind, we are actually reading news like fiction. We believe news to be real but sometimes would rather it be as unreal as fiction. We believe fiction to be unreal but sometimes would rather it be as real as news. From this we derive an interesting conclusion: based on the reader's attitude—whether "knowing it to be real but wishing it were unreal" or "knowing it to be unreal but wishing it to be real"—reading is not a passive process but an active form of control.

A reader who cannot verify the objectivity of a news report often asks: "Is this piece of news made up? By the same token, a reader who cannot verify the source of fiction asks: Is the fiction alluding to something?" Now let us see how active an inquiring reader can be, and what kind of control he can have.

It is impossible for a completely passive reader to exist because anyone can raise questions about the piece of writing in front of him based on his memory, the only difference being the size of the memory bank. A reader who remembers the Manchu slaughters of the Han people in the seventeenth century is shocked when he reads in the news that a certain minister of the Executive Yuan—you may remember his name consists of three characters and he speaks with a heavy Zhejiang accent—says: "The Manchu government didn't apologize for slaughtering the Han people, so why should . . ." (Can you fill in the ellipsis?) Did he misspeak? How could he say such a thing? But a reader who doesn't know history would not recognize the minister's faux pas; the news is no different from blank space on the page. [. . .]

On the other hand, being a fiction reader requires no less memory than being a news reader. At the most basic level, a reader of detective fiction would not understand why a character was arrested by the police if he forgot that the story was about the search for a murderer. A reader of a romance novel would not understand why the heroine was pregnant and getting bigger and bigger if he forgot the night of stormy passion.

Of course, just as in reading news, it is not just memory that prompts fiction readers to ask questions persistently; other kinds of material, such as specialized knowledge, history, and news, are also at work. Those who know something about the law would ask: "Will the villain be arrested?" Those who know something about biology would ask: "Was the baby conceived on that night of stormy passion?" As for more intelligent readers, the questions asked are more intelligent too, such as: In Zhu Xining's "The

Tale of the Broken Tongue," why does the author move the setting of the story in volume six of *Shocking Tales from the Desk* from a convent to a pawnshop? If no answers to his questions surface during reading, the reader will experience suspense; when the answers are revealed, the reader will be satisfied; when the answers are unexpected, the reader will be surprised—then go on to raise new questions.

In asking questions prompted by memory, a reader carries a dialogue with both news and fiction. Memory and dialogue interact with each other. Sometimes we visit the world of fiction with the memories derived from reality; sometimes we question reality with memories derived from fiction. Regardless, the act of reading is not as well defined as we idealize it in such simple terms as truth and fiction. Through the dialogue between the work and the reader, reading entwines reality with fiction in an ever more complex way. Our active control originates from the questions based on our memory, but when we stop asking questions due to a lack of memory, we lose such control.

The so-called news fiction—a genre I have invented—is in essence an attempt to interweave "reality" with "fiction," while at the same time constructing "fiction" with "reality" by manipulating memory. The moment news is made public, the fiction writer starts questioning: "How do I let this piece of news infiltrate my fiction?" The moment a work of fiction appears in print, the reader starts questioning: "What would the fiction be like without the infiltration of news?" When a piece of news no longer exists in anyone's memory, the fiction writer and the reader will ask together: "Is this news or fiction?" All three questions are related to "creative writing"; they belong to the author as well as the reader. More to the reader, I'd say. So long as the reader keeps asking questions, he will not accept the superficial dichotomy of reality versus fiction, and will understand that all is "creative writing." Reading is creative writing, so is memory. Even the question of reality versus fiction is our creation.

*Translated by Michelle Yeh*

# Yu Hua

*(b. 1960)*

Yu Hua was born in Hangzhou, and both of his parents were doctors. He grew up during the Cultural Revolution with little access to books. He learned dentistry and worked for five years but disliked the constricting lifestyle. One day he noticed people at a cultural center who seemed to have more relaxed jobs. When he asked them how he could work there, they suggested that he write novels. In 1983 he gave up dentistry to pursue fiction. A year later, he published his first short story, "Star," and three years later his first novel, *Leaving Home at Eighteen*, shook up the Chinese literary scene. His depictions of violence, as well as his linguistic experimentation, stood out. Since 1984, he has written thirteen books: four novels, six collections of stories, and three collections of essays. His novels include *Cries in the Drizzle* (1991), *To Live* (1992), *Chronicle of a Blood Merchant* (1995), and *Brothers* (2005), and his short stories are available in *The Past and the Punishments* (1996) and *World Like Mist* (2003). *To Live* received widespread acclaim and was awarded the Grizane Cavour Award in Italy in 1998. It was also made into a renowned film by Zhang Yimou.

Yu Hua's evolution as a writer is marked by three successive stages, where he focused first on the short story, then on the novel, and then on the essay. In recent essays, he has written about Kawabata, Kafka, García

Márquez, Faulkner, and Lu Xun. In the following excerpt from "Autobiography," which is published here for the first time, as well as the excerpt from the author's postscript for *To Live*, Yu Hua writes about becoming a writer and the magic of literature.

## Excerpt from "Autobiography"

[. . .] I fell in love with the big character posters in the street. By then I was already in middle school. Every day when I got out of school I'd idle away an hour or so reading those posters. By the 1970s, all the big character posters had turned into personal attacks. I wondered how all these people, whom I knew, could use such venomous language to curse one another, hurting each other with vicious rumors. Some of them went as far as digging up the graves of their enemies' ancestors; others made up stories of erotic decadence to which they would attach cartoons. The content of these cartoons was even more wide-ranging. They'd draw anything, even depict people having sex.

During the years of the big character posters, the realm of the imagination was explored on an almost unprecedented level. Every literary device was utilized and developed: fiction, exaggeration, metaphor, satire, they used it all. This was my earliest contact with literature. There in the street, before the layers upon layers of posters, I began to enjoy literature.

By the time I actually began to write, I had already become a dentist. After graduating from middle school, I entered the town's public-health school to become a dentist. All my classmates were sent to work in factories. The fact that I wasn't was completely attributable to the strings my father pulled. He hoped that I, like him, would seek a career in medicine.

Afterward, I spent a year studying at the public-health school, and that year was especially difficult for me. Especially difficult was physiology class, in which the positions and names of muscles, nerves, and organs all had to be memorized. The excessive amount of tedious and mechanized study caused me to begin to feel an air of disgust toward my future career.

I wanted a job with a higher degree of freedom, a job in which I could explore and develop my imagination, a job in which I could follow my heart's desire. However, being a doctor (strictly speaking I never became a true doctor, it was only my job title), one can only equal one, two can only equal two. You can never imagine the heart to be inside a thigh, just as you can't mix up teeth and toenails. This kind of work was too strict, and I felt it unsuitable for me.

It also was difficult for me to become accustomed to working eight hours a day. Going to and getting off work at a set time was simply too confining. And so my earliest motivation for writing professionally grew out of a desire to cast off the environment I was ensnared in. At the time my greatest wish was to join the county cultural center. I saw that most of the people at the cultural center were lazy and carefree, leading me to think this was an appropriate job for me. So, I began writing; moreover, I was assiduous to this end.

After five years of being a dentist, writing enabled me to finally realize my wish and join the county cultural center. From then on, it seems that all the changes in my life have been related to writing, including my departure from Haiyan to Jiaxing and my voyage from Jiaxing to Beijing.

Although I have left Haiyan, my writings will never leave there. I lived in Haiyan almost thirty years, and I am familiar with everything there. As I grew up, so I also watched the streets and the river grow. Each and every corner of Haiyan is alive in my mind; sometimes when I'm talking to myself, the local dialect spoken there sneaks out of my mouth. That's where the spirit of my past is from, and from today on, that's where my inspiration arises from.

*Translated by Michael Berry*

## Excerpt from "Author's Postscript"

In the introduction to the 1993 Chinese edition of *To Live,* I wrote: "I once heard an American folk song entitled 'Old Black Joe.' The song was about an elderly black slave who experienced a life's worth of hardships, including the passing of his entire family—yet he still looked upon the world with eyes of kindness, offering not the slightest complaint. After being so deeply moved by this song, I decided to write my next novel—that novel was *To Live*."

For an author, the act of writing always begins with a smile, a gesture, a memory on the verge of being forgotten, a casual conversation or a bit of information hidden in the newspaper—it is these tiny pearl-like details that sometimes transform one's fate and spread like waves into magnificent vistas and scenes. The writing of *To Live* was no exception. An American slave song with only the simplest lyrics grew into Fugui's life—a life imbued with upheavals and suffering, but also tranquility and happiness.

Old Joe and Fugui are two men who could not be more different. They live in different countries and different eras; they are of different nationalities and cultural backgrounds; even their fundamental likes and dislikes are different, as is the color of their skin—yet sometimes they seem to be the same person. They are both so very human. Human experience, combined with the power of the imagination and understanding, can break down all barriers, enabling a person truly to understand that thing called fate at work in his life—not unlike the experience of simultaneously seeing one's reflection in two different mirrors. Perhaps this is what makes literature magical; it is precisely this magic that enabled me—a reader on the other side of the world in China—to read the novels of Nathaniel Hawthorne, William Faulkner, and Toni Morrison, and through them, to discover myself.

*Translated by Michael Berry*

# Mo Yan

*(b. 1956)*

Mo Yan was born into a peasant family in Gaomi, in Shangdong province. In his childhood, he experienced bitter poverty. During the Cultural Revolution, he worked as a farmer and then in an oil-producing factory. In 1976 he joined the People's Liberation Army and, a few years later, began writing fiction. In 1981 he published his first short story, "Rain Falling Thick and Fast in the Spring Night." In 1986 he graduated from the People's Liberation Army Art Academy and joined the Writers' Association. *Red Sorghum*, his most famous work, was published in that year. He served in the People's Liberation Army until 1997, when he accepted an editorial position at the *Beijing Procuratorial Daily*. He is the author of many novels, novellas, short stories, essays, and film scripts. His works in English translation include *The Garlic Ballads* (1995); *The Republic of Wine* (2000); *Shifu, You'll Do Anything for a Laugh* (2002); *Big Breasts and Wide Hips* (2005); and *Life and Death are Wearing Me Out* (2008).

Mo Yan consciously draws inspiration from his hometown, and his fictions often entwine local flavor with social commentary. For instance, in *The Republic of Wine,* Mo Yan depicts Chinese farmers, amid changing traditional lifestyles and values, obsessed with food and sex. He creates remarkable characters, often utilizes stark, violent images, and develops plots rich with symbolic meaning. In 2006 he received the Fukuoka Asian Cultural Prize. In

March 2009 Mo Yan was awarded the inaugural Newman Prize for Chinese Literature for his novel *Life and Death Are Wearing Me Out* and was subsequently featured in the July 2009 issue of *World Literature Today*. Several of his novels, including *Red Sorghum*, have been adapted for film.

Of the two talks that follow, the first was given when Mo Yan visited the Tattered Cover Book Store in Denver in March 2000. The second was delivered when he received the Newman Prize at the University of Oklahoma in March 2009.

## My American Books

My first novel translated into English was *Red Sorghum*. Before it was rendered into English, it was made into a movie by China's renowned director Zhang Yimou and won a major prize at the Berlin International Film Festival. The novel became famous because of the movie. In China, when my name is mentioned, people say, "Oh, *Red Sorghum*!" Forgive my immodesty, but, as a matter of fact, *Red Sorghum* evoked strong reactions in China before it was made into a movie. So Zhang Yimou benefited from my novel, and then my novel benefited from his movie.

I wrote *Red Sorghum* when I was still at the PLA art college. It was the early 1980s, the so-called "golden age of contemporary Chinese literature." An enthusiastic readership inspired writers to become passionate about literature. People were no longer content to create or read stories written in traditional styles. Readers demanded that we be more creative, and we dreamed of nothing but becoming more inventive. A critic quipped that Chinese writers were like a flock of sheep being chased by a wolf—a wolf whose name was Innovation.

At the time, I had just crawled out of mountain ditches and didn't even know how to use a telephone, let alone possess any knowledge of literary theories. So the wolf of innovation was not chasing me. I hid out at home, writing whatever I felt like writing. Now that I have some rudimentary knowledge of theory, I realize that slavishly following trends is not true innovation; real creativity is writing honestly about things you're familiar with. If you've had unique experiences, then what you write will be unique. And being unique is new. If you write something different, you will have developed a unique style. It's like singing: training can change your technique, not your voice. No matter how diligently you train a crow, it can never sing like a nightingale.

In other talks I've given, I've brought up my childhood. While city kids were drinking milk and eating bread, pampered by their mothers, my friends and I were fighting to overcome hunger. We had no idea what sorts of delicious foods the world had to offer. We survived on roots and bark, and were lucky to scrape together enough food from the fields to make a humble meal. The trees in our village were gnawed bare by our rapacious teeth. While city kids were singing and dancing at school, I was out herding cows and sheep, and got into the habit of talking to myself. Hunger and loneliness are themes I've repeatedly explored in my novels, and I consider them the source of my riches. Actually, I've been blessed with an even more valuable source of riches: the stories and legends I heard during the long years I spent in the countryside.

In the fall of 1998, when I visited Taiwan, I participated in a roundtable discussion on childhood reading experiences. The other writers on the panel had read many books in their childhood, books I haven't read even now. I said that my experience was different, because while they read with their eyes as children, I read with my ears. Most of the people in my village were illiterate, but such words flew from their mouths that you'd have thought they were educated scholars. They were full of wondrous stories. My grandparents and my father were all great storytellers. But my grandfather's brother—we called him Big Grandpa—was a master storyteller, an old Chinese herbal doctor whose profession brought him into contact with people from all walks of life. He was very knowledgeable and had a rich imagination. On winter evenings, my brothers, sisters, and I would go to his house, where we'd sit around a dusky oil lamp, waiting for him to tell us a story. He had a long, snowy-white beard, but not a single hair on top. His bald head and his eyes glinted under the lamplight as we begged him to tell us a story. "I tell you stories every day," he'd say impatiently. "How many do you think I have? Go on, go home and go to bed." But we'd keep pleading, "Tell us a story—just one." And finally, he'd give in.

I've memorized some three hundred of his stories, and with minor changes, every one of them could become a pretty good novel. I haven't even used fifty of them. I doubt I could ever use up all the stories he told us. And the ones that haven't been written down are far more interesting than those that have. It's like a fruit peddler who tries to sell the wormy fruit first. Someday, when the time is ripe, I plan to sell those stories of his.

Most of Big Grandpa's stories were told in the first person, and they all sounded like personal experience. Back then we believed they were his own stories, and it wasn't till much later that I realized he'd made them up as he went along. His stories sprang from the fact that he was a country doctor who often saw patients in the middle of the night. They always started like this:

"A couple of nights ago, I went over to Old Wang the Filth's house in East Village to check on his wife. On my way back, as I passed that small stone bridge, I saw a woman in white sitting on the bridge and crying. I said to her, 'Big Sister, it's the middle of the night. Why are you out here all alone, and what are you crying about?' She said, 'Mister, my child is sick, he's dying. Would you go take a look at him?' I said to myself, 'I know every woman in Gaomi, so this one has to be a demon.' I asked her, 'Where do you live?' The woman pointed under the bridge and said, 'There.' I said, 'You can't fool me. I know you're that white eel demon under the bridge.' Seeing that her ploy had failed, she covered her mouth and smiled. 'You've got it again.' Then, with a jerk of her head, she leaped under the bridge."

Legend had it that a white eel the size of a bucket lived beneath the stone bridge. It had transformed itself into human form to seduce Big Grandpa. We asked him, "Big Grandpa, why didn't you go with her since she was so pretty?" He just said, "Dopey kids, if I had, I'd never have come back."

Then he would go on to another story. A few nights earlier, he said, a man came to see him, leading a little black donkey with one hand and holding a red lantern in the other. The man said that someone in his family was very sick. Now, Big Grandpa was a very conscientious doctor, so he got dressed and left with the man. The moon was out that night, and the little black donkey shone like fine silk. After the man helped him onto the donkey, he asked, "Sir, are you all set?" Big Grandpa said he was, so the man slapped the donkey on the rump. Big Grandpa said, "You can't believe how fast that little donkey flew. How fast? All I heard was the wind whipping past my ears, and all I saw were trees on both sides of the road whizzing backward." We were dumbstruck. That donkey must have been like a rocket. He said he knew something wasn't right, and he must have run into demons again.

What kind of demons? He didn't know, so he made up his mind to wait and find out. Before long, the donkey descended from the sky and landed in a magnificent mansion, all lit up by lamps. The man helped Big Grandpa down as a white-haired old lady came out of the house and led him to the sickroom. It turned out to be a woman about to give birth. Country doctors had to take care of every illness in the world, so delivering a baby was no big deal. He rolled up his sleeves to help the woman deliver her baby. He said this woman was also very pretty, unsurpassingly beautiful—that was his favorite phrase in describing a pretty woman. And not only beautiful, but amazingly fertile. As soon as he grabbed hold of a hairy, furry baby, out came another head. Big Grandpa thought, "Hey, twins!" But then another furry head poked out, and he thought it must be triplets; then out came another. Just like that, one after another, she delivered eight babies, all furry, with little tails. Cute as can be. It suddenly dawned on him what they were. "Foxes!" he shouted, but the word was barely out of his mouth when ghost-like cries and wolfish howls erupted and darkness descended around him. Scared witless, he bit his middle finger—a fabled way of exorcising demons—and found himself in a tomb, surrounded by furry little foxes. The adults had fled.

I also heard stories from my grandmother, my father, and other talented storytelling relatives. I've committed many of them to memory. Since they were told by different people, they have distinctively different flavors. If I were to relate all the stories they told, my talk today would be as long as the Great Wall. So now I'll tell you about my novels.

On the surface, *Red Sorghum* seems to be about the war against Japan. But in reality, it's about the folklore and legends told by my kin. Of course, it's also about my longing for the contentment of love and a life of freedom. The only history in my head is the legendary type. Many famous historical figures were actually ordinary people, folks like us. Their heroic accomplishments were nothing but the result of embellishment over a long period of oral transmission. I've read some American reviews of *Red Sorghum*. They struck a chord when they characterized my novel as folklore. This story, which I wrote in the ancient form of storytelling, has been viewed by Chinese critics as a fantastic innovation, and I can't help but chuckle to myself. If this is innovation, then being innovative is the easiest thing in the world.

My second novel in English was *The Garlic Ballads*, which I wrote in 1987. In the early summer of that year, a major incident occurred in a Shandong county famous for its garlic. The farmers had a great harvest that year but were unable to sell their crops, owing to the corruption of officials. Tons of garlic lay rotting in the fields. So the outraged farmers trashed the county government building. There was widespread fallout and lengthy newspaper reports. In the end, the officials were dismissed, but the farmers who led the rebellion were also arrested and jailed. This incident enraged me. I may look like a writer, but deep inside I'm still a peasant. So I sat down and wrote the novel; it took me a month. Of course, I moved the setting to the kingdom of my literary production: Northeast Gaomi Township. In reality, this is a book about hunger, and it is a book about rage. I wasn't thinking about innovation when I wrote it, because I felt the need to vent the anger welling up inside me. I wrote it for myself and for all my peasant brethren. But after the book was published, critics continued to insist that I was striving for innovation. They pointed out that the novel was told from three perspectives: first, that of a blind man, a balladeer; second, the objective viewpoint of a writer; and finally, the perspective of the official voice. And they called *that* innovation!

In my hometown, there were indeed balladeers, most of them blind men. They generally performed in groups of three: one to play the Chinese lute, one to beat a drum, and the third to sing. Some were very talented men who wove current affairs into their songs and improvised as they went along. As a child, I admired them greatly and considered them to be true artists. When I was writing *The Garlic Ballads*, their hoarse, sad voices echoed in my ears. That, not innovation, was my muse.

My third novel was *The Republic of Wine*. I began writing it in 1989 and finished it in 1992. It was published in 1993, to deafening silence. The clamoring critics had suddenly turned mute. I guess these noisy "experts" were shocked. They had been promoting innovation all along, but when true innovation arrived, they turned a blind eye to it.

There are still many improvements that could be made to both *Red Sorghum* and *The Garlic Ballads*, and if I were to rewrite them, I believe they'd be better. But with *The Republic of Wine*, I couldn't improve it, no matter what I did. I can boast that while many contemporary Chinese writers can produce good books of their own, no one but me could write a novel like *The Republic of Wine*. I know that even though I may look like a middle-aged man on the outside, my heart is still as young as when I was listening to Big Grandpa's stories. I realize I'm getting older only when I look in the mirror. When I'm facing a piece of paper, I forget my age, and my heart is filled with the joy of a child. I hate evil with a passion, I ramble, I mutter as if dreaming, I rejoice, I raise hell, I feel drunk.

*Translated by Sylvia Li-chun Lin*

## Six Lives in Search of a Character: The 2009 Newman Prize Lecture

*Norman, Oklahoma, March 5, 2009*

It seems ironic to ask someone called "Mo Yan" to speak in front of so many people. Thirty years ago, when a man with the name "Guan Moye" took a character from his given name, Mo, split it into two characters, and changed it into Mo Yan, he did not fully realize the implications of this rebellious act of changing both family and given names. Back then he was thinking that he should have a pen name, since all major writers had one. As he stared at the new name that meant "don't talk," he was reminded of his mother's admonition from way back. At that time, people in China were living in an unusual political climate; political struggles came in waves, one more severe than the one before, and people in general lost their sense of security. There was no loyalty or trust among people; there was only deception and watchfulness. Under those social conditions, many people got into trouble because of things they said; a single carelessly uttered word could bring disaster to one's life and reputation as well as ruination to one's family. But at a time like this, Mo Yan, or Guan Moye, was a talkative child with a good memory, an impressive ability to articulate, and, worst of all, a strong desire to express his views in public. Whenever he felt like showing off his eloquence, his mother would remind him, "Don't talk too much." But as the saying goes, it's easier for a dynasty to rise and fall than for a man to change his nature. As soon as he was away from his mother's watchful eye, out came a torrent of words.

In *Life and Death Are Wearing Me Out*, the novel that won the Newman Prize, there is a Mo Yan who spews incessant nonsense and incurs everyone's displeasure. Though I cannot say that this Mo Yan is the real Mo Yan, he isn't far off.

Literature comes from life. This is, to be sure, an apt description, a sort of eternal truth. But life encompasses boundless experience, and all a writer can use is a sliver of his personal life. If a writer wants to continue to write, he must strive to expand his life experience and fight the desire to pursue wealth and leisure. Instead, he must search for suffering, which is the salvation of an established writer, even though in the pursuit of suffering one can stumble upon happiness. Therefore, the greatest wealth of a writer is the suffering he happens upon in his search for happiness. This, of course, is purely coincidental, not something that can be planned. So I believe that, in addition to talent and hard work, fate is indispensable to one's literary success.

A writer can produce many works in his lifetime, but only one or perhaps a few will be remembered by his readers. As of now, I've written ten novels and nearly a hundred novellas and short stories. I cannot say for sure which one, or ones, might pass the test of time and continue to be read. The jury, in a way, made that judgment for me when they awarded the Newman Prize to *Life and Death Are Wearing Me Out*. So if two of my novels will be read by later generations, I believe that *Life and Death Are Wearing Me Out* will be one of them, partly because it won the prize, but especially because it brings into play some of the most important experiences of my life. I have said elsewhere that the novel was written in the short span of forty-three days, but it took forty-three years to germinate and develop. In the early 1960s, Guan Moye was still in elementary school. Every morning during the calisthenics broadcast after second period, he would see an independent farmer with the surname Lan pushing a cart with wooden wheels, something that was no longer in use even then. It was pulled by a gimpy donkey accompanied by Lan's wife, a woman with bound feet. The wooden wheels grated shrilly against the dirt path by the school, leaving deep tracks. Guan Moye remembered all this. Back then, like all the other kids, Guan Moye felt nothing but disgust and disdain for this stubborn farmer who had insisted upon working independently instead of joining the commune, and even joined them in the evil act of pelting him with stones. Lan Lian resisted the pressure until 1966, when, under the cruel persecution of the Cultural Revolution, he could no longer hold out and took his own life.

Many years later, after Guan Moye became Mo Yan, he wanted to turn the independent farmer's story into a novel. The commune system was abolished in the 1980s, when peasants were allotted parcels of land, essentially making them independent farmers again. Mo Yan was particularly impressed by Lan Lian, an exceptional peasant who dared hold to his own views and wage a war against society, to the point of sacrificing his life to preserve his dignity. There has never been another character like him in contemporary Chinese literature. But Mo Yan delayed writing the novel because he had yet to find the right narrative structure. It was not until the summer of 2005, when he saw in a famous temple the mural of the six transmigrations of life, that he had an epiphany. He decided to let a wrongly executed landlord pass through the lives of a donkey, an ox, a pig, a dog, and a monkey before being reborn as a big-headed baby with an incurable, congenital disease. The loquacious baby recounted the many strange and uncommon experiences of his lifetimes as domestic animals, while examining, from the perspectives of those animals, the transformations of the Chinese countryside over the past fifty years.

Someone once asked me about the connection between the Mo Yan in the novel and the real-life Mo Yan. My response was: the Mo Yan in the novel is a character created by the writer Mo Yan, but is also the writer Mo Yan himself. In fact, this is the connection between a novelist and all the characters in his novels.

*Translated by Sylvia Li-chun Lin*

# Wang Ping

*(b. 1957)*

Wang Ping was born in China and came to the United States in 1985. Her publications include *American Visa* (short stories, 1994), *Foreign Devil* (novel, 1996); *Of Flesh and Spirit* (poetry, 1998), *The Magic Whip* (poetry, 2003), and *The Last Communist Virgin* (stories, 2007), all from Coffee House Press. *New Generation: Poetry from China Today* (1999), an anthology she edited and co-translated, is published by Hanging Loose Press. She graduated from Beijing University and received her Ph.D. in comparative literature at New York University. Her dissertation on the history of foot binding in China was published under the title *Aching for Beauty: Footbinding in China* (2000) and was selected for the Eugene Kayden Award for the Best Book in Humanities.

Wang Ping has also had two solo photography and multimedia exhibitions: "Behind the Gate: After the Flooding of the Three Gorges," at the Janet Fine Art Gallery, Macalester College, in 2007, and "All Roads to Lhasa," at the Banfill-Lock Cultural Center, in 2008. She is the recipient of fellowships from the National Endowment for the Arts, the New York Foundation for the Arts, the New York State Council of the Arts, the Minnesota State Arts Board, the Bush Foundation, and the Lannan Foundation. She is an associate professor of English at Macalester College.

"Writing in Two Tongues" discusses writing in Chinese and English and how it "walks the tightrope between languages and cultures." The essay also incorporates a discussion of the composition of Chinese characters to show how they consist of "a compound with multiple units, with image within image, image upon image, a flowing, complex contour."

## Writing in Two Tongues

Seventeen years ago, I walked into a creative-writing class by accident and started writing. I wrote in two languages, Chinese, my mother tongue, and English, which I studied in my early twenties before I came to the U.S. There was a huge gap between my Chinese poems and the English ones, and I couldn't see it until I tried to translate the English poems into Chinese and found the task nearly impossible. Putting them side by side, I realized that when I wrote in Chinese, I automatically walked the line of three thousand years of poetic tradition: cultured, flowery, cluttered with historical allusions, images, and metaphors. However, my English poems were simple, bold, and straightforward, both in form and content, playful paintings by a child who knows no fear or inhibition, who never hesitates to point and shout, "The emperor has no clothes!"

> I was a virgin till twenty-three, then always had more than one lover at the same time—all secret.
>
> . . . . . . . . . . . . . . . . . .
>
> The asshole in Chinese: the eye of the fart.
>
> . . . . . . . . . . . . . . . . . .
>
> The most powerful curse: fuck your mother, fuck your grandmother, fuck your great-grandmother of eighteen generations.
>
> . . . . . . . . . . . . . . . . . . .
>
> We don't say "fall in love," but "talk love."
>
> When I left home, my father told me: "never talk love before you're twenty-five years old." I waited till twenty-three. Well, my first lover was a married coward. My first marriage lasted a week. My husband slept with me once, and I never saw him again. (from "Of Flesh and Spirit")

Such vulgarity! Such horror! My mother tongue would never allow them to surface to my consciousness, let alone let them out in writing as a poem.

It is simply unimaginable, unthinkable, and unspeakable—and, therefore, untranslatable.

The discovery shook me. True, mother tongue soothes and nurtures like a cradle, but it's also a pointing finger, telling me what to see, where to go, how to think and feel. It provides the ground for my imagination while setting the boundary. It works subtly, unconsciously, and ubiquitously. I speak, write, and think in Chinese without a second thought, taking it for granted. It's like going home through a forest path so old and familiar that I can do it with my eyes closed. And I often do; therefore, I no longer see.

To write poetry in a second tongue, however, I do not have such luxury. I have to keep my eyes, ears, and mouth open all the time for new sounds, new expressions, new meanings. I constantly stop a conversation and ask, "What does it mean?" or "What are you really trying to say?" Most of the time, people laugh kind-heartedly, give me the definition of the word, then go on. Sometimes they get annoyed for being interrupted, or become condescending. My questions force them to reexamine the words they use, revealing unintentionally that they don't really know what they are saying, or don't mean what they are trying to say. Some people would feel threatened, and start mocking my accent and my grammatical mistakes. But I don't care. Marked forever as a linguistic child by my foreign accent, I have a giant playground full of endless toys to play with. I can break rules, challenge the authority of the language, and bypass the old ways of seeing and thinking. And I feel no shame to stumble and fall.

SYNTAX

She walks to a table
She walk to table

She is walking to a table
She walk to table now

What difference does it make
What difference it make

In Nature, no completeness
No sentence really complete thought

Language, like woman
Look best when free, undressed

A word is not just a word, but a universe pulsing with the lives and histories of the people who speak it, write it, and live it. Yet it can also become stagnant from the forced rules, become grimy and clichéd from careless use. A poem must first of all yank us out of the familiar ground we stand on to make us see things in a new light. It must challenge the thinking patterns a mother tongue has ingrained in our brains so that we can think out of the box. A poem must bring words closer to the origin of things, back to the fundamental reality of time and space, which is neither linear nor flat. It must make words speak at once with the vividness of painting and the mobility of sounds. In a poem, words must come alive, bloom, fruit, and every sound must echo and vibrate, summoning souls, stories, passions of the past and present and future from all directions.

Since my writing walks the tightrope between languages and cultures, there's no old word for me, be it English or Chinese. Every time I use a word, I enter a virgin forest. I cut and chop to open new paths. I sniff and taste each exotic plant, mushroom, flower, fruit. . . . I dig for roots, hidden treasure, forgotten history. I wander, look, poke. I trip, get lost, fall into traps. I encounter beasts and monsters that sometimes befriend me, other times tear me apart. But no matter, in the forest of language, I'm always Alice in Wonderland, the little Red Riding Hood who chats with the Big Wolf, enters his stomach, then tumbles out with double axes.

One axe is my Chinese sense of time, which is ruled by the moon instead of the sun, which doesn't always run a linear line of logic. Unlike English, in which a word is spelled out horizontally with alphabetic order, which predetermines the linear quality of image, time, and thought process, a Chinese character is an ideogram, a direct and indirect copy of images from nature. Each word stands as a square unit built with straight vertical and horizontal lines, long and short curves, angles, hooks, dots, and so on, laid out with positions and movements of up and down, left and right, inside and out. And each unit is put together with different parts, with their own meanings and sounds, their own units of positions, directions, and movements. The word bright 明 is made of two parts: the sun and the moon standing next to each. For wife, 婦, it is a woman holding a broom. Forest, 森, comes into being when three trees grow together and on top of one another. Unlike a phonetic word, a Chinese character is not written as a single line along which image and thought are flattened into a neat, straight order. It is a compound with multiple units, with image within image, image upon image, a flowing, complex contour. Its roots, trunk, and branches are always visible and available to be taken apart and reassembled to form new meanings, new perspectives, new horizons.

> Home—家—*Jia:* a roof under which animals live.
>
> . . . . . . . . . . . . . . . . . . . .
>
> House—房—*fang:* a door over a square, a place, a direction.
>
> . . . . . . . . . . . . . . . . . . . . . . . . .
>
> Room—屋—*wu:* a body unnamed and homeless until it finds
> a destination.
>
> —my tangled roots for home. (from "Mixed Blood")

Without my other axe of English, however, I'd be walking, like most native speakers, in the forest of three thousand years of Chinese tradition and poetics, my eyes closed and ears plugged. Home would just be a place where I eat, sleep, and grow old. I would not have seen the roots or searched for the secret doors. I would not have discovered the beasts under its roof, or seen the directions outside its door. I'd have remained an unnamed and homeless body without a destination.

A deconstructed kiss 親 吻 goes like this:

> Parents kiss mouth not.
> Parents, do not kiss mouth.
> Don't kiss parents' mouth.
> Mouth kiss parents? Don't!
> Kiss parents, not mouth.
> "Do not kiss," mouthed the parents.
> (from "Oral")

As I make a new path in my virgin English forest, I also clear the old road in my Chinese one. When the two roads converge, I arrive at a new world of space and time, where the sun and moon shine together in the sky, and I swim in many rivers and run along many paths at the same time. Words, freed from grammar and clichés, become flexible and fluid. A noun is a verb is a preposition is an adjective is a conjunction at once and all times. Words are no longer abstract signs or signifiers. They're concrete, alive, full of sap from nature and pregnant with possible meanings and nuances. And the poem becomes an electric field where motion leaks everywhere, charging and entangling until the ground is no longer a mere existence, but a forest bursting with the noise, drama and myth of life.

> 愛—*ai*—the hand comes first, then the roof, then the heart—心—*xin*. Its three dots spurt and drip like blood over a standing leg. For decades, the heart has been erased from books, papers, magazines. But its pulse has never stopped. It's been pulsing in my grandmas' stories, my sister's waiting for the reunion with her long-lost daughter, in the shafts of sunlight, moonrise, fallen leaves, in the whip my mother carefully placed behind the bedroom door. (from "Ways to Ai 愛")

I write in English, and Chinese always runs as the undercurrent in the process. The two tongues gnash and tear, often at each other's throat, but they feed on each other, expand, intensify and promote each other. They keep me on my toes, opening new doors and taking me to places I'd never have imagined otherwise.

A poetry critic told her Chinese daughter-in-law, "You can be a top lawyer, top essayist, even top fiction writer with English as a second language, but keep poetry to your mother tongue."

After twenty years in America, my English is still broken, full of holes, and I have fallen through them many times. But I've learned to fall with grace, and turned each fall into an adventure. One never knows what lies at the bottom, what world awaits us when we come through the other end. That's the beauty of language and poetry: to see the invisible, to reach the unknown through our gracious fumble and tumble.

A poem must tear away from the mother tongue's zealous cling, must clear the overgrowth, debris, grime, dust, sometimes set a fire, in order to revitalize the forest. A second language gives us new eyes and tools. A poem is not about completion, but process. It is an ocean with mammals and fish and plants, with islands and corals and volcanoes. In this living ocean, we swim and sail, by boat, raft, ship, life-preserver currents of metaphors, between the continents of cultures and languages.

Poetry may indeed belong to the mother tongue, but it also belongs to the heart that no logic or rules can bind, to the myth of life that sings with multiple voices.

# Chen Li

*(b. 1954)*

Chen Li was born and raised in Hualien, Taiwan. After graduating from the English department of National Taiwan Normal University in 1976, he returned to his hometown and taught in junior high school. In recent years he has taught creative writing at National Dong Hwa University and has been the organizer of the annual Pacific Poetry Festival in his hometown. Chen Li started writing poetry in the 1970s, under the influence of modernism. He turned to social and political themes in the 1980s and, from the 1990s onward, has explored a wide range of subjects and styles, combining formal and linguistic experiments with concern for indigenous culture and formation of a new Taiwanese identity. He has published more than ten books of poetry, including *Animal Lullaby* (1980), *Love Song of Buffet the Clown* (1990), *Traveling in the Family* (1993), *The Edge of the Island* (1995), *The Cat at the Mirror* (1999), *The Well-Tempered Clavier of Anguish and Freedom* (2005), and *Microcosmos: Two Hundred Modern Haiku* (2006). Compared with the poets of the generation of Ji Xian who advocated "horizontal transplantation," Chen Li's generation not only borrows and learns from both Western and Oriental (Japanese) poetics, but also cherishes the heritage of Chinese poetry and redefines the culture of Taiwan. Chen Li is also a prolific prose writer and translator. In collaboration with his wife Chang Fen-ling, he has translated into Chinese the works of many poets, such as Plath, Heaney, Neruda, Paz, Sachs, and Szymborska, and has published over a dozen volumes of translations, including *Anthology of Modern Latin American Poetry* (1989) and *One Hundred Famous Love Poems of the World* (2000).

In this new essay, Chen Li describes the influences of translation on his own work, how it has affected his evolution as a poet, and how linguistic experimentation is at the heart of what he does.

## Traveling Between Languages

*0*

Language is communication of feeling, thought, etc., through a set or system of formalized symbols, signs, sounds, or gestures. Chinese, English, and dialects in Taiwan (Min Nan and Hakka dialects, for example) are languages; music, painting, and mathematics are also languages. While notes and colors are the languages used by composers and painters, words are the language I use to write; while some writers use other systems of words, I write in Chinese.

I also translate works written in other languages into Chinese. To me, translation is a substitute for reading and writing. I'm not an active reader. To translate, I force myself to read more widely or attentively. I am not an active writer, either. Through translating others' works, I get some compensation and stimulation—in translating a work, I mistake it for my own, feeling that I'm writing again; during or after the process of translation, I inevitably acquire some inspiration or dynamic for my writing by getting closer to others' works.

I sometimes feel writing is another form of translation: while writing, I integrate or transform into my works my experiences of reading, translating, or having access to other languages (English, Japanese, etc.; music, painting, etc.)—either consciously or unconsciously. Therefore, I, as a writer, travel from language to language frequently.

*I*

I was born in Taiwan after the Second World War and brought up in Hualien, a small city in eastern Taiwan. My parents grew up in the period while Taiwan was occupied and governed by Japan. Therefore, in my childhood and youth, I spoke Chinese (Mandarin) at school and Taiwanese (Min Nan dialect) at home, and my parents talked to each other in Japanese most of the time. My mother is a native speaker of Hakka dialect, so I could often hear her talk in Hakka dialect with her relatives living in the neighborhood. After graduating from the university, I returned from Taipei to my hometown and worked as an English teacher in a junior high school. In a class of forty students, there were two or three aboriginal (mostly Amis and Atayal) students. They spoke Chinese just like the other students.

When I studied in the English department of the National Taiwan Normal University in Taipei, I started to read literary works of foreign writers in the original or in translation, including those of Yeats, Eliot, Rilke, Baudelaire, Rimbaud, and some Japanese haiku poets. Since my graduation from the university, I, in collaboration with my wife, Chang Fen-ling, have translated into Chinese many poems of foreign poets, such as Larkin, Hughes, Plath, Heaney, Sachs, Vallejo, Neruda, Paz, Szymborska—they all have had an influence on me. Among them, Neruda's influence seems the most obvious because we have translated at least three books of his poems.

In my university days I chose Spanish as my second foreign language and came to take an interest in Latin American literature. I was not a good learner of Spanish, but I found Spanish sounded delightful, which motivated me to read Spanish poems. I bought some bilingual (Spanish and English) collections of Latin American poetry; they seemed not too hard to comprehend. In 1978 I set about translating an anthology of modern Latin American poetry. It had been completed by 1985. However, not until 1989 was the book published. Included in it (more than six hundred pages) are nearly two hundred poems by twenty-nine poets.

Since my high school days, I have enjoyed listening to music. Composers like Bartók and Debussy influenced and inspired me when I was very young. Later, Webern, Janáçek, Messiaen, and Berio also became my favorites. After attending university, I started to read books about painting and to appreciate the works of many cubist, surrealist, and expressionist painters—Picasso, Braque, Dalí, Magritte, Ensor, and Kokoschka, for instance. They too played a part in my aesthetic development. In my university days, a school librarian gave me an old issue of *Chicago Review* (a special issue on concrete poetry), published in September 1967. This issue left quite a deep impression on me and contributed to my later writing of concrete poetry to a certain extent.

*2*

For the past few decades, the Chinese language used by the people in Taiwan has been in many ways different from that used by the people in mainland China. The differences lie not only in its expressions, accents, pronunciations, and characters but also in its linguistic "temperament." In my opinion, the Chinese language used in Taiwan has some sort of vitality different from that used in mainland China. For one thing, whereas mainland China made great efforts to wipe off its traditions, started the Great Cultural Revolution, and implemented a simplified form of Chinese characters, Taiwan, under the rule of the KMT after the Second World War, advocated the "Movement of Reviving Chinese Culture," continued to use the traditional complex form of characters, and put Chinese classical literature and history on the examination list—the result of the different policies is that people or writers in Taiwan are likely to have a more profound understanding and a subtler perception of "the beauty of Chinese" than people or writers in mainland China. For another, being an island, Taiwan enjoys more liberal and freer living environments, which enables people in Taiwan to assimilate more naturally and freely diverse elements of language (Taiwanese, Japanese, and English in particular) and elements of daily life to form a more flexible, energetic, hybridized, and colorful language.

Chinese, with its pictographs, monosyllables, homonyms, and characters with multiple meanings or similar pronunciations, has a savor that is rarely found in other languages. A Chinese poem written in traditional complex characters is likely to lose part of the savor if one should transcribe it in simplified characters. Thus, I feel that the Chinese or the Chinese poem I write in Taiwan has absolutely a savor that may be absent in works written by users of other languages or Chinese users in other areas. Judging from what modern poetry of Taiwan has achieved for the past few decades, the Chinese language in Taiwan has indeed evolved and created new sensibility, interest, and vitality.

In my poem "Breakfast Tablecloth of a Solitary Entomologist" I collect all the Chinese characters with "虫" (meaning "insect") as their radicals. This character tablecloth, made of numerous strokes and swarmed with insects, would be out of shape or lose its savor if it were printed in simplified characters. For example, the traditional complex character "蝟" would be simplified into "猬"—the radical "虫" would be turned into "犭" (meaning "dog"); "蠱" and "蠶" would become "蛊" and "蚕"—several insects would be missing:

虭虮虯虰虱虳虴虷虹虺虻虼蚅蚆蚇蚊
蚋蚌蚍蚎蚐蚑蚓蚔蚕蚖蚗蚘蚙蚚蚜蚝
蚞蚡蚢蚣蚤蚥蚧蚨蚩蚪蚯蚰蚱蚳蚴蚵
蚶蚷蚸蚹蚺蚻蚼蚽蚾蚿蛀蛁蛂蛃蛄蛅
蛆蛇蛈蛉蛋蛌蛐蛑蛓蛔蛖蛗蛘蛙蛚蛛
蛜蛝蛞蛟蛢蛣蛤蛦蛨蛩蛪蛫蛬蛭蛵蛶
蛷蛸蛹蛺蛻蛾蜀蜁蜂蜃蜄蜅蜆蜇蜈蜉
蜊蜋蜌蜍蜎蜑蜒蜓蜘蜙蜚蜛蜜蜞蜠蜡
蜢蜣蜤蜥蜦蜧蜨蜩蜪蜬蜭蜮蜰蜱蜲蜳
蜴蜵蜷蜸蜺蜻蜼蜾蜿蝀蝁蝂蝃蝆蝌蝍
蝎蝏蝐蝑蝒蝓蝔蝕蝖蝗蝘蝙蝚蝛蝜蝝
蝞蝟蝠蝡蝢蝣蝤蝥蝦蝧蝨蝩蝪蝫蝬蝭
蝮蝯蝳蝴蝵蝶蝷蝸蝹蝺蝻螁螂螃螄螅
螇螈螉融螏　螐螑螒螓螔螖螗螘螚螛
螜螝螞螟螢螣螤螥螌螬螭螮螯螰螲螳
螴螵螶螷螸螹螺螻螼螽螾螿蟀蟂　蟃
蟄蟅蟆蟈蟉蟊蟋蟌蟑蟒蟓蟔蟗蟘蟙蟚
蟜蟝蟞蟟蟠蟡蟢蟣蟤蟥蟦蟧蟨蟪蟫蟬
蟭蟯蟳蟴蟶蟷蟹蟺　蟻蟼蟾蠀蠁蠂蠃
蠅蠆蠈蠉蠊蠋蠌蠍蠐蠑蠓蠔蠕蠖蠗蠙
蠛蠜蠝蠟　蠠蠡蠢蠣蠤蠥　蠦蠨蠩蠪
蠫蠬蠮蠯蠰蠱蠲蠳蠶蠸蠹蠻蠼蠽蠾蠿

Years ago I wrote a poem, "A War Symphony," which consists of many lines but only of four characters—"兵", "乒", "乓", and "丘" (you may even say it's composed of only one character, "兵", since the other three characters can be seen as its transformations):

兵兵兵兵兵兵兵兵兵兵兵兵兵兵兵兵兵兵兵兵兵兵兵兵
兵兵兵兵兵兵兵兵兵兵兵兵兵兵兵兵兵兵兵兵兵兵兵兵
兵兵兵兵兵兵兵兵兵兵兵兵兵兵兵兵兵兵兵兵兵兵兵兵
兵兵兵兵兵兵兵兵兵兵兵兵兵兵兵兵兵兵兵兵兵兵兵兵
兵兵兵兵兵兵兵兵兵兵兵兵兵兵兵兵兵兵兵兵兵兵兵兵
兵兵兵兵兵兵兵兵兵兵兵兵兵兵兵兵兵兵兵兵兵兵兵兵
兵兵兵兵兵兵兵兵兵兵兵兵兵兵兵兵兵兵兵兵兵兵兵兵
兵兵兵兵兵兵兵兵兵兵兵兵兵兵兵兵兵兵兵兵兵兵兵兵
兵兵兵兵兵兵兵兵兵兵兵兵兵兵兵兵兵兵兵兵兵兵兵兵
兵兵兵兵兵兵兵兵兵兵兵兵兵兵兵兵兵兵兵兵兵兵兵兵
兵兵兵兵兵兵兵兵兵兵兵兵兵兵兵兵兵兵兵兵兵兵兵兵
兵兵兵兵兵兵兵兵兵兵兵兵兵兵兵兵兵兵兵兵兵兵兵兵
兵兵兵兵兵兵兵兵兵兵兵兵兵兵兵兵兵兵兵兵兵兵兵兵
兵兵兵兵兵兵兵兵兵兵兵兵兵兵兵兵兵兵兵兵兵兵兵兵
兵兵兵兵兵兵兵兵兵兵兵兵兵兵兵兵兵兵兵兵兵兵兵兵
兵兵兵兵兵兵兵兵兵兵兵兵兵兵兵兵兵兵兵兵兵兵兵兵

兵兵兵兵兵兵兵乒兵兵兵兵兵兵兵乓兵兵兵兵兵兵兵乒
兵兵兵乓兵兵乒兵兵兵乒乒兵兵乒乓兵兵乒乓兵兵乓乓
乒乒兵兵兵兵乓乓乓乓兵兵乒乒乓乓乒乓兵乓兵兵乓乓
兵乒兵乒乒乒乓乓兵兵乒乒乓乓乓乓乒乒乓乓乒兵乓乓
乒兵乓乓乒兵乓乓乒乒乓乓乒乒乓乓乒乒乓乓乒乒乓乓
乒乒乓乓乒乒乓乓乒乒乓乓乒乒乓乓乒乒乓乓乒乒乓乓
乒乒乓乓乒乒乓乓乒乒乓乓乒乒乓乓乒乒乓乓乒乒乓乓
乒乓乒乓乒乓乒乓乒乓乒乓乒乓乒乓乒乓乒乓乒乓乒乓
乒乓乒乓乒乒乓乓乒乓乒乓乒乒乓乓乒乓乒乓乒乒乓乓
乒乒乒乒乒乒乒乒乓乓乓乓乓乓乓乓乒乒　乒乒乒　乓
乓乓　乒乓乒乒　乒　乓　乒乒　　　　乒乒　　乓乓
乒乒　　乓乒　乒　乓　乒　乓　乒乒乒　　乓　乒
　乒乒　乓　乓乓　乒　　乒　乓　　乒　乓　　　乒
乒　　　　　　乓乓　　　　　　乓　　　　乒　乓
　乒　　　乓　　　　乒　　　　　乓　　　　乓
　　　乒　　　　　　　　　　　　　乓

丘丘丘丘丘丘丘丘丘丘丘丘丘丘丘丘丘丘丘丘丘丘丘丘
丘丘丘丘丘丘丘丘丘丘丘丘丘丘丘丘丘丘丘丘丘丘丘丘
丘丘丘丘丘丘丘丘丘丘丘丘丘丘丘丘丘丘丘丘丘丘丘丘
丘丘丘丘丘丘丘丘丘丘丘丘丘丘丘丘丘丘丘丘丘丘丘丘
丘丘丘丘丘丘丘丘丘丘丘丘丘丘丘丘丘丘丘丘丘丘丘丘
丘丘丘丘丘丘丘丘丘丘丘丘丘丘丘丘丘丘丘丘丘丘丘丘
丘丘丘丘丘丘丘丘丘丘丘丘丘丘丘丘丘丘丘丘丘丘丘丘

丘丘丘丘丘丘丘丘丘丘丘丘丘丘丘丘丘丘丘丘丘丘丘丘
丘丘丘丘丘丘丘丘丘丘丘丘丘丘丘丘丘丘丘丘丘丘丘丘
丘丘丘丘丘丘丘丘丘丘丘丘丘丘丘丘丘丘丘丘丘丘丘丘
丘丘丘丘丘丘丘丘丘丘丘丘丘丘丘丘丘丘丘丘丘丘丘丘
丘丘丘丘丘丘丘丘丘丘丘丘丘丘丘丘丘丘丘丘丘丘丘丘
丘丘丘丘丘丘丘丘丘丘丘丘丘丘丘丘丘丘丘丘丘丘丘丘
丘丘丘丘丘丘丘丘丘丘丘丘丘丘丘丘丘丘丘丘丘丘丘丘
丘丘丘丘丘丘丘丘丘丘丘丘丘丘丘丘丘丘丘丘丘丘丘丘
丘丘丘丘丘丘丘丘丘丘丘丘丘丘丘丘丘丘丘丘丘丘丘丘

"兵" (*bing*) signifies a soldier. "乒" (*ping*) and "乓" (*pong*) are onomatopoeias that sound like gunshots but look like one-armed or one-legged soldiers; when combined, they are associated with ping-pong (table tennis). "丘" (*qiu*), meaning small hill, has the implication of "tomb." This poem may be my best-known work, but I think it is hard to translate. Most translators simply translate its title and attach to it an annotation, but leave the original intact. However, one day I surfed the Internet and found that Bohdan Piasecki, a Pole who taught translation in England, had translated it into English. In the first stanza, he substitutes "A man" for "兵". In the second stanza, "Ah man" and "Ah men" are used to replace the scattered "乒" and "乓". And in the third stanza, "丘" is replaced by "Amen," which may be interpreted as a prayer at the funeral. It is an interesting translation. Through translation, the translator re-creates the poem.

I often tell others that I am not the real author of this poem. I was simply possessed by "Chinese characters": one morning I woke up, turned on the computer, took five minutes to key in and duplicate those four characters, and then it was completed. In my prose "The Delight of Animations," I mentioned "Konflikt" (Conflict), an animation made by the Russian animator Garry Bardin (b. 1941) in 1983. A green match troop comes into conflict with a blue match troop; they burn each other to death. This animation never crossed my mind when I was writing "A War Symphony." Not until a female artist in Taiwan re-presented it in the form of animation did it occur to me. You may say my poem translates Bardin's film. Some reader mentioned on the Internet that there might be some relation between "A War Symphony" and the poem "Ping Pong," written in 1953 by the German poet Eugen Gomringer (b. 1925). I searched for the poem immediately and found I had never read it before. Yet this poem is very much like a translated version of part of the second stanza of "A War Symphony":

ping pong
        ping pong ping
        pong ping pong
                    ping pong

I think this may be regarded as a coincidental encounter of two writers while they are traveling in languages. And such a happy encounter transcends time and space.

*3*

In 1983, in collaboration with Chang Fen-ling, I translated and published *Selected Poems of Nelly Sachs* and *The Divine Arias: Dante*. Translating works by Nelly Sachs and Dante was a very peculiar experience for me. Before that, I knew nothing about Jewish mysticism, and had little interest in imagined afterlife or heavenly blessing. But translating forced me to read; after reading, I got confused, started to ponder, and was greatly touched. I can never forget the thrill I felt while reading the last few cantos of "Paradise" of *The Divine Comedy*. What a great and magnificent imagination! What abstract and pure order! Neither can I forget the peculiar joy I felt when my heart was pierced with Sachs's pure, mysterious, persevering lyricism, even though I am still an atheist. These marvelous imaginations and creations are concerned not only with religion (or one religion), but with all mankind. Besides being realistic, I learn to see things in other ways. To me, translation means conveying concretely and clearly to others the touching experience I have had through reading. And it is a translator's job to transform the experience into a motive force with a clear direction. The translation that enables readers to fully feel what you have felt is a good translation.

Comparatively speaking, Latin American literature can more easily touch the hearts of people growing up in Taiwan. This may be partly because the Third World countries are in a similar situation when faced with the impact of Western literary trends. I have always felt the development of modern poetry in Taiwan is actually the epitome of the history of modern Latin American poetry, except that their progress or problems came twenty years earlier than ours. The ultimate question is: How do we preserve or manifest the local characteristics in the process of westernization or modernization? Magic realism is the distinct answer Latin America has given. But there is more than one answer, and each answer has its own meaning. No doubt, surrealism allows many poets in Latin America and in Taiwan to have more ways of viewing the world. Reading and translating Latin American literature teaches me to combine elements of Taiwan with modern or postmodern art. To put this into practice, I appropriate or re-create (or de-create) the myths and legends of Taiwanese aborigines in some of my poems. The following is an example: "A fly has flown onto the sticky flypaper below the goddess's navel. / Just as the day hammers gently on the night, / my dear ancestor, hammer gently with the unused Neolithic tool between your thighs." (According to the Atayal myth of the creation, there were a god and a goddess in very ancient times who were ignorant of love-making until one day a fly landed on the private part of the goddess; the Amis have a similar myth.) Words like "flypaper" and "Neolithic tool" integrate the past with the present, adding to the poem a postmodern interest and making it both legendary and contemporary, tribalistic and erotic.

The first poem I translated of Neruda's is "Explico algunas cosas" (I Explain a Few Things), taken from *Residencia en la tierra* (Residence on Earth). This poem states the reason for the transformation of his poetic style—because of the outbreak of the Spanish civil war, his poetry begins to move away from the obscure, hermetic, and fanciful to a clearer and more accessible style. The last few lines are very touching: "You will ask: why doesn't your poetry tell us / about dreams, about leaves, / about the great volcanoes of your native land? // Come and see the blood in the streets, / come and see / the blood in the streets, / come and see the blood / in the streets!"

As a writer, I think my poetic language and concepts are evidently influenced by my experience of translating Neruda. However, I am not sure whether my poetic language—with Chinese as its tool—is influenced by Neruda's original poems or by my Chinese translation of his poems. The poetic strategy and ideas in some of my poems indeed derive from

Neruda. In 1979 I translated his "Alturas de Macchu Picchu" (The Heights of Macchu Picchu), a long poem in *Canto General.* The theme of death and birth, of oppression and rising, and the idea that poets should be sufferers' spokesmen have since been deep-rooted in my heart. In this poem Neruda piles up a litany of seventy-two noun phrases, which inspires me to boldly juxtapose thirty-six noun phrases in "The Last Wang Mu-Qi," a long poem written the next year about a mining calamity. Later, in the poem "Taroko Gorge, 1989," I apply the technique of cataloging, listing forty-eight names of places in the Atayal language, and in the poem "Flight over the Island," I list ninety-five names of mountains of Taiwan deriving from different languages. All these can be seen as an extension of Neruda's writing techniques. But they may also be traced back to another poem in *Residencia en la tierra:* "Como era España" (What Spain Was Like). In the first four stanzas, Neruda describes how he loves the tough land and the humble people of Spain; in the last six stanzas, he lists fifty-two names of Spanish towns. I didn't translate this poem because I didn't think it was successfully written since the names were cataloged in a rather flat way (when the famous English translator of Neruda, Ben Belitt, translated this poem, he omitted the last six stanzas, which impressed me). In "Taroko Gorge, 1989" or "Flight over the Island," I try to make the groups of nouns form a certain dialectic relationship to the other part of the poem. Reading them over is like undergoing a ritual of identity, a return to the native land where different races are reunited. Neruda's cataloging, in turn, may have been influenced by another Chilean poet, Vicente Huidobro (1893–1948), who listed 190 noun phrases with "Molino" (Mill) as the initial word in canto V of his 600-line-long avant-garde epic poem *Altazor.*

In *Anthology of Modern Latin American Poetry*, I translate five poems of Huidobro's. Among them, "Nipona" (Japanese), printed in the shape of a double arrowhead, is the only concrete poem in the anthology. I found it quite interesting the first time I read it.

### *4*

Although I can't read Japanese, even so I have read and translated some Japanese haiku and tanka through English translation and the original, because there are many Chinese characters in Japanese and because I can always consult my father, who knows Japanese. Reading these Japanese poems inspires me to write about contemporary life in similar poetic forms. The result of such experimentation is my book of three-line poems: *Microcosmos: Two Hundred Modern Haiku*, whose title comes from Bartók's *Microcosmos*, a musical composition containing 153 piano pieces. Patterning after or imitating senior masters (or using allusions) is in itself part of the convention of haiku. Some of my "modern haiku" are tributes to or variations of classical haiku or other art classics; others are evolved from poems written by senior writers, fellow poets, or myself. Whether they are metamorphosed thoroughly, reshaped, or implanted, traveling in the family of poetry forms the most substantial and warmest link on the lonesome journey in the universe. ("Traveling in the Family," the title of one of my poems and of one of my books of poetry, comes from the Brazilian poet Carlos Drummond de Andrade [1902–87], whose poem of the same title is translated in my *Anthology of Modern Latin American Poetry*.) My three-line poems are "Taiwanese" rather than "Nipona." They manifest the savor of "Taiwanese Chinese": at once Chinese and Taiwanese, classical and contemporary, just like the island of Taiwan, which constantly assimilates and converges all the surrounding elements because of its geography and history. Take, for example, some poems I've read, translated, or written:

> Picking chrysanthemums by the east hedge, at ease I see the south mountain. (T'ao Ch'ien, 365–427)
>
> At ease he sees the south mountain—this frog. (Kobayashi Issa, 1763–1827)
>
> Resting on the temple bell, asleep, a butterfly. (Yosa Buson, 1716–1784)
>
> Resting on the temple bell, glowing, a firefly. (Masaoka Shiki, 1867–1902)
>
> He washes his horse with the setting sun on the autumn sea. (Masaoka Shiki)
>
> He washes his remote control / with the moonbeams infiltrating / between two buildings. (Chen Li, *Microcosmos*, I: 1)
>
> I wait and long for you: / a turning die in the empty bowl of night / attempting to create the 7th side. (*Microcosmos*, I: 14)
>
> A turning die in the empty bowl of the night / creates the 7th side: / oh God, you do exist. (*Microcosmos*, II: 25)

> Multiplication table for kids of clouds: / mountains times mountains equals trees, mountains times trees / equals me, mountains times me equals nothingness . . . (*Microcosmos*, I: 51)
>
> The story of marriage: a closet of loneliness plus / a closet of loneliness equals / a closet of loneliness. (*Microcosmos*, I: 97)

Just as the "frog" in Issa's haiku defamiliarizes and freshens the perspective of the ancient Chinese poet T'ao Ch'ien, I use the "remote control" to translate and update the elegantly lonely life scene of Shiki. Both are resting on the temple bell—Shiki's glowing firefly vividly stirs the serenity of Buson's soundly sleeping butterfly. And in my poems the same die tosses out a different imagination at a different time and space, attesting to the ambiguity of the existence of God or miracles and to the anxiety and fragility of man. The last two poems are written based on "pseudo-arithmetical" formulas. Maybe they could be seen as examples of how modern poetry in Taiwan creates surprise out of the commonplace.

## 5

In 1976 I wrote a ten-line poem, "Footprints in the Snow," whose title comes from a piano piece by the French composer Debussy (*Preludes*, book 1, no. 6). I attempted to translate Debussy's musical work into poetry: "Cold makes for sleep, / deep / sleep, for / a feeling soft as a swan. / Where the snow is soft, a hastily scrawled line is left / in white, white / ink, / hastily because of his mood, and the cold: / the hastily scrawled / white snow." Several composers have set this poem to music; by so doing, they have translated it back into music. In 1995 I wrote another "Footprints in the Snow." You may say it was a translated version of the previous poem, but this time I used noncharacter symbols and punctuation marks only:

%

%

%

%

•

.

.

A similar self-translation appears in *Microcosmos:*

> Your voices suspend in my room
> cutting through silence, to become
> a bulb speaking with heat or chill.
> (*Microcosmos*, II: 47)

> ……
> 。
> ，
> (*Microcosmos*, II: 48)

The latter poem can be viewed as a translation or visualization of the former poem. The Chinese punctuation mark "。" (a period) is very much like a bulb that gives off sound in silence or with silence.

Is writing some kind of translation, traveling between languages? Or do all writers create the same work, the pure blankness and the empty fullness overwritten again and again? Recently I wrote a poem called "White." The first half consists of two Chinese characters, "白" (white) and "日" (day); the other part is made up of noncharacters. After this poem was completed, the paintings of Mark Rothko (1903–70), an American painter whom I like very much, came into my mind:

白白白白白白白白白白白白白白白白白白白白白白白白
白白白白白白白白白白白白白白白白白白白白白白白白
白白白白白白白白白白白白白白白白白白白白白白白白
白白白白白白白白白白白白白白白白白白白白白白白白
白白白白白白白白白白白白白白白白白白白白白白白白
白白白白白白白白白白白白白白白白白白白白白白白白
日日日日日日日日日日日日日日日日日日日日日日日日
日日日日日日日日日日日日日日日日日日日日日日日日
日日日日日日日日日日日日日日日日日日日日日日日日
日日日日日日日日日日日日日日日日日日日日日日日日
日日日日日日日日日日日日日日日日日日日日日日日日
日日日日日日日日日日日日日日日日日日日日日日日日
凵凵凵凵凵凵凵凵凵凵凵凵凵凵凵凵凵凵凵凵凵凵凵凵
凵凵凵凵凵凵凵凵凵凵凵凵凵凵凵凵凵凵凵凵凵凵凵凵
凵凵凵凵凵凵凵凵凵凵凵凵凵凵凵凵凵凵凵凵凵凵凵凵
凵凵凵凵凵凵凵凵凵凵凵凵凵凵凵凵凵凵凵凵凵凵凵凵
凵凵凵凵凵凵凵凵凵凵凵凵凵凵凵凵凵凵凵凵凵凵凵凵
— — — — — — — — — — — — — — — — — — — — — — — —

— — — — — — — — — — — — — — — — — — — — — — — — —
— — — — — — — — — — — — — — — — — — — — — — — — —
— — — — — — — — — — — — — — — — — — — — — — — — —
..........................................................................................
..........................................................................................
..........................................................................................
..........................................................................................
..........................................................................................
..........................................................................................

*Translated by Chang Fen-ling*

# Leung Ping-kwan (Liang Bingjun)

*(b. 1949)*

Leung Ping-kwan grew up in Hong Kong, and his family home had many books that ranged from classical Chinese poetry to modern fiction. Exposed to a unique combination of highbrow and popular culture, he began to write in the late 1960s and learned his craft by translating contemporary French fiction, Latin American fiction, and American literature into Chinese. In 1972 he and some friends began editing a new journal, *Four Seasons*. He has now published more than ten volumes of poems, including such bilingual editions as *City at the End of Time* (1982), *Foodscape* (1997), *Clothink* (1998), and *Travelling with a Bitter Melon* (2002). He was writer-in-residence in Berlin in 1998 and published two volumes of poems in German translation. In the summer of 2006 his residency in southern France coincided with the publication of *De ci de là des choses,* a volume of poems in French translation. He also writes fiction and has published a novel and four collections of stories, among them *Islands and Continents* in English (HKU Press, 2007) and in French translation (*Îles et Continents*, Gallimard, 2002). He was awarded the Hong Kong Urban Council's Biennial Award for Literature in 1991 (fiction) and 1997 (poetry). He teaches literature and film studies at Lingnan University, and his extensive publications on urban culture and film studies include *Hong Kong Culture* (1995) and *Hong Kong Literature and Cinema* (2005). He has collaborated with various visual and performing artists, fashion designers, and cultural workers, and had his poetry and photograph exhibitions, "Food and the City" and "East West Matters," shown in Hong Kong, Frankfurt, and Bern.

His essay below was written in 1998 for a special issue on contemporary Chinese culture in the German journal *Lettres*.

## Confronting the Multiple Deaths of the Chinese Language

My impression of my father is blurred. I can only recall the day that Mother held me up so that I could stick a sheet of yellow paper onto his cold forehead. I was four. I remember the joss paper burning in the flames—what turned into ashes had once been the sudden dart of fiery tongues among dark symbols, along with the dread of that unspeakable name in the alien stillness. Afterward, bits and pieces leaked from grown-ups' whispers led me to vaguely understand that he was upset: Mother hadn't stayed to keep him company when his soul returned home three nights later, so in a fit of anger he knocked the sacrificial offerings off the table. Immediately, people scurried to arrange the food and drink as nicely as before; more than one claimed to have heard the toppling of the table and chairs, the loud clear rattle of plates and cups shattering onto the floor. I could only learn the truth from such adult gossip. In the end what I gleaned was that behind the immediate reality, there was another unknown world.

At that time, my mother wasn't in the room. She'd heeded the advice of relatives and was staying somewhere not too far from her family's home. She was a filial child who'd devoted her whole life to caring for her parents and brothers, following the traditional teachings of how to be a dutiful eldest daughter. My maternal grandfather had been a government official in the Nationalist Party. When the political situation changed in 1949, he left Guangdong for British-ruled Hong Kong. In the spirit of an ancient scholar who has retreated from public life after suffering misfortune, he made a living running a small farm on the southern end of Hong Kong Island. Plucking papayas and pomegranates from eastern hedges, he leisurely planted crops and raised chickens near Nam Lang Hill.[1] My young but earnest father couldn't find work and eventually moved with my mother to a little place next to the farm, where they grew their own vegetables. Disheartened, and afflicted with a chronic illness that remained too long untreated, in the end he died of despair. My maternal grandfather was the master of the house, ordering the rest of the family around. In his free time he either recited classical prose or recounted treatises by Cantonese geniuses such as Chan Mung-kat that were filled with witty couplets and tales of twisting wordplay.[2] Grandfather excelled at calligraphy, and at each New Year's celebration the neighbors would call on him to dash off a few antithetical couplets on spring. Proud, he was fond of talking about the glorious history of those years in the Mainland. In the old days, subordinates would deliver presents on such holidays; my mother and her brothers remember how back in China, the rooms of their spacious house would be stacked high with gifts of mooncakes, and my eldest uncle would secretly dig out the egg-yolk centers, devouring them without getting caught. Restless, Grandfather roamed the small islands of Hong Kong, somewhat despising this place for its lack of culture. He cherished the memory of people and customs of a bygone era, yet he also felt that in this tiny present realm, the model of earlier times still endured. But as a child I began to rebel against these practices as soon as I realized that they wouldn't allow my mother to cross the threshold of their ancestral home on New Year's Day. They disliked the fact that their daughter was a widow, fearing she would bring bad luck.

1. Nam Lang Hill (Nam Lang Shan), also known as Brick Hill, is located on the south side of Hong Kong Island, overlooking the South China Sea. Here, Leung references a couplet from Tao Yuanming's (365–427) famous poem "Drinking Wine": "I pluck chrysanthemums from the eastern hedge / Leisurely gazing at South Mountain" (*Nam Shan* in Cantonese). Tao Yuanming (also known as Tao Qian) was dissatisfied with officialdom and withdrew to the countryside; he has come to represent the paradigm of a poet who has eschewed a political career in favor of cultivating a carefree, eremitic lifestyle.

2. Chan Mung-kat (Chen Mengji) was a famous Cantonese lawyer and scholar during the Qing dynasty who was renowned for his wit and is considered one of the four greatest lawyers of Guangdong province.

If my father were alive, perhaps he too would have rebelled against these small-town superstitions. In an iron building on the farm, I discovered an entire attic's worth of used books, all of which had been brought to Hong Kong by my parents and uncles. Among them were writings by Lu Xun and Tao Fen, translations of Shakespeare and old Russian novels, fairy tales and classical fiction, as well as popular martial arts, detective, and humor magazines that had been all the rage in 1950s Hong Kong. I read them intermittently. Whenever I was unhappy I would hide in the book world, thinking that among the hodgepodge of words, I might find things nonexistent in the real world. These linguistic conglomerations also offered alternative attitudes toward perceptions of reality. I fumbled about the cracks, checking out the collected works of some left-wing writers whom my father supposedly adored, but I had to put them down. I preferred reading love stories, translated fiction, and Eileen Chang.

My maternal grandfather read the right-leaning *Hong Kong Times* and *Overseas Chinese Daily News*. Each October 10, these papers would display the symbols of the Nationalist Party flag: blue sky, white sun, the ground completely red. Moreover, they also featured Chiang Kai-shek's presidential address in Taiwan and predictions of "counterattacks against the Mainland," inciting my grandfather to excitedly rise, asserting, "For sure it'll be this year!" He was familiar with *yin* and *yang* and the five elements, with geomancy and *fengshui*, and yet each year he still contemplated "victory," estimating the distance between country and individual. Like a majestic high priest of meandering words, with a writing brush, he foretold fates on sheet after sheet of rice paper, but I always half-believed, half-doubted his prognostications. Yet while I resisted the language of Grandfather's politics and superstitions, I didn't completely buy into Father's venerated utopian discourse, either. Those convoluted sentences comprised of arcane diction, inciting arbitrary attacks, seemed to belong to a departed era; it's as though the language had been buried along with my father. What remained were the spectral characters and plots of translated literary works, as well as fiery-tongued sentences that would ooze from the ashes if poked with a dusty stick.

Nevertheless, I was most familiar with the sounds of Mother and Auntie competing to recite ancient poetry and prose as they worked from home pasting matchbooks and stringing chains of beads. Bai Juyi's "Song of Everlasting Sorrow," Du Fu's "Ballad of the Army Carts," Tao Yuanming's "The Return," Li Ling's "A Reply to Su Wu," Zhuge Liang's "First Memorial on Dispatching the Troops," and Su Dongpo's "Former Red Cliff Rhapsody" and "Latter Red Cliff Rhapsody"—it was a game of you say a line, then I deliver the next, sometimes starting over because of the other person's mistake, sometimes forgetting then vying to make corrections, an archaic narrative unfurling before one's eyes, breathing vitality into an otherwise tiring and inconsequential workday. It was different from how Grandfather clung to the glory of the past, or how Father died of severe depression. Mother was practical, earning a living from a tedious job, delighted by words used to describe life's different plights and attitudes.

When Mother put me in elementary and middle school, however, I was unable to find such delight from school education. Growing up in Hong Kong, we spoke the Cantonese dialect of Guangdong; the books we studied in school were written in vernacular Chinese, and then official and important matters were all in English. This state of two written and three spoken languages attested to our chaotic cultural condition, but still, this wasn't the most serious problem. The biggest issue was the gap between our school textbooks and actual lives. For example, the books for English class used teaching materials from India and Malaysia: nowhere in Hong Kong are there plantations of rubber trees or tropical fruits. The history department avoided post–Opium War history. The use of English-language science books caused poorer students to be stuck memorizing abstruse vocabulary, never able to connect the scientific concepts with everyday life. In Chinese literature and language courses, textbooks were compiled by educators who'd come from southern China after 1949, featuring esoteric classical prose, or pieces filled with the didacticism of early May Fourth writers, revealing their nostalgia for the motherland mixed with a vague apolitical admiration for Chinese culture. Under conservative teaching methods and a strict examination system, students were trained to study arcane terms, to analyze rhetoric, and to memorize facts of the authors' lives and their talents for allusion, with no regard to critical thinking or the ingenuity of language. Students listened to a generation of teachers from southern China droning about "Beijing in a Snowstorm" or

"The Qinhuai River Amidst the Sound of Oars and Lamplight" who knew absolutely nothing about the places mentioned in the texts. Growing up in this type of educational system, I began observing and writing about the city in which I lived, finding it particularly difficult to locate a precedent to guide me.

The China artificially constructed from the language of textbooks was a symbol of the flickering shadow of the empire. I cut class to wander the city streets of Hong Kong, pondering the relationship between the faces and signs in front of me and that other far-off world hanging above my head. In 1950s and '60s Hong Kong, the airwave novels broadcast on radios gave way to newspapers and serializations of varying political persuasions. In the newly established *Ming Pao*, I read the popular martial-arts stories of Jin Yong. The author used his classical literary training and knowledge of Chinese culture to weave fresh tales of vivid characters and dramatic plots. The more he wrote, the more his work distanced itself from nationalist themes and conventional heroism. Back then, it seemed as though only the cultural setting of Hong Kong was capable of inheriting and reinventing Chinese culture. Around this time, through reading *New Life Evening Post*, I learned that in Kaohsiung, Taiwan, Cantonese was the language used to narrate Hong Kong city life in *Broker La's Diary*. Aside from language and literary form, its content and subject matter demonstrated an attitude that differed from past Mainland Chinese literary works. At the time, what I really liked, however, was reading Eileen Chang's serialized stories in *Sing Tao*. There was also Liu Yichang, who on the one hand published installments of popular fiction in newspapers, and on the other composed experimental stream-of-conscious novels. His works "for entertaining others" and "for entertaining himself"—i.e., both his popular and his avant-garde pieces—coexisted in the space of Hong Kong mass media. In Mother's women's and housekeeping magazines I read even more trendy urban romances, and in recently launched literary journals I encountered modern poetry. Yet in the classroom, whenever I searched for a type of new Chinese language that was conducive to conveying the experience of the modern metropolis, my elderly teachers who'd graduated from Peking University routinely supplied me with four-character idioms that were intended to make my Chinese seem more seasoned. They also always gave me a grade of C-.

Hong Kong in the 1960s and '70s marked an era of fervent nationalism, as well as the city's most westernized phase. Whether we passionately embraced or strongly despised these trends, both failed to bring us closer to the language. In 1974 a friend about my age and I set off to the just-opened Mainland to visit family; each of us emerged disturbed in our own way. In my eyes, the real China and the China I'd read about in books were entirely different. At night, the façades of food stalls were arranged into long troops; inside, people bowed their heads and ate beneath dreary cloth banners criticizing Lin Biao and Confucius. On a chilly night, inside the hotel I spread out the books I'd purchased that day from Xinhua Bookstore. There wasn't a page whose words I could decipher! On my way back, customs officers looked over the photographs I'd taken and claimed that I'd cut off part of one of the slogans, and as a result, they planned to confiscate the picture. I protested, "It wasn't my intention to photograph the slogan to begin with!" The other party remained silent. I increasingly felt the distance between us. As for Chinese slogans, whether they were broken or intact, I found it impossible to feel that they had any vitality. The Chinese language has had multiple deaths. There's no guarantee it won't be pasted as a talisman on someone's forehead, mourning its own passing.

In 1960s Hong Kong, I learned how to write in Chinese. Naturally, I felt the looming pressure of the language piling on me. Strolling through my newly acquainted city, I wondered how to transform outdated words into something that could describe this gritty modern metropolis. Because of the comings and goings of travelers, this port city harbored a wealth of information. In the large bookshops of Central and Tsim Sha Tsui, between colorful book jackets I discovered *Evergreen Review*, *Village Voice*, *Avant-Garde*, and the even rarer *Poland*, all these fugitives! I subscribed to small journals and academic book series, listened to folk music and political protests, and watched European films shown by both cultural associations and private individuals. They expanded the scope of our educational shortcomings and taught us what other contemporary cultural figures were able to accomplish with language. During the 1960s, I began translating many avant-garde works from France, the U.S., and then Latin America—perhaps it was to experiment with the possibilities of Chinese. This also helped me to develop and remold my own writing, making it more colloquial, folklike, and accented with magical symbols, testing my city from various angles.

Strangely, these languages from foreign lands surprised me with marvelous hidden threads that lured me back to Chinese. It didn't matter whether it was the Beat poet Gary Snyder or the clear meditations of Mexican poet Octavio Paz, not to mention Fenollosa and Pound, whom I later devoured with interest. Curiously, their remarks on the Chinese language, beginning with their foreign misreadings, prompted me to rethink previously analyzed classical Chinese texts. Had the unique imagery and the ambiguities of Chinese characters turned the language into a gravestone and a talisman? Or was it a secret paw print, a smoke signal? If even more cultures shared their misinterpretations, would it cause us to lose our noble purity? Or would it urge us to transform our stagnant language into something more vibrant?

The Chinese presently used in Hong Kong is at even greater risk of facing unknown peril among the trends of commercialization and politicization. Both of these cause language to be dulled by monotony and imagination to wither. There are many words that spark complex emotions, but due to educational oversights and the monopoly of the publishing industry, they gradually vanish from our lives. Last year, the celebrated Cantonese opera star (the rich language and imagination of Cantonese opera is also an art form that has been forced into obscurity) Tang Wing-Cheung (known by his stage name of Sun Ma-Sze-Tsang) passed away. Day after day, page after page, the tabloids broadcast his family's disputes over his estate, summing up everyone's wrongdoings. Reporters trailed an undercover detective, making groundless accusations and exaggerating unconfirmed scandals, to the point of creating controversy and fabricating news just to get a rise. Today's language is wasted on chronicling the ostentation of funerals, how the paper gardens and Western-style buildings are spread out, burned, and presented to the dead, along with brand-name cars and all sorts of extravagant offerings. Death has the potential to become a kind of landscape. At the other end, watching Mainland Chinese collectively and unaffectedly waving their hands in front of TV sets as they judge death-row inmates, we outsiders feel that death seems almost trivial, no more than some sort of set design. In blockbuster films and politics, people's deaths are reduced to nothing. If we don't respect death, then how can we respect life?

Recently, artists on Oil Street in North Point, an area the government had developed into studios and galleries, have been using the pluralism of the metropolis to broaden the cultural scene. A future show will incorporate an original government burial chamber into an exhibit on death. Unfortunately, while the space is something novel, the actual exhibit lacks thought and imagination. Images of death are confined to skeletons and memorial tablets, the language stagnating in commonplace four-character idioms. In the past couple of years, although the freedoms of press and speech haven't been quelled in Hong Kong, narrow viewpoints and the depletion of creative powers are revealed beneath the confusion of language and exposure of past misdeeds. Language is as susceptible to being reduced to slogans of commercial sales promotions as it is to slogans of political propaganda. In today's papers, with our own eyes we witness these never-ending deaths of language. Under such circumstances, several different places use Chinese to manufacture people, precisely confronting the initial creation of this kind of death.

*Translated by Jennifer Feeley*

# Xi Chuan

*(b. 1963)*

Xi Chuan is a poet, essayist, and translator. He was born in the city of Xuzhou, Jiangsu Province. From 1981 to 1985, he received his education in the English Department at Beijing University. After graduation, he became an editor of *Globe* magazine, compiled by the Xinhua News Agency, and he currently teaches classical and modern Chinese literature at the Central Academy of Fine Arts in Beijing.

Xi Chuan started writing poetry in 1981 and, in 1988, along with his friends, started an unofficial poetry magazine, *Tendency.* He was on the editorial board of another unofficial magazine, *Modern Han Poetry* (1990–95). In 1989, after his poet-friend Haizi committed suicide, Xi Chuan championed Haizi's work by collecting and collating the posthumous works of the poet. Xi Chuan was awarded the October Prize for literature by the *October Bimonthly* (1988), the prize of *Shanghai Literature Monthly* (1992), the prize of the *People's Literature Monthly* (1994), the Modern Chinese Poetry Prize (1994), the Anne Kao Prize for Poetry (1995), and the Aiwen Prize for Literature (1999). In 2001 he received the national Lu Xun Prize for Literature and, in 1993, the Zhuang Zongwen Prize for Literature. He is the author of many books of poetry, including *Secret Convergence* (1997), *A Fictitious Family Tree* (1997), *Roughly Speaking* (1997), and *Selected Poems of Xi Chuan, 1986–1996* (2002). His essays are published in several volumes, including *Let the Masked*

*Speak* (1997), *Water Stains* (2001), and *Depth and Shallowness: A Selection of Xi Chuan's Poems and Essays* (2006). In the fall of 2002 Xi Chuan was at the International Writing Program at the University of Iowa, and he has also read his poetry at many universities across the United States.

"Chinese as a Language in a Neighborhood," rearranged and rewritten from comments at the Columbia University Poetry and Translation Conference in April 2007, was completed in February 2008. In this essay, Xi Chuan makes many interesting points regarding the evolution of the Chinese language.

## Chinese as a Language in a Neighborhood

*I*

For Chinese to be an independent language, or else to be a language contiguous with other languages, is for us a matter of different significance. Before the language of Ancient Chinese that originated in the central plains had its translated introduction via the archives of Buddhism as Chinese, Chinese had nearly no neighbors. "Nearly," because it had a few small neighbors. In the "Fine Persuasions" in his *Garden of Persuasions,* Liu Xiang recorded a "Song of the Viet,"

> 滥兮抃草滥予昌枑泽予昌州州湛州焉乎秦胥胥漫予乎昭澶秦踰渗惿随何湖

—which is the earliest pigeon-like pidgin recorded in the archives of the Chinese language. Translated into Chinese, it would read:

> What eve is this eve, ho?
> Adrift amidst the River Qian (*variant:* A boat drifts amidst the Qian)
> What day is this day, ho?
> That I share a boat with the Prince
> Conceal me in my shyness, ho,
> I say naught for I'm shy
> Such stupor in my heart and never will it die, ho,
> That I may know my Prince
> A tree is on the mountain, ho, branches on the tree,
> My heart delights at you, ho, and here you know not me.

The archives also contain a number of other non-Han lyrics, such as "The Song of the Huns" recorded in "Old Tales of the Western River," buried in the *Records of the Grand Historian* in the index of "The Tale of the Huns":

> Lost we have the Qilian Mountains,
> Leaving no land to graze for our six herds.
> Gone it is our Yanzhi Mountain,
> Leaving no color on the faces of our wives.

(Two variant texts are contained in the *Collection from the Music Bureau* and the *Collected Gazetteers.*) "The Chronicles of the Southwest Yi and the Southern Min" in the *History of the Latter Han Dynasty* have texts transliterated into Chinese characters of the songs "Distant Barbarians Delight in Virtue," "Distant Barbarians Yearn for Virtue," and "Distant Barbarians Embrace Virtue." In the North and South Dynasties the Northern Dynasties' "Streams of Chi-le" is very famous, but whether the oblique metrics of its singers were in Sienpian, the Chi-le language, or else in Turkic, no one has ever been clear. Though the poetries of these other nationalities appear in the Chinese archives, in terms of writing poetry in Chinese they cannot be said to have brokered any influence. The translation of the Indian sūtras was a big event for the Chinese language. It had influence on the themes of Chinese poetry. Even a thoroughly Chinese poem such as Cao Cao's "Short Song,"

> Looking at liquor and singing,
> How short is this thing called Life!
> Just like the morning dew,
> With many sorrows at the close of day.

may have been influenced by *The Six Paramitas. The Six Paramitas* says,

> Just as the morning dew, dripping on the grass, disappearing with sunup, brief and ephemeral, so is the life of man like the morning dew. (as translated by Kang Senghui)

In terms of prosodic regulation, without the awareness of Sanskrit, Chinese would never have established a theory of "four tones," would have no knowledge of initial consonants and final vowels, could never have grasped the reverse-cut spelling system, and classical Chinese poetry could have founded no prosodic system. Certain classical Chinese poets knew Sanskrit, and it is said that Xie Lingyun was one of them. But that Buddhism was largely sinicized after its entry into China is an uncontested fact. No one has ever heard the expression "overall Indianization." From this can be seen the strength of ancient China's self-complacency. Mongolians and Manchus both ruled China, but their language, rather than affecting Chinese, was instead more aptly influenced by Chinese. Mongolians seem to have been troubled by the effects of Chinese on them, so they invented the 'Phagspa script with the assistance of the Tibetans, but 'Phagspa ultimately died.

When Chinese really found itself inside a neighborhood was after the May Fourth Movement of 1919, which was when Ancient Chinese became Modern Chinese. The written and spoken forms of Ancient Chinese had existed in parallel. To read Wang Fanzhi's poetry from the Tang is to be able to sense how deep and far the roots of colloquial Chinese plunge. The colloquial (recorded in written form as the vernacular) is everyone's language, and is not only limited to the Buddhist clergy and the commoners. The Song dynasty vernacular of *The Discourses of Master Zhu* are actually not that far from our language today. *The Discourses* are the lecture notes of Zhu Xi's students. For such a great thinker to be speaking a language so similar to ours is interesting. But once Zhu Xi began writing articles, he would go back to official written Classical Chinese. From this we can know how weighty, how grand a language Classical Chinese is. And although this grand written language had its own path of advancement, its forms are for the most part stable and guarantee an immutability within ancient Chinese morality, legality, and scholasticism over thousands of years. While the not-so-weighty has cropped up within the history of weighty writing that is Classical Chinese, including such particularly unweighty erotic fiction as *The Story of Sir Asyouwish*, fiction is ultimately a thing of the brothels and back alleys, and naturally would have the vernacular as its language. And then the vernacular became Modern Chinese. The distinction between Modern Chinese and the vernacular can be located in the fact that the vernacular faces written Classical Chinese, whereas Modern Chinese does not. Starting from the vernacular, it has received the influence of foreign languages. In terms of vocabulary, the influence of Japanese cannot be overlooked; in terms of sentence structure, Western languages, especially English, have left their mark all over Modern Chinese.

Beginning in the final years of the Qing dynasty, Chinese people became aware with headaches and heartbreak that Chinese was in fact a language within a neighborhood; and being a language within a neighborhood, the importance of translation became manifest. Only with translation could we "participate in the methods of the West so as to save China" (Liang Qichao, *On the Translation of Books*). But once the work of translation spread, Chinese could no longer not be influenced by the languages of the West. In *On the Translation of Names,* Hu Yilu writes: "Society cannot be independent; language is an implement of intercourse; there naturally can be no land wherein the folk arrive at old age or death with neither comings nor goings, and consider the Esquimaux, whose people's speech could not avoid the encroachment of foreign tongues." And to make Chinese accept the influence of Western languages, and thereby arrive at the goal of reshaping the Chinese language, was the conscious program of certain individuals. In December 1931 Qu Qiubai wrote in a letter to Lu Xun, "Translation—aside from being able to introduce the content of source texts to Chinese readers—also has an important function; this is to help us create a new modern language for China. The Chinese language (writing) is so impoverished [that] all expression of exquisite distinction or complex relationships amongst adjectives, verbs, and prepositions, is practically nil. The excesses of the feudal Middle Ages tightly enfetter the living language of Chinese people (and not only the masses of workers and peasants!), under which circumstances, the creation of a new language is a task of extreme importance."

From the Chinese of Lin Shu to the modern Chinese in use nowadays, under the catalysis of translation, inclusiveness has spread far within Chinese. The inclusiveness and expressiveness of Chinese in turn function for translation, allowing the poorly translated or untranslatable elements of foreign source texts to be able, finally, to enter into the Chinese language smoothly. This was unimaginable when Lin Shu first started translating Western books in the Tongcheng style of Classical Chinese. In a certain sense, only with the catalysis of translation did Chinese achieve its "modernity," did it become modern Chinese. The poet Ouyang Jianghe insists on calling Modern Chinese "Mandarin," so as to distinguish "Chinese" from "Classical Chinese," intending to emphasize the modernity of Chinese, which does not seem invalid. However, along with this understanding of the use of Chinese today comes immediately another question: after ninety years of use, amid all its intermittent conscious and unconscious alterations, is Chinese losing its "Chineseness"? Already many blame contemporary literature, especially certain linguistic practices in modern Chinese poetry, for deviating from Chineseness. Here, we can take a look back at the course of development for modern Chinese, whose basic track has been as follows: vernacular writing → individualized Chinese, as well as Chinese with Europeanized coloration → the modern Chinese of collectivization → the modern Chinese of ideologization. After this, to cast off the ideologization of modern Chinese, writers have brought Chinese in three directions: (1) a return to pure modern Chinese; (2) a return to dialect; (3) a search for and employment of the physicality of language. Of these, the return to dialect is a counter to the Europeanization of modern Chinese, one of whose possibilities is to return to the vernacular; whereas neither the return to pure modern Chinese nor the employment of the physicality of language can ever cast off translation. This requires an assessment of to how great a degree modern Chinese has already become Europeanized. And to reply to such a question, first it will be necessary to face the question of whether Chinese is with or without "Chineseness." If so, where are the specific properties of Chinese? The ancients never asked themselves such questions, because Classical Chinese had nearly no neighbors. It did not need a linguistic other to help it know itself. What is ironic is that the quest to nativize Chinese (which some are doing) is a quest filled with modernity. Li Bai and Du Fu never pursued nativization.

So what kind of language is modern Chinese? I would like to speak from my own individual experience. In October 1996, in Saskatchewan in central Canada, I lived in a monastery. The monks in the monastery had to sing hymns. The sight of them, wearing black robes and singing hymns, I had previously only read about in novels. At the time I mingled among them, singing along with them. I'm not a Christian, but I am interested in the ceremonies of religion. While singing, I had an experience, which was that I could go somewhere in English that, whether in Classical or vernacular Chinese, or even in Modern Chinese, I had never been able to reach. I expect that in Latin I could travel even further on the road toward God; in Greek further still; and in Hebrew I could make it nearly all the way to be at God's side (which is not to cast aspersions on Christians in Chinese, as they must have their means, which I do not possess). This all reminded me of the

Taiping Rebellion. Hong Xiuquan called God "Heavenly Father," and called Jesus "Heavenly Elder Brother," while he himself was the younger brother of Jesus. This probably in part came about from his speaking Chinese. Yang Xiuqing's spiritual smoke and mirrors, frothing at the mouth, falsely transmitting the Heavenly Brother's Holy Writ to punish Hong Xiuquan, was probably completely because he spoke Chinese. Concerning all the absurdity, ignorance, irrationality, wildness, and brutality of the Taiping Rebellion, scholars today have disclosed almost everything, and not much more need be said. But to date I have seen no attempts from the standpoint of linguistics to discuss the forms of discourse of the Taiping Rebellion. Rather than an approach toward Christianity, the Taiping Rebellion was instead closer to the White Orchid and Luo sects in terms of its organization, activity, and political aspirations. No language does not carry at each instant a cultural memory symbiotic with that language. And this is the angle from which we observe the modern world. Modern hermeneutics has a set of theories which put forth that non-Hebrew congregations tend to betray their own language in guessing at the meaning of the Bible, in guessing at God, whereas Hebrew congregations can approach God based on their own language, because it can be said that the Hebrew Bible is the selfsame as God. In this, among readers of the Hebrew Bible, the notion of God has become plural, because all readers can read forth their own God. And those who do not read the Bible in Hebrew, in order to approach their singular God, cannot but raise up the translated Bibles in their hands, cannot but cautiously infer, cautiously seek verification, so as not to be pulled away from the correct interpretive track by translations of the Bible. In the history of thought the significance of this phenomenon is of extreme interest. Therefore have scholars indicated that the multiplicity and postmodernism of the world today actually conform to the cultural modes of Hebrew, rather than a Greco logocentrism.[1] I seem to have digressed a little, but this digression was necessary. My point has been to point out that different languages might indicate different views of truth.

Let's come back and analyze my feelings when singing hymns in that

1. For more discussion about this question, see Liu Yiqing, *A Literary Hermeneutics of the Bible* (Beijing University Press, 2004), 9.

monastery. Once I put the two languages of Chinese and English together, the differences between them became evident. Several elements of English (similar to other Western languages), such as its multiclausal structure and its logical structure, do not exist in Classical Chinese, while the multiclausal structure of Modern Chinese is precisely the outcome of the influence of Western languages. Mandarin has, from Classical Chinese through to right now, valued short sentences. Although the sentences of Modern Chinese have had their growth, they are still not able to achieve the length of Charles Dickens's sentences. In long sentences, the vocabulary itself constitutes a progression of layers, a state of upward or downward or advancing spirals. This linguistic state can perfectly fulfill language's directionality of logos, or the directionality of God. In other words, the only language with ultimate aim in logos or God can be an alphabetic language. This is a language that necessarily observes logic, that necessarily observes rationality, that necessarily observes its interior system; this is a self-determined language. People tend to think that faith is a-rational, and indeed it is. But what is meant here by faith is the precondition of faith. Locke once said of Berkeley: If you don't get rid of the precondition of Berkeley, then you'll never be able to refute Berkeley. And this is just to say, if you use the rigid method of Berkeley's logic you will never be able to refute the rigid Berkeley of logic. Faith in God belongs to the a-rational, but at the heights of Christian faith in God, the high-density, high-quality, super-meticulous rationality of Thomas Aquinas has been praised as "divine." The revolt set off against this logical language—counterlogical, counterrational—was actually its self-contained necessity. This is not the morphology of Chinese. Nor is it the problem of Chinese. The short sentence of Chinese may be related to the Chinese character's origins in hieroglyph and ideogram. From recordings in symbols to recordings in writing, the written morphology of Chinese was regulated; and its earliest poetic forms were based on the four-character line. In prose its most florid, most formalistic written form was four-six parallel prose. This is how the short sentence came to be. In Modern Chinese some people attempt the long sentence, such as Gao Xingjian, but that is not a successful long sentence (though in his failed long sentences Gao Xingjian has accommodated thought that short sentences could not accommodate, which is another matter). In the styles of Chinese writing, the natural numerical limit of characters per sentence forces its leaps, with the ultimate emergence of these leaps being something satori-like. Through the morphology of logic, English and other Western languages achieve the goal of verbalization and the truth of the matter, while through leaps Chinese spreads from its goal of verbalization and touches the truth of the matter. In this sense, the view of truth emergent from the Chinese short sentence and the view of truth emergent from the long sentence (at least the long sentence of the past) of English (as well as other Western languages) are not the same. Given that Modern Chinese has been influenced by Western languages, its view of truth, in comparison with Classical Chinese, has been somewhat muddled, though inasmuch as it is still based on the medium of the Chinese character, it is still not the same as Western languages. In linguistic difference is cultural difference.

Within China, the question of linguistic Chineseness is not especially prominent, but in the field of languages with neighbors, this question must be raised. The poet Zhai Yongming has spoken of reading classical poetry after returning to China from abroad. She is not unique in this experience. Many people have increased awareness of being Chinese speakers of Chinese amid the environment of another language and culture. This is how one's sense of identity is formed. No matter whether you want it or not, your cultural identity continually exists within your self. You have this sense of identity because you live in a neighborhood.

*2*

From Classical Chinese to Modern Chinese, the endeavor to alter Chinese has been sustained. For example, with court Mandarin's harmonious Bible, what was employed was neither Classical Chinese, nor what we now call Modern Chinese, but rather a special language intermediary between the two. A man-made language. This conforms to the identity of the Bible—it's God's language, or language bestowed by God. Gradually, Modern Chinese and Classical Chinese were pulled apart; Classical Chinese with its primary linguistic unit, the monosyllabic character, and Modern Chinese with its primary linguistic unit, the bisyllabic word. From character to word, the rhythms and music of Chinese underwent change, the verbal center of gravity underwent change, Chinese sentence structure and the life and world that Chinese must face underwent change, and with the world and life that Chinese expresses undergoing change, the kind of world that it could pursue spread open, all undergoing change. Classical Chinese is the product of an agricultural society, or precisely put, it is the language of the elite echelons of an agricultural society, while Modern Chinese cannot but, even as it faces agricultural society, also face industrial society, democratization, urbanization, globalization, informatization, often needing to remind itself as well not to stray too far from the life of the masses. Modern Chinese cannot simply return to Classical Chinese and has, put plainly, become a "foreign language" with respect to Classical Chinese. Though because of their linguistic consanguinity, returning to Classical Chinese from Modern Chinese would be easier than entering Western languages from Modern Chinese. Nevertheless, Modern Chinese could be taken out, both in its position as neighbor to Classical Chinese and in its position as neighbor to Western languages, even if it is as a slightly frail neighbor. When compared with Classical Chinese, it may be especially more so. Narrow cultural conservationists certainly would not agree with our views: How could you split Modern Chinese from Classical Chinese? I would also like to say, you can't. But the problems encountered in translating Classical Chinese to Modern Chinese are so many, are so great, that they are in no way secondary to the problems encountered in translating English or other languages into Modern Chinese. In the translation of poetry this is especially the case.

Several years ago at a conference on Classical Poetics and Writing Modern Poetry at Capital Normal University, I picked up a book and read a passage to everyone:

> In life everybody has their likes, oh,
> And I like only cleanliness and love nice smells.
> Tearing me to shreds wouldn't change me, oh,
> Who could ever dash my hopes?

After I finished reading, I asked everybody: What do you think of this poem? Among the participants not one disagreed that it was a lousy poem, expressing only an ambition, without any formal elements, so how could it compare with classical poetry in grace or succinctness? And the rhythm of the first two lines reads comically, like a hurdy-gurdy. When they had finished I revealed my hand: this was the Modern Chinese translation of

In a person's life each has his pleasure, ho,
I alone take love of cultivation as obtain
Though my form be disfigured would I yet not alter, ho,
How could it be that my heart suffer scorn?
(from "On Encountering Sorrow")

The translator was Mr. Xiao Bing, author of the thick *Deciphering "Songs of Chu" Culture*. He read the *Songs of Chu* through the methodology of cultural anthropology, with much innovation. His research on the *Songs of Chu* cannot be considered shallow, and while he is an expert, his Modern Chinese translations are patent failures, and do not meet the poetic needs of readers of modern Chinese poetry. Are other translations any better? Mr. Chen Zizhan's translation reads:

In life everybody's got their delight, yeah,
But I go on loving beauty as a rule.
And even if I were torn to shreds I wouldn't change, yeah,
Or did you think my gentle-heartedness could be reproved?

In comparison, Xiao Bing's translation is more terse, and is *ad sensum* translation. But though both Xiao Bing and Chen Zizhan have rhymed their translations, their rhymes cannot guarantee that their translations are poems. Obviously, fine cultivation in Classical Chinese does not guarantee that they can write fine poems. Who is responsible for these problems? Were Qu Yuan's original poems not very good (no one would dare think this)? Or were Xiao Bing and Chen Zizhan overconfident in their facility with Modern Chinese? Or can Modern Chinese not be used as a language for poetry? Of course, this is not a very important section of Qu Yuan's poem, but why is it a passable section in Classical Chinese, only to become a pile of trash in Modern Chinese? A possible explanation: poetry is untranslatable. But then we've seen several brilliant translations of foreign poetry into Modern Chinese. If Modern Chinese cannot translate classical poetry, then it shouldn't be able to translate foreign poetry. So Modern Chinese cannot be to blame. Some would say that classical poetry doesn't need to be translated, but I'm afraid that in some places there's still a need to translate, such as Du Fu's

Fragrant rice   plucked by leftover   parrot kernels
Emerald tung trees   perched on by   phoenix branches

—what does that mean? Modern readers can't figure out what it means. If we try to translate it into Modern Chinese, perhaps we will even enable Modern Chinese to achieve the force of Classical Chinese. Generally speaking, classical poems were built within the context of Classical Chinese, not built in Modern Chinese. Of contemporary translations of classical poetry, in China, so far, I have not seen any successful examples. This part has led us to a deification of classical poetry. Are Modern Chinese and Classical Chinese the same language? Do they have the same structure? Or is their charm in the same place?

Du Fu's "Spring Longings":

States will crumble    yet mountains and rivers remain
The city Springs    as grass and trees deepen

Feeling the times    flowers splash with tears
In remorse at parting    birds startle the heart

Beacon fires    have linked three months
A letter from home    would be worth ten thousand in gold

My white hair    has been scratched yet thinner
So that it    cannot bear a pin

The Mexican poet Octavio Paz's Spanish translation, as translated back into Mandarin:

CAPTIVE SPRING

The empire has crumbled, mountains and rivers remain;
March, the green tide, covers streets and squares.

Harshness of these times: tears in the flowers,
the flights of birds sketch goodbyes.

Towers and battlements speak the language of fire,
powdered gold the price of a letter to my family.

I scratch my head, thin and white my hair
no longer holds the little pin of my cap.

The particular sentences in this translation raise the points I brought up in my discussion of translation elsewhere. As seen from this translation back into Modern Chinese, it largely upholds the poem's sensibility—not only the sensibility of the image, but the sensibility of thought as well, which in certain places are inventions, such as "March, the green tide, covers streets and squares" in the second line. If this were only a word-for-word translation of the original poem, to translate "The city Springs as grass and trees deepen" into "the city's spring, grass and trees flourishing," would be to produce yet another line of trash. "The city Springs as grass and trees deepen" works, and "the city's spring, grass and trees blossoming" does not work. We can point out Paz's inaccuracy: why must "Spring" be "March"? Did ancient China have our modern "squares"? This may have to do with the differences between the ancient Chinese concept of city and the concept of city in Mexican culture (while Mexico is a Latin American country, culturally speaking it beckons back to Western culture). But these problems do not mitigate the fact that Paz's translation is a translation that has achieved modernity. "March" is more accurate than "Spring," because "March," the third month, is a diversion from the "three months" of "Beacon fires have linked three months." "Streets and squares" contains a more modern sensibility than "city." Even if what we are reading here is a doubly translated Du Fu poem, Du Fu has nonetheless been stirred awake. And in this line, Paz turns "grass and trees" into "the green tide"—so deviant, yet so interesting! He didn't translate "deep" into an equivalent adjective or verb, but actually "deep" in Modern Chinese would have no way of being translated into a verb. The equivalent nonequivalent word that he used is "to cover." Seemingly from this "cover," the entire structure of the sentence is different from the original, as the translated sentence in contemporary meaning has become effective. To compare, in *The Complete Translation of the Three Hundred Tang Poems*, the Chinese scholar Sha Lingna translated this line as, "The Spring approaches, only seeing the woods in their boundlessness / the tufts of grass sprouting up, dilapidating into a field of emptiness." It should be said that Sha Lingna's translation is one hundred times more accurate than Paz's, and that Sha Lingna employs the tone of New Poetry from the first half of the twentieth century, but concerning how Modern Chinese poetic writing has advanced to today, her translation brokers no meaning. Other places of Paz's translation can likewise be highlighted: "Feeling the times flowers splash with tears" can be explained either as human tears, or else explained as the tears of the flowers, and Paz "invented" it as "tears in the flowers." Sha Lingna translated it as "In remorse over the instant, seeing the flourishing blossoms wither and wilt, / rather makes my tears soak my sleeves," which is too clumsy, in addition to being a cliché of literary parlance. The later line "the flights of birds sketch goodbyes," in Sha Lingna's translation: "Grief over parting, hearing the spring birds cooing in harmony, only feeling that my heart is startled." The source of Sha Lingna's translation problems is that she's too literary, too eager to translate Du Fu into a modern poet, so that she translates him into a *littérateur* from the 1940s. She has no other choice, because what she grasps and comprehends is only the linguistic tools of the 1940s. This is also exactly the standard linguistic repertoire that the average poetry readers can understand of Modern Chinese poetry. So if they read Paz's translation, "Towers and battlements speak the language of fire," the foolish will fume but the bright will delight, because Paz directly turned Du Fu into a surrealist poet (despite the birth of surrealism being in the era of World War I, or earlier, in the sphere of Chinese poetry the boat did not moor until the 1980s, and non-expert readers may yet be unclear about the meaning of surrealism even today). The last two lines of Du Fu's poem in Paz's translation are: "I scratch my head, thin and white my hair / no longer holds the little pin of my cap," a method of translation that might make us laugh out loud. I'm sorry, let me tell the truth: Du Fu as translated by Sha Lingna (if foreign translators translated Du Fu this way) could never achieve the admiration of the world. Only by approaching Paz's means of translation could Du Fu become as great a poet as he is today. Paz's Spanish translation, when translated back into Chinese, is of no mean fascination, giving us no small amount of enlightenment on how to establish a Modern Chinese language. If our hearts doubt it, we can ask again whether Paz's Du Fu is a Spanish-language poet. If you've read a bit of modern and contemporary Spanish-language poetry (from Spain or from Latin America), you will know that, even in Spanish, Du Fu is always a Chinese poet. Paz did not consciously seek out his linguistic Chineseness, but his linguistic Chineseness here is nonetheless indelible. And simultaneously, going through this kind of translation, Du Fu has attained modernity, in harmonious rhythm with world culture.

The size of the rift between Classical Chinese and Modern Chinese is beyond imagination for non-Chinese writers. In Western languages—

English, for example—English can also be divided into three periods: from the fifth century to the twelfth century is the period of Old English, from the twelfth century to the fifteenth century is the period of Middle English, and from the fifteenth century to today is the period of Modern English. Among these, Modern English began with Chaucer, six hundred years ago, and has undergone all sorts of transformations. In comparison, our ninety-year course of Modern Chinese is exceedingly brief (not mentioning that in such a short period it has still managed to come up with an array of clichés), despite the fact that the history of our linguistic resources is much longer by far. So, the different plights of language and language will emerge. An English writer today can still write a sonnet, no matter how modern, how postmodern, the writing, but in Modern Chinese it is already impossible to write classical quatrains or regulated verse, and to force one out would be to approach ditties and doggerel. As has been mentioned already, in Modern Chinese the principal linguistic unit, rhetorical method, syntax, rhythm, and musicality are all at a great remove from those of Classical Chinese. Under these circumstances, if Modern Chinese can fully acknowledge its identity as a language in a neighborhood, from Classical Chinese to foreign languages (not limited to Western languages) to be inserted into our creativity (and not merely our cultural cultivation), then Modern Chinese might be able to achieve unprecedented possibilities. To say this might sound like endlessly hitting the same old notes, but what I am concerned with is concrete behavior. We've wasted too much breath talking about continuing tradition and platitudes about absorbing nourishment from all the world's cultures, while the work we have actually done remains pitiably little. Of all the work that should be done, the deficiency in the transition from the Classical Chinese archives to Modern Chinese (and not simply in so-called translation) is particularly stunning. In comparison, W. B. Yeats achieved his elder Standish O'Grady's sturdy Modern English to rewrite the sagas of ancient Irish folklore. Seamus Heaney retranslated the Old English *Beowulf.* Modern Western writers' continuation and replication of ancient writers has long been a constant: the Greek poet and novelist Kazantzakis, for instance, starting from midway through Homer, wrote a new version of the epic *Odyssey.* The Italian poet and filmmaker Pasolini rewrote cantos from Dante's *Divina Commedia.* The English poets Michael

Hofmann and James Lasdun invited forty English language poets to re-do Ovid, and in 1996 published the volume *After Ovid: New Metamorphoses*. But Chinese writers and scholars have not performed work like this. Chinese classical literature demands that an effective transformation into Modern Chinese be achieved. Modern Chinese likewise demands an effective transformation toward world literature. This is work for the masses, and these are the linguistic possibilities everyone within the realm of Modern Chinese needs. In the praxis of language, the triad of effective translation, effective explication, and effective transformation is one, and the creativity of our era is to participate within it.

*Translated by Lucas Klein*

# Yang Lian

*(b. 1955)*

Yang Lian was born in Switzerland in 1955 and grew up in Beijing. He began writing when he was sent to the countryside in the 1970s. On his return to Beijing, he became one of the first group of young "underground" poets who published in the literary journal *Jintian* (*Today*). Yang Lian's poems became well known and influential inside and outside of China in the 1980s, especially when his poem "Norlang" was criticized by the Chinese government during the "Anti-Pollution" movement. He was invited to visit Australia and New Zealand in 1988 and became a poet in exile after the Tiananmen massacre. Since that time, he has continued to write and speak out as a highly individual voice in world literature, politics, and culture. He has published seven selections of poems, two selections of prose, and many essays in Chinese. He was awarded the Flaiano International Poetry Prize (Italy, 1999), and his book *Where the Sea Stands Still: New Poems* won the Poetry Books Society Recommended Translation award (UK, 1999). His three volumes of collected works, *Yang Lian Zuo Pin 1982–1997* (2 vols.) and *Yang Lian Xin Zuo 1998–2002,* were eventually published in China. His translations into English include *Where the Sea Stands Still*, a collection of poems (Bloodaxe Books, 1999); *Yi*, a book-length poem (Green Integer, 2002); *Notes of a Blissful*

*Ghost*, a selection of poems (Renditions Paperback, 2002); *Concentric Circles*, another book-length poem (Bloodaxe Books, 2005); *Unreal City*, a selection of poems and prose (Auckland University Press, 2006); and *Riding Pisces: Poems from Five Collections*, a selection of poems (Shearsman Books, 2008). He currently lives in London.

"Island (#2)," part of a five-poem sequence, shows Yang Lian's distinctive vision and poetry, which utilizes surprising tonal shifts. His new essay offers a close reading of a classic poem by Du Fu. He describes the aesthetic pressures on contemporary poetry and, returning to Du Fu, muses, "He is marvelous—but what about us?" After more than a century of social and literary transformations, it is an appropriate way to end this collection.

## Island (#2)

You're right    in life's chamber music
either listen with total attention    or else switch off
Water    one drop can perfectly lock up these shores

The crash of waves has no gap    is like a tailored body
still sitting on the rock    the lilac-scented surrounding ocean
still striking at a little girl's unceasing gaze into distance

Purple or white    petals are stored in the eyes
all through the springtime night, dark rings around the eyes
keep opening    torn by where she looks far away

Suffering is that waiting, underwater pearl
what turns old is salt    low sobbing in every wave
The fierce wind is a jade bracelet on the wrist

Island    like a boat sailing since the day you were born
never slowing down its disconsolate speed
always arriving yet, underfoot, drawn away by the ebbing tide

Purple     wounds the turbulent, close-up scene
sets off white     the horizon like land cutting, above snowline, into fate
exposing the snow flower you've caught for life

Still wet     tears run halfway down the girl's cheeks
After so many years play the cold rain you've brought back
A seagull plunges     then flies back up     You hear clearly this kiss

*Translated by Arthur Sze*

## The Poetics of Space, and More: Aesthetic Pressures on Classical Chinese Poetry and a Contemporary Solution

*London, June 28, 2008*

### *Part 1: Classical Poetry*

#### THE AESTHETICS OF SPACE IN THE GENES OF CHINESE CHARACTERS

The forms of classical Chinese poetry are extensions of the aesthetic genes of Chinese characters. A close look at Du Fu's "Dēng Gāo," known as the exemplary specimen of seven-syllable regulated verse,[1] will make the point. This poem was written in the Tang dynasty, about 1,200 years ago. Composed of eight lines, each of seven syllables, this masterpiece demonstrates the characteristics of classical Chinese poetry: vision / image, tones / music, syntax / structure, synchrony / space, text / transcendental experience. Moreover, it can be understood as autobiography, history, politics, philosophy, poetry, and as a unique interpretation of time and space, and of the universe, even. In terms of the aesthetics of classical Chinese poetry, it has not yet been comprehensively interpreted; as one of mankind's intellectual resources, its potential has not yet begun to be tapped. Du Fu remains alone.

I will show the whole poem below, with *pinyin* transcription and literal trot, before discussing its aesthetics on several levels, as well as its philosophical connotations.

1. *Translators' note:* a classical poem of eight seven-syllable lines with a strict tonal pattern and strict rhyme scheme.

登高 DĒNG GĀO / *CLIMB HİGH*

1 風急／天高／猿嘯哀 feng jī / tian gao / yuán xiào aì
*wind gust / sky high / gibbon moan sorrow*
2 渚清／沙白／鳥飛回 zhü qing / sha bái / niäo fei húi
*shallows clear / sand white / bird fly back*
3 無邊／落木／蕭蕭下 wú bian / luò mù / xiao xiao xià
*without end / falling tree / rustle rustle fall*
4 不盡／長江／滾滾來 bú jìn / cháng jiang / gün gün lái
*no limit / Yangtze River / roll roll come*
5 萬里／悲秋／常作客 wàn lï / bei qiū / cháng zuò kè
*10,000 mile / grief autumn / always be stranger*
6 百年／多病／獨登臺 bäi nián / duō bìng / dú deng tái
*100 year / much illness / alone climb tower*
7 艱難／苦恨／繁霜鬢 jian nán / kü hèn / fán shuang bìn
*trouble strife / suffer regret / many frost hair*
8 潦倒／新停／濁酒杯 liáo däo / xin tíng / zhuó jiü bei
*down and out / new stop / cheap wine cup*[2]

For the sake of convenience, the original verse is shown above with different images separated by a forward slash. On the right are the *pinyin* tran-

2. *Translators' note:* The diacritics represent the following pitch contours: ¯ high level; ´ rising; ˇ dipping; ` falling. For prosodic purposes, they are divided into *level* and *oblique:* this distinction is an ancient one, but note that we do not know the exact contours in the Chinese of Du Fu's time (which had five tones, rather than the four of modern Mandarin). This is a rough sketch of *Deng Gao* that may help the reader imagine at least something of the depth and complexity of Du Fu's masterpiece:

FROM HIGH ABOVE
a rising gale, a high sky
gibbons moan and wail
clear shallows, white sand where
birds fly home to roost
no end of failing trees, leaves
fallen in the whistling wind
no rest for the long Yangtze River
rolling and roiling downstream
a million miles of miserable autumns—
an eternal outcast, me
a long life of sickness too—
climbing the tower alone
troubles, cares, and bitter regret
frosting my old brow
down and out, done for—and just given
up the bloody booze

scriptions with tones (the diacritic marks that represent the four possible pitch contours of each syllable) and beneath, a literal trot. I'll explore the aesthetics of it below, on several levels.

### THE FIRST AESTHETIC OF CLASSICAL POETRY: TONAL PATTERN—PERFECT MUSICAL DESIGN

Every Chinese character is an integration of form, sound, and meaning and a combination of many separate parts. Among these elements, sound is the most difficult to apprehend. The syllables of Chinese characters are separated into sounds and tones.[3] Unlike phonographically written languages, the sound of Chinese characters is not spelled out, since the pronunciation of a character is rarely apparent, and the four tones of Chinese syllables are all the more singular for this. From its birth with the *Book of Songs* and *Songs of the South* to Han dynasty rhyme-prose, or ancient ballads with their five- or seven-syllable lines, ancient Chinese continually explored the musical patterns of Chinese characters, and what I call "the formalistic tradition of Chinese characters": these all established this musical system. The tonal patterns of poetry formulate a specific rhythm for the verse even before it has been composed. When a verse strictly follows the tonal pattern, slowing and stretching its sounds and tones turns recitation into song. On the other hand, if the poet fails to follow the pattern, he is like an opera singer singing off key, and like the opera singer, the poet too will be thrown off the stage. For more than a thousand years, the rule of "four sounds and eight errors" has been used to diagnose errors in musical design, which shows that the musical design of ancient Chinese poetry has always been conscious. In my opinion, rhythmic design is not merely attributable to the pursuit of musical aesthetics, but is also part of the cohesive and coherent connection between the [syntactically] loosely connected characters. Suppose that there were no integration of these musical patterns in "Dēng Gāo," then there could be no necessary grammatical connections between the "bottomless skies," "howling gibbons," and "gusting wind" of the first line. These would simply be three disparate images set side by side, which the reader could hardly combine to form a visual image. So it is with the remaining lines of this poem. Thus, the visible images are integrated into

3. *Translators' note:* That is to say, the syllable sound (e.g., *ba*) plus its associated pitch contour.

the poetic whole by invisible musical patterns. This also explains why I often talk of the musical pattern of a Chinese poem as "a mysterious power."

"Dēng Gāo" is a good example of the poet drawing with sound, and its "terrible beauty." The words *xiāo xiāo* at the end of the third line perfectly mimic the sound of dry leaves falling. And the following word, *xià*, in accord with its meaning of "falling," uses a falling tone, so sight, sound, and meaning are combined into a harmonious whole. Likewise, the dipping tone of *gǔn gǔn*, in the next line, is compatible with the sound of rolling waves: along with the rising tone *lái* that follows it, the words create an image of the Yangtze River coming from far away and rising up from below, and overwhelming the reader. The poet as composer: isn't that amazing?

### THE SECOND AESTHETIC OF CLASSICAL POETRY: ANTITHESIS—MULTILAYERED IMAGES

Under Pound's influence, the visual images of classical Chinese poetry have come to be seen as its unique specialty, and this has led to a dreadful overuse of the notion in our own time. However, a close look at classical Chinese poetry will reveal the fact that the arrangement of images is not random. Within one line, images are bound by the artistic conception of the whole poem and have clear implications when they are set side by side. Between two lines, images are challenged by the antithesis peculiar to classical Chinese poetry. Like two lines of honor guards or two mirrors, antithesis requires the parallelism of words in the same position in two different lines (i.e., nouns paralleled with nouns, verbs with verbs, adjectives with adjectives, adverbs with adverbs, even colors with colors and numbers with numbers, so as to form an echo effect). This is a word game playable only by using the square characters of Chinese. The characters, sentences, couplets, and the whole poem are built up into a multilayered image structure, which forms a crystal-clear architecture in the eye and mind of the reader. In addition, the sounds and tones of each line also help to make this structure pleasing to both the eye and the ear. Hence, every image has to be able to meet the tests of eye, ear, and mind. "Dēng Gāo" shows Du Fu's incomparable skills and his mastery of antithesis. "Dēng Gāo" is not only in accordance with the rule for "seven-syllable regulated verse" that requires the parallelism of two couplets in the middle, but parallelism is also featured in the four "run-on pairs" within the eight lines. This quadruple-image pattern shows an extremely high level of human creativity and skill, even approaching the beauty of nature itself, demonstrating, in Du Fu's own words, that "until my words amaze men, I will never die." This is no random "natural beauty" but the result of painstaking effort by the poet.

Besides the above-mentioned *xiāo xiāo xià* and *gŭn gŭn lái*, there is another amazing antithesis in the fifth and sixth lines of this poem. Sun Zhu, the eighteenth-century editor of *Three Hundred Tang Poems*, added to the poem the footnote "fourteen syllables, but ten layers [of meaning]," which puzzled me a great deal when I first read it. Not until I myself was in exile did I understand how much sadness Du Fu put in the seven syllables of each line.

> Line 5: *be a stranger — often be a stranger — often be a stranger in autumn — often be a stranger in autumn's grief (not golden autumn) — often be a stranger in autumn's grief, thousands of miles from home.*
>
> Line 6: *climb high — climb high alone — climb high alone when ill — climb high alone when very ill — climb high alone when very ill within such a short life.*

Du Fu's loneliness was borrowed from Chen Zi'ang's, as implied in Chen's poem "On Climbing Youzhou Tower"—loneliness was already written in Chen's famous lines of a thousand years ago: "Where are the sages of the past, and the sages still to come?"

### THE THIRD AESTHETIC OF CLASSICAL POETRY: NONLINEAR NARRATION—SYNCHRONIC SPACE

Since Chinese verbs have no tense, sentence patterns remain unchanged even when person, time, and number change. This feature of "synchronic space" is a limitation as well as an opportunity, as it leads Chinese to give up linear narration and to focus on the building of the poem's internal space.

This can be clearly seen through a contrast between the multilayered spiritual structure in Qu Yuan's "Encountering Sorrow" (*Lí Sāo*) in *Songs of the South* and the chronological narrative of Western epics.[4] In "Dēng Gāo," there is not a chronological but a spatial connection between lines. The whole poem centers on the high place where the author stands, and is built into a microcosmic model:

4. *Translators' note:* See David Hawkes's magisterial translation in his *Songs of the South* (Harmondsworth: Penguin Classics, 1985), 67ff.

Line 1: looking up high;
Line 2: looking down at the valley;
Line 3: hearing (autumn wind with falling leaves);
Line 4: sight (tidal waves of Yangtze River);
Line 5: space (thousands of miles away);
Line 6: time (within a hundred years);
Line 7: deep into the heart;
Line 8: back to the present.

The organization of four pairs of antithesis into four corresponding couplets makes us feel almost as if we are listening to four duets on the same theme.

A closer look will find both horizontal and vertical directions in the verse: the first and the last couplets are complementary, both describing the scenery while standing high; the middle two couplets further extend the theme by elaborating on hearing, sight, space, and time. The vertical intensity and the horizontal extension empower the poem with huge tensile force. Finally, our sight falls on the tiny winecup the poet is holding in his hand, the focal point of the vast universe. I want to point out that it is not depreciatory to regard the "synchronic space" in classical Chinese poetry as merely a rhetorical device. Its connotations are more philosophical. What is the illusion of time? How has history been fabricated over and again? Besides the deep insights of the heart, what can be called "innovation"? In the concentric circles of the text, is there an eternal rotation? One poem comprises the theory of evolution.

### THE FOURTH AESTHETIC OF CLASSICAL POETRY: TEXT—THE TRANSCENDENTAL EXPERIENCE OF POETRY

This is an extension of the previous idea: the forms of classical Chinese poetry inherit the genes of Chinese characters and take the building of nonchronological texts as their ultimate goal; for instance, "Dēng Gāo" is still the slogan of every poet in exile nowadays, but we must, however, eliminate a misconception: "nonchronological" doesn't mean "having no chronology." In contrast: it includes *all time*. Chinese characters have been used for over three thousand years and "seven-syllable regulated verse" composed for more than a thousand years, and how many generations of poets have been born and died since then?

Classical Chinese poetry stresses the use of allusion (as I mentioned Chen Zi'ang previously) and even requires the principle of "no word but has a source." In modern terms, it is the intertextuality that constantly adjusts and rewrites the whole system. In the transcendental space created by the text, *this moment* is connected to the real conditions of life by aesthetics, while both past and present reality are contained in the text. I wonder, when Ezra Pound was putting segments of different cultures and histories together on a large scale, whether he thought of trying to break with *diachronic* life and language in order to reach the *synchronic*? When "Dēng Gāo" illustrates to the fullest extent the pain of exile, does it matter if I call the author Du Fu or Yang Lian?

## *Part 2: A Contemporary Solution*

### THE PERSONAL POETIC SPACE

The more elegant the aesthetic system, the more terrible the pressure it will produce. One general misconception is that the tradition of classical Chinese poetry is like a straight line connecting ancient poetic creativity and contemporary innovation. This misconception originates from a visual illusion: this is the impression that, since through time Chinese characters remain almost unchanged visually, any person with some knowledge of Chinese has no difficulties in reading Laozi or Confucius, works written more than two thousand years ago. However, some hold that the difference between Modern Standard Chinese and Classical Chinese is no less than that between Chinese and a foreign language. This seems exaggerated, but, on second thought, it makes sense. It's worth noting that more than 40 percent of the Chinese we use today is actually an interpolated "foreign language"—Western vocabulary was first translated into Chinese characters by the Japanese, then borrowed into written Chinese. There are numerous examples, such as "democracy," "science," "materialism," "idealism," "human rights," "law," "politics," "sports," "socialism," "capitalism," and even "self," "psychology," "time," "space," etc., without which the modern mentality would lose its roots. Because of their belief that meaning inheres in the visually stable character, Chinese people tend to think there have been few changes from classical monosyllabic words to modern polysyllabic ones, but actually there have been dramatic changes. For example, the Chinese word *rénmín* is an indivisible concept in Japanese, corresponding to English "the people," but to us, it corresponds to two Chinese characters: *rén* as the abstract name for human beings, and *mín* specifically referring to the citizens, as opposed to *guān* or officials. When to use which word might need no detailed pondering, or might rely entirely on intuition. Here, monosyllabic words are emotional and connected to our tradition; polysyllabic words are conceptualized, translated, and imported. The separation of these two layers is a major cause for the weak cornerstone of much contemporary Chinese poetry. Though they borrowed characters from Chinese, Japanese people are more open-minded, viewing the combined characters as the temporary carriers of Western concepts. But how can we write poems with this second-hand foreign language that is Modern Standard Chinese? How can we acknowledge that these beautiful square characters are not even as old as American English? What's worse, the aesthetics of classical poetry exert very little pressure on us, or no pressure at all—it's too far away to reach us. We should therefore spare no effort to seek out and rebuild a real connection with the aesthetics of our classical poetry, but to invite that pressure is no easy task.

What I call the first Poetic Mini-Theory of our generation is what post–Cultural Revolution poets did by consensus: they eliminated the boring and meaningless, politically conscious, high-register vocabulary from the language of poetry; but to describe the nightmare of reality, the disaster of rebirth, and the destruction of the inner self, we went back to images such as the sun, the moon, water, earth, darkness, and the sea. What was called "Misty poetry" was a simple return to favoring a pure and classical Chinese.[5] What was different was that it sounded strange to politically conscious ears. This also brings a way of thinking: energy comes from hardship; nightmares can also inspire us. What's exciting about contemporary classical Chinese poetry lies in the deeply buried dilemma of Chinese culture: the transformation of modern society means neither merely going

5. *Translators' note:* Misty poets—the group of poets who published their work in *Today* magazine (1978–80), which included Yang himself as well as Duo Duo, Bei Dao, Gu Cheng, Mang Ke, Shu Ting, and others.

back to the ancient classics nor purely plagiarizing the West. On the contrary, we must root ourselves in the individual, to break out of East-West divisions, and integrate all our intellectual resources. In a word, the ultimate principle of poetry is this: to express one's own feelings in one's own words. "One's own words" must contain the aesthetic power of Chinese characters, while "one's own feelings" must relate to the in-depth thinking of all humanity. Thus, "Chinese" and "contemporary" are inseparable. The depth of the thinking relies on the innovation in expression. Given this huge question mark about what is "Chinese," every contemporary Chinese poem is in fact an extremely experimental poem, regardless of whether you are conscious of it or not.

Our solution started with building a *creative connection* between contemporary and classical poetic aesthetics. Consanguinity is not inherited from the ancestors but created after birth, and Ezra Pound is still inspiring us: the individual is the energy that rediscovers language and tradition. Maybe it's fate that, due to the historical vicious circle brought about by the Cultural Revolution, my writing had to start from "the pain of timelessness"—the tenselessness of the Chinese verb—which is much worse than "the pain of time." Such a tenselessness was only very awkwardly established in my life. My early works *Banpo* and *Dunhuang* do not deal with historical materials but contain nonhistorical themes—antihistorical, even. The long poem *Yi*, which I wrote in the five years before leaving China, also tries to eliminate time by establishing multilayered textual spaces: by combining the ancient *Book of Changes* and contemporary writing, by adopting the spontaneous rhythms and musical patterns of Chinese characters, and by building connections between images and structure (not creating single, isolated images), by creating a final work "in symmetry with death," I allowed the roots of poetry to suffuse me and relate me to the general experience of mankind. The massacre in Tiananmen Square in 1989 led me to write "1989," whose last line, "this is no doubt a perfectly ordinary year," appalled all my friends.

However, as opposed to many memories of death and an emptiness worse than death, isn't this timelessness actually the only truth? The works I finished during exile—such as *Where the Sea Stands Still*, *Concentric Circles*, *Notes of a Blissful Ghost*, *Lee River Poems*, and even the collection of erotic poetry *Dark Blue Poems*—are more of a series of projects than poem collections, each adding more and deeper layers to the space of Yang Lian's poetry. The only thing they amplify is the weight of my thought.

Contemporary Chinese poetry must lie in the interaction between in-depth thinking and creative forms. With "the Tao (way) that can be spoken is not the unchanging Tao," Laozi long ago made these breakthroughs: to surpass language within the limits of language; to penetrate to the self through constant self-reflection; to remain in the now until the acceptance of the idea that "the now is farthest away." Poems never simplify themselves: images full of darkness and pain shine out because of their creativity; words that inherit nothing from classical poetic forms are beautiful because of their man-made music and tones. The synchronic/spatial feature of Chinese characters develops into a unique structural element of every work, forming expressions more profound and complete than a single image or line. The ambiguity of Chinese, the vagueness of Chinese grammar, the basic nature of Chinese being "abstract as soon as written," the use of classical stories and the intertextuality of classical poetry, and the ludic element in the evolution of the forms of classical Chinese poetry: these can now be transformed into the concepts behind my work, to lay the groundwork for the artistic installation of the text. When I say "there is no pure poetry, but we have to take every poem as pure as we write it," I mean we must deal with our thoughts in a "formalistic" way. We must guard against the cheap and commercialized propaganda of "politics" and try to surpass it, as we must surpass every "subject" in a philosophical and aesthetic (i.e., literary) way. Form is never enough, even if it is necessary. The more extreme the original work is, the bigger the challenge it poses, the more valuable the conversation it will create between poems all over the world. "Spatial aesthetics" is my own writing tactic; it penetrates and transforms all my different works, causing the work to blossom into multi-layered "concentric circles."

The difficulty of contemporary Chinese poetry lies not only in the challenges posed by our classical tradition and Western tradition, but also in our own works, which build themselves on a fractured slope. I once described this terrible situation as "a tower built from the top down": a tower of poems, just like a banyan-tree, has to send its tendrils downward to seek earth and seek the ground. But can *we* really find the ground? Can what we find be not only exotic local specialties in the supermarket but also an organic part of humanity's contemporary thinking?

In other words, can the ancient Chinese characters and the classical language inspire the contemporary world? That is to say, do we still have the power to ask ourselves the *Heavenly Questions*?[6] In some sense, I'm very pessimistic about it. But I still believe in "starting from the impossible": the more "impossible" it is, the more powerful the "start" will be. Isn't every poem reincarnated as each line finishes?

Returning to Du Fu—his work has been honored as "poetic history": neither history written in verse, nor a Western epic, but history enclosed in poetry. The eight short lines of "Dēng Gāo" mark a space big enough for a thousand years of reincarnation. He is marvelous—but what about us?

*Translated by Brian Holton & Xie Guixia*

6. *Translators' note:* See Hawkes, *Songs of the South*, 122ff.

# *Translators*

Joseph R. Allen
Alison Bailey
John Balcom
Jody Beenk
John Berninghausen
Michael Berry
Steve Bradbury
Chang Fen-ling
Aaron Crippen
Kirk A. Denton
Murray Edmond
Jennifer Feeley
Matthew Fryslie
Karen Gernant & Chen Zeping
Howard Goldblatt
Brian Holton & Xie Guixia
Ted Huters & Feng-ying Ming
Andrew F. Jones
Lucas Klein
Leo Ou-fan Lee
Mabel Lee
Pu-mei Leng
Peter Li
Sylvia Li-chun Lin
Andrea Lingenfelter
Gerald Maa
Denis Mair
Ruth Nybakken
Simon Patton
Peng Wenlan & Eugene Chen Eoyang
Pascale Petit
David E. Pollard
Arthur Sze
Zona Yi-Ping Tsou
Wang Ping
Yang Xianyi & Gladys Yang
Michelle Yeh

# *Permissions*

Every effort has been made to identify the copyright holders of previously published materials included in this collection; any incorrect attributions will be corrected in subsequent printings upon notification to the publisher.

AI QING, excerpts from "Author's Preface," in *Ai Qing: Selected Poems*, ed. Eugene Chen Eoyang. Copyright © 1982 by Foreign Languages Press, Beijing. Reprinted by permission.

BEI DAO, first publication of "Drifting," translation copyright © 2010 by Jody Beenk. Excerpts from "Reciting," in *Blue House*, translation copyright © 2000 by Ted Huters & Feng-ying Ming. Reprinted by permission of Zephyr Press. Excerpts from "Paris Stories," "Midnight's Gate," "Empty Mountain," and "King Martin," in *Midnight's Gate: Essays*, translation copyright © 2005 by Matthew Fryslie. Reprinted by permission of New Directions Publishing Corp.

BIAN ZHILIN, first publication of preface to *A Historical Record of Carved Critters*, translation copyright © 2010 by Lucas Klein.

CAN XUE, "A Particular Sort of Story," in *Blue Light in the Sky and Other Stories*, translation copyright © 2006 by Karen Gernant & Chen Zeping. Reprinted by permission of New Directions Publishing Corp.

EILEEN CHANG (ZHANG AILING), "Writing of One's Own," in *Written on Water*, trans. Andrew F. Jones. Copyright © 1968 by Eileen Chang. Translation copyright © 2005 by Columbia University Press. Reprinted by permission of Columbia University Press and Crown Publishing Co., Ltd.

CHEN LI, first publication of "Traveling Between Languages," translation copyright © 2010 by Chang Fen-ling.

DAI WANGSHU, "Dai Wangshu's Poetic Theory," trans. Kirk A. Denton, in *Modern Chinese Literary Thought: Writings on Literature, 1893–1945*, ed. Kirk A.

Denton. Copyright © 1996 by the Board of Trustees of the Leland Stanford Jr. University. All rights reserved. Reprinted by permission of Stanford University Press, www.sup.org.

DING LING, "We Need the Zawen Essay," trans. Ruth Nybakken, in *Modern Chinese Literary Thought: Writings on Literature, 1893–1945*, ed. Kirk A. Denton. Copyright © 1996 by the Board of Trustees of the Leland Stanford Jr. University. All rights reserved. Reprinted by permission of Stanford University Press, www.sup.org.

GAO XINGJIAN, first publication of "The Art of Fiction," translation copyright © 2010 by Mabel Lee. Chapter 72 from *Soul Mountain*, translation copyright © 2000 by Mabel Lee. Reprinted by permission of HarperCollins Publishers.

GU CHENG, "Poetry Lessons" and "Misty Poetry: An Interview," in *Sea of Dreams: The Selected Writings of Gu Cheng*, translation copyright © 2005 by Joseph R. Allen. Reprinted by permission of New Directions Publishing Corp. Sections 10, 11, 12, 15, 23, and 31 from "A Brief Self-Introduction," in *Nameless Flowers: Selected Poems of Gu Cheng*, translation copyright © 2005 by Aaron Crippen. Reprinted by permission of George Braziller, Inc.

HAIZI, first publication of excerpts from "The Poet I Most Love—Hölderlin," translation copyright © 2010 by Gerald Maa.

HSIA YÜ (XIA YU), excerpt from "Hsia Yü: Interview by Steve Bradbury," in *Zoland Poetry: An Annual of Poems, Translations and Interviews*, no. 2. Reprinted by permission of Steve Bradbury. "Brokenhearted time and ordinary daily moment" [two versions], in *Zoland Poetry: An Annual of Poems, Translations and Interviews*, no. 2. English poem and back-translation from Chinese copyright © 2008 by Hsia Yü. Reprinted by permission of Hsia Yü.

HU SHI, excerpt from "Some Modest Proposals for the Reform of Literature," trans. Kirk A. Denton, in *Modern Chinese Literary Thought: Writings on Literature, 1893–1945*, ed. Kirk A. Denton. Copyright © 1996 by the Board of Trustees of the Leland Stanford Jr. University. All rights reserved. Reprinted by permission of Stanford University Press, www.sup.org. "Dreams and Poetry," in *Anthology of Modern Chinese Poetry*, ed. & trans. Michelle Yeh. Copyright © 1992 by Michelle Yeh. Reprinted by permission of Yale University Press.

JI XIAN, "Six Tenets," trans. Leo Ou-fan Lee, from Lee Ou-fan Lee, "'Modernism' and 'Romanticism' in Taiwan Literature," in *Chinese Fiction from Taiwan: Critical Perspectives*, ed. Jeannette L. Faurot. Copyright © 1980 by Indiana University Press. Reprinted by permission of Indiana University Press.

JIA PINGWA, excerpts from "Life Is Changing: Even in Hilly Shangzhou," trans. Peter Li, in *Modern Chinese Writers: Self-Portrayals*, ed. Helmut Martin & Jeffrey Kinkley. Translation copyright © 1992 by M. E. Sharpe, Inc. Reprinted by permission.

LAO SHE, first publication of "How I Wrote My Short Stories," in *An Aging Ox and Dilapidated Cart*, translation copyright © 2010 by Howard Goldblatt.

LEUNG PING-KWAN (LIANG BINGJUN), first publication of "Confronting the Multiple Deaths of the Chinese Language," translation copyright © 2010 by Jennifer Feeley.

LI ANG, excerpt from "Protest of a Woman Author against Reckless Accusations: Another Self-Interview, This Time from Taipei," trans. Pu-mei Leng, in *Modern Chinese Writers: Self-Portrayals*, ed. Helmut Martin & Jeffrey Kinkley. Translation copyright © 1992 by M. E. Sharpe, Inc. Reprinted by permission.

LIANG SHIQIU, excerpt from "Literature and Revolution," trans. Alison Bailey, in *Modern Chinese Literary Thought: Writings on Literature, 1893–1945*, ed. Kirk A. Denton. Copyright © 1996 by the Board of Trustees of the Leland Stanford Jr. University. All rights reserved. Reprinted by permission of Stanford University Press, www.sup.org.

LO FU (LUO FU), first publication of "Innovation and Continuity in Poetry," in *The Essential Lo Fu*, translation copyright © 2010 by John Balcom.

LU XUN, "Preface to *Call to Arms*" and "The True Story of Ah Q," in *The Complete Stories of Lu Xun*, translation copyright © 1980 by Yang Xianyi & Gladys Yang. Reprinted by permission of Indiana University Press.

MAO DUN, "Literature and Life," trans. John Berninghausen, in *Modern Chinese Literary Thought: Writings on Literature, 1893–1945*, ed. Kirk A. Denton. Copyright © 1996 by the Board of Trustees of the Leland Stanford Jr. University. All rights reserved. Reprinted by permission of Stanford University Press, www.sup.org.

MAO ZEDONG, excerpts from "Talks at the Yan'an Forum on Literature and Art," in *Selected Works of Mao Tse-tung*, translation copyright © 1996. Reprinted by permission of Foreign Languages Press, Beijing.

MO YAN, "My American Books," trans. Sylvia Li-chun Lin, *World Literature Today* 74, no. 3 (Summer 2000): 473–76. Translation copyright © 2000 by Sylvia Li-chun Lin. "Six Lives in Search of a Character: The 2009 Newman Prize Lecture," trans. Sylvia Li-chun Lin, *World Literature Today* 83, no. 4 (July–August 2009): 26–27. Translation copyright © 2009 by Sylvia Li-chun Lin. Reprinted by permission of the translator and *World Literature Today*.

SHANG QIN, excerpt from "Preface to *Dream or the Dawn and Other*" and "The Lock Electric," in *Feelings Above Sea Level: Prose Poems from the Chinese of Shang Qin*, translation copyright © 2006 by Steve Bradbury. Reprinted by permission of Zephyr Press. Excerpts from "A Conversation with Shang Qin," trans. Zona Yi-Ping Tsou, *Fascicle* 3 (Winter 2006–2007). Copyright © 2006 by Zona Yi-Ping Tsou. Reprinted by permission of the author.

WANG ANYI, first publication of "Why I Write," translation copyright © 2010 by Michael Berry.

WANG PING, "Writing in Two Tongues," *Manoa: Beyond Words: Asian Writers on Their Work* 18, no. 1 (2006): 12–16. Copyright © 2006 by Wang Ping. Reprinted by permission of the author.

WEN YIDUO, first publication of "Form in Poetry," translation copyright © 2010 by Andrea Lingenfelter. "Dead Water," in *The Silk Dragon: Translations from the Chinese*, translation copyright © 2001 by Arthur Sze. Reprinted by permission of Copper Canyon Press, www.coppercanyonpress.org.

XI CHUAN, first publication of "Chinese as a Language in a Neighborhood," translation copyright © 2010 by Lucas Klein.

XI XI, first publication of "Goatskin Raft—In Lieu of Preface," in *Xi Xi, Volume in Hand*, translation copyright © 2010 by Michelle Yeh.

YAN LI, "Thanks for That," in *Pamirs Poetry Journey: The First Chinese-English Poetry Festival at Huangshan Mountain, China, 2007*, translation copyright © 2008 by Denis Mair. Reprinted by permission of the translator.

YANG LIAN, "Island (#2)," in *Poetry,* translation copyright © 2009 by Arthur Sze. Reprinted by permission of the translator. First publication of "The Poetics of Space, and More: Aesthetic Pressures on Classical Chinese Poetry and a Contemporary Solution," translation copyright © 2010 by Brian Holton & Xie Guixia.

YANG MU, first publication of "Further Reflections on the Headwaters of Poetry in Taiwan," translation copyright © 2010 by Andrea Lingenfelter. First publication of "The Song of Bishop Wort," translation copyright © 2010 by Andrea Lingenfelter.

YU HUA, first publication of excerpt from "Autobiography," translation copyright © 2010 by Michael Berry. Excerpts from *To Live*, trans. Michael Berry. Copyright © 1993 by Yu Hua. Translation and afterword copyright © 2003 by Michael Berry. Reprinted by permission of Anchor Books, a division of Random House, Inc.

YU JIAN, excerpts from "The Brown Notebook: Rejecting Metaphor," trans. Wang Ping, in *New Generation: Poems from China Today*, ed. Wang Ping. Copyright © 1999 by Wang Ping. Reprinted by permission of Hanging Loose Press. Additional passages translation copyright © 2010 by Wang Ping. Excerpts from "They Tattoo Their Bodies for the World: Yu Jian Interview, November 2007–February 2008," in *Full Tilt*, *http://fulltilt.ncu.edu.tw,* translation copyright © 2007 by Simon Patton. Reprinted by permission of the translator.

ZANG DI, first publication of excerpt from "Toward a Writerly Poetry," translation copyright 2010 by John Balcom. First publication of "A Charm about Things," translation copyright © 2010 by Murray Edmond.

ZHAI YONGMING, first publication of "Black Night Consciousness," translation copyright © 2010 by Andrea Lingenfelter. "The chrysanthemum lantern is floating over me," in *The Treekeeper's Tale*, translation copyright © 2008 by Pascale Petit. Reprinted by permission of the translator and Seren Books.

ZHANG DACHUN, first publication of "All Is Creative Writing—News, Fiction, News Fiction," in *Zhang Dachun's Literary Views*, translation copyright © 2010 by Michelle Yeh.

ZHANG ER, first publication of "A Female Voice from the Past: An Alternative Tradition of Chinese Poetry," copyright © 2010 by Zhang Er.

ZHOU ZAN, first publication of "Musings on Poetry," translation copyright © 2010 by Jennifer Feeley.

ZHOU ZUOREN, excerpts from "My Own Compositions," in *Zhou Zuoren: Selected Essays*, translation copyright © 2006 by David E. Pollard. Reprinted by permission of Chinese University Press.

# *Writers/Works Index*

ARTHUR SZE is the author of nine books of poetry, including *The Ginkgo Light*, *Quipu*, *The Redshifting Web: Poems 1970–1998*, *Archipelago*, and *The Silk Dragon: Translations from the Chinese*, from Copper Canyon Press. He is the recipient of numerous awards, including two National Endowment for the Arts Creative Writing fellowships, a Guggenheim fellowship, a Lannan Literary Award, an American Book Award, and a Lila Wallace–Reader's Digest Writers' Award. He is professor emeritus at the Institute of American Indian Arts and lives in Santa Fe, New Mexico.

TRINITY UNIVERSITY PRESS strives to produce its books using methods and materials in an environmentally sensitive manner. We favor working with manufacturers that practice sustainable management of all natural resources, produce paper using recycled stock, and manage forests with the best possible practices for people, biodiversity, and sustainability.